# SAILING SCHOOL

# SAILING SCHOOL

## DOUG SCHRYVER

# BARRON'S

Woodbury, New York

*To my father, Gerry Schryver,*
*who taught me to love the water and who helped me keep a course*
*— D.S., NYC.*

A QUARTO BOOK

First edition for the United States published 1987
by Barron's Educational Series, Inc.

Copyright © 1987 Quarto Publishing Ltd

All inquiries should be addressed to:
Barron's Educational Series, Inc.
113 Crossways Park Drive
Woodbury, New York 11797

International Standard Book No. 0-8120-5813-5

Library of Congress Catalog Card No. 86-26604

Library of Congress Cataloging-in-Publicaton Data

Schryver, Doug.
   Sailing school.

   Includes index.
   I. Sailing. I. Title
GV811.S364 1987      797.1'24      86-26604
ISBN 0-8120-5813-5

This book was designed and produced by
**Quarto Publishing Ltd**
**The Old Brewery, 6 Blundell Street**
**London N7 9BH**

**Senior Editor** Stephen Paul
**Editor** Adrian Morgan

**Designers** Julian Dorr, Robin Nicholl, Mick Brennan
**Art Editor** Anne Sharples

**Illustrators** Trevor Ridley, Mick Hill
**Photographer** Jonathan Eastland

**Editorial Director** Jim Miles
**Art Director** Alastair Campbell

Typeset by Facsimile, Coggeshall, Essex
Manufactured in Hong Kong by Regent Publishing Services Limited
Printed by LeeFung Asco Printers Ltd, Hong Kong

**Editor's Note**
Sailing is a sport which is strongly dependent on the forces of nature.
Because the demands of wind and water are constantly changing,
because the different localities present different challenges to the sailor,
and because different readers interpret instructions in different ways, no
single volume can act solely to prepare an individual for the sport of
sailing. One must spend time in the study of sailing with qualified
instructors to be fully prepared to participate safely. Therefore, we, the
producers and author of this book, strongly counsel the reader to enroll
in a certified course of instruction in his or her own community.

# CONTENTS

# INTRODUCTION

**S**ailing is a high-level sport. At the top end it requires much in the way of equipment — and knowledge of that equipment — to master. Unlike track and field or swimming, both of which rely almost solely on muscular activity and endurance, sailing demands great concentration and knowledge of external forces. The sailor must be aware of the wind and weather, the condition and performance of the boat, the location and activities of other boats, and the dynamics of the water.

The rewards of the good sailor's endeavors are the sense of control he gets when his boat performs flawlessly, the perfection of balance between natural forces and the sheer beauty of the environment in which all this activity takes place.

The sailboat is an almost perfect invention. It uses the natural forces of wind and sea, creating order and direction from relative chaos. How it does this is a matter of great concern to the sailor, by understanding the theory behind a boat's performance he can handle any eventuality on the open water.

This book will explore the sailboat in all its forms, and while we examine the boat itself, we will also learn to understand how and why everything fits together.

The next step is to go sailing and

*Balance and control are two crucial skills in all dinghy sailing.*

understand how all the components of a sailboat *work* together, and apply the terminologies and principles to the real world of wind and water.

### CAVEATS

There are several things you should know immediately. Sailing does not come easily. Everything from "learning the ropes" to keeping her moving in light winds to setting a recalcitrant spinnaker will need to be learned. All it takes is the will and the time. There is no evidence that any one person has more of a "natural gift" for sailing than another.

Mastery of one type of sailing does not necessarily mean being capable of entering another phase of the sport without so much as a blink of the eye. Keelboat sailing is a quantum leap from dinghy sailing in both scale and complexity. You will need to study and then apply the lessons learned to the new level of activity.

And lastly, sounder skills will develop if the sport is shared with others. Local club classes are excellent ways to upgrade or maintain skills. Racing sharpens the eye and intuition. Joining a group of like-minded people helps to get a perspective on one's own capabilities and weaknesses.

*Sailing at the highest level — an Admiral's Cup fleet speeding through the Solent.*

# 2 | THE HISTORY OF SAILING

*The Chinese junk — a rig that has changed little in centuries.*

**W**hile today's sailboat is actually quite perfect as machines go, this was not always the case.

Some of the earliest known boats were the open log canoes or dugouts of the primitive peoples of the tropics, the skin-covered coracles of northern climes, and the bark-plated and woven canoes of the Indians in the Western Hemisphere.

All these were paddle-driven in their earliest forms, but there is reason to believe that some early inventors tried rigging some crude forms of sail.

It is well known that the early Polynesians used sail power extensively on their dugouts and outriggers and even on their large ocean-voyaging war canoes. Much of the Pacific was settled in these vessels long before the European explorers arrived, and possibly long before anyone in Europe had the technology to wander to see farther than the next inshore bay.

It is also widely known that at about the same time the Polynesians were exploring far and wide, the Chinese were plying the coastal trade routes in Asia in their seaworthy and able junks. So advanced was the junk as a sailing machine, that the Chinese are believed to have explored as far north as what we now call Alaska. Much later, the British settled in Hong Kong only with the permission of the warlords of

China, whose junk fleets were far superior in speed and maneuverability to Her Majesty's men-of-war.

Nevertheless, the early sailboat was far less than the perfection we see today.

There are two reasons why sailboat design has come such a long way in the intervening eight centuries. The first is that materials have been developed which permit greater strength and lighter weight in the structure. But far more important is that man's thinking has taken that long to evolve on the subject.

## WORKING WITH WIND

Early sails were most likely made of either pounded or rolled skins sewn together in large sheets, or of woven fiber mats, depending on the region of their use. These sails were no doubt crudely fashioned, and rigged to the most basic of spars. Solid masts hewn from trees supported them and ropes twisted together out of flax or sisal (or leather thongs pieced from the hides of animals) controlled the angle of the sails to the wind.

The earliest sailing vessels relied on their sails only for going downwind; they hoisted sail only when the wind was blowing in the direction of their travel. The primitive sailor would hoist his sail in a favorable breeze, square-off before it and get a free ride to his downwind destination. It was certainly better than paddling, and sail power soon became popular. A trader or trapper could load his canoe with grain or pelts and wait for a following wind to sail him and his cargo to market.

But if he wanted to travel upwind, he had to get out the paddle. Obviously this was no trouble when small quantities of goods were being shipped, but when boats got larger, more and more men were needed to paddle or row the extra weight.

Viking ships and Roman galleys sprouted banks of oars and stout crewmen were needed to manage them. Polynesian dugouts carried the whole tribe, paddles foaming in the sea.

Man needed a way to sail upwind, and the Eastern world was far ahead of the West in this, designing workable sailing vessels capable of transoceanic travel — some of which was, of neccessity, upwind.

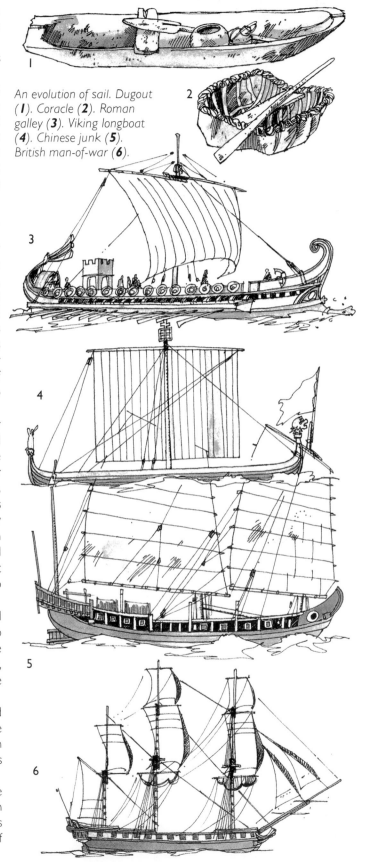

An evolution of sail. Dugout (*1*). Coracle (*2*). Roman galley (*3*). Viking longboat (*4*). Chinese junk (*5*). British man-of-war (*6*).

## FORE AND AFT

One only needs to look at the types of early rigs seen in the East and West to see the differences. Western sails hang from horizontal poles or *yards*. These *squaresails* are really most effective when pushed by the wind downwind, and they display a symmetry when rotated around their mast. Eastern sails, by contrast, have *rotational asymmetry*; their area is over-balanced to one side of the vessel's mast. Although they hang from yards, they are shaped so that they present a better aerodynamic surface to the wind on angles other than downwind.

The sails of these Eastern vessels are the forerunners of today's *fore-and-aft* rigs. The Chinese lug rig, or "junk" rig, had woven fibre sails that were stretched tightly between upper and lower yards, and had many lateral intermediate yards. Lines attached to the main and intermediate yards controlled the shape of the sail. Because the dimensional stability of the junk sail was so good, it could be set at any angle, catching the full force of the wind and using it to drive the ship.

Similarly, the Persian and Egyptian dhow had long asymmetrical yards from which hung its large triangular sails. These sails had no lower or intermediate yards, however, but were *loose-footed* at their lower edges, and controlled by lines attached to the yards and to the lower corner of the sail. Like the Chinese lug, the Persian lug or "lateen" rig could be angled in the best way to catch the wind.

The "fore-and-aft" lug rig works by holding its shape at any angle to the wind. Because of its yard, the lateen rig can be pointed quite closely to the wind's eye before it fails to capture the breeze effectively. Because of its stiffness and intermediate yards, the Chinese lug can also point closely without losing the wind.

By contrast, the Western squaresail has two identical loose edges, port and starboard. If either is brought too close to the wind's eye by over-rotation of the boat's yard, the sail will collapse, because there is nothing to stabilize the cloth.

Centuries of cross-pollination through trade brought fore-and-aft sail design to the Western world, and it wasn't long before coastal traders and fishermen began using

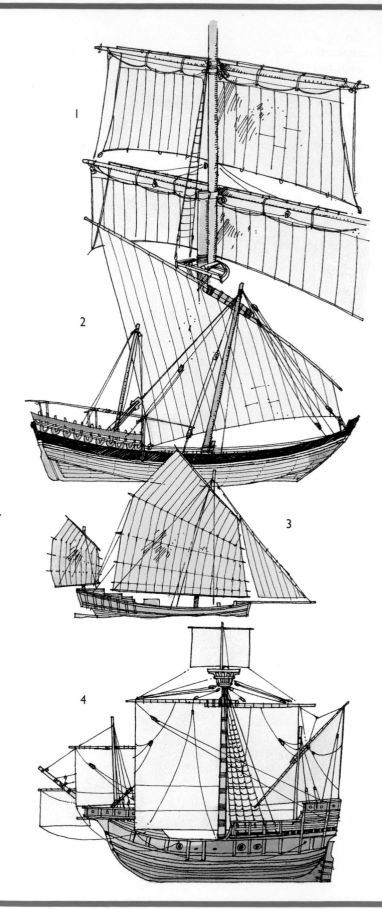

the rig. By the time of the great western explorations, Spanish and Dutch and English ships carried enough fore-and-aft sails on their tall masts to make reasonable headway across the wind and even slightly to windward. Columbus's ships, for example, had lug sails on their rearmost masts, and other derivations forward.

Nevertheless even through the age of commercial sail (well into the 19th and even 20th centuries) the squaresail held sway on the world's trade routes. Because the technology was so firmly entrenched, and because the world's winds were, and are, so stable and reliable, the *square-rigger* was the highest development in mercantile sail power. It took a completely different form of power — steam — to render it obsolete.

Ironically, the technology to compete with steam existed for centuries before the culmination of sail in commerce, but no designers ever used it to any great degree.

## EARLY YACHTS

By the time man began to sail for pleasure, the technology was well developed. Both coastal fishing and trading vessels as well as pleasure boats used the fore-and-aft rig.

In fact, the earliest pleasure boats (dubbed "yachts" by the English after the small Dutch working vessels called *jaghtschips*) were simply adaptations of lowlands working boats. By the 17th century, there were shipbuilders on both sides of the English Channel who specialized in the construction of yachts.

*A modern junk-rigged charter yacht in the Caribbean (**below left**).*

*The square-rigger Christian Radich (**below**) at the start of a Tall Ships Race.*

*Squaresails (**left**) were developed in the West while fore-and-aft rigs, like the lateen rigged dhows, were of Eastern origin; the latter are the precursors of modern rigs. Squaresails set on yards (**1**). Lateen rigged dhow from Arabia (**2**). Chinese junk (**3**). Columbus's Santa Maria (**4**).*

Charles II's pleasure yacht — the forerunner of the sport of yacht racing.

Bristol Channel pilot cutter — a fast and seaworthy working craft.

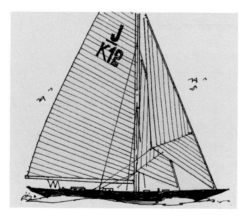

A J-class racing yacht of the 1930s.

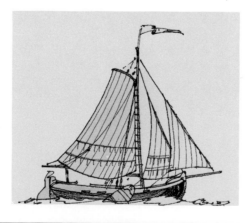

Dutch boeier — an efficient working vessel for shallow waters.

Charles II of England was the first royalty to take an interest in yachting as a sport, and it is Charles to whom we owe much of the sport's aristocratic character. Charles, with his brother James, Duke of York, competed against each other, and invited members of the Court to play along.

The earliest of these regattas would have been ludicrous, as the boats must have been lumbering beasts of great weight and poor handling characteristics, not to mention poor windward capability. But something in the adventure fascinated the king and his friends, for Charles went on to establish the sport of yachting as it stands today — a sport of competition and camaraderie popular throughout the world.

By the 18th century, coastal working craft and yachts began to develop rapidly. Technology had come through its slow evolution from skins and logs to woven cloth and ship's planking, but most importantly, man's thinking had expanded to take in all of the known world. Western Man now had all the intellectual tools in hand and was ready to use them without restraint.

### THE MODERN ERA

The fore-and-aft rig held the promise for the future of sail as it provided the capability of sailing closer to the direction of the wind — to *windward* — and this allowed commercial craft flexibility. As history has proved, the best generator of progress is commercial gain.

Both England and America contributed greatly to the development of fore-and-aft rigged sail during the 18th and 19th centuries. The weatherly and swift Bristol Channel pilot cutters of the period bear witness to the level of sophistication of the deep, narrow, heavily ballasted type. A similar look at the Yankee fishing schooner shows how highly developed the shallow, light, broad-beamed workboat had become in America.

Both these types of craft used variants of the *gaff-headed rig*. Gaffs were spars hoisted up the boat's masts on which were laced the principal driving sails of the vessel. These sails were also laced or otherwise *bent* to the masts. At the mainsail's lower edge or *foot* was another long spar called the *boom*.

In the gaff rig, the mast provided the leading edge of the mainsail, unlike the lug sail which extended some short distance forward of the mast. The boom and gaff pivoted from the mast to provide the sail's rotation. With the canvas sailcloth of the period, sail shape could be controlled to maximize efficiency.

Forward of the mast were sails similar to those seen on early sailing ships. These tall, triangular sails called *jibs*, were hoisted on fixed hempen lines, called *stays*, and were also designed to catch wind at an efficient angle.

## STATE OF THE ART

The last thing eliminated on the way to modern rig design was the gaff. A vestige of the yards of square and lug sails, the gaff served only to create weight aloft and diminish the aerodynamic efficiency of the top of the sail. The next step would be tall, narrow triangular sails.

Designers needed only slightly stronger and lighter materials technology to create the optimum rig. Just a slight leap in materials, and a great leap of faith generated this progress.

The first step was to create rigging strong enough to bear the loads of taller masts. This came in the form of wire cables to replace the tarred hemp of the clipper ship era. With wire, designers could build taller, more complex masts that were thinner in section and therefore lighter as well. *Spreaders* — short perpendicular protrusions from the mast — splayed the cables out and away from the mast, making them even better at support.

Glues were then developed to enable mast builders to fashion tall, thin, lightweight masts that were hollow in section, yet just as strong as the old solid spars.

The result, in the middle of the Modern Era, was the *marconi rig*, so named because it resembled the tall radio tower designed by the famed inventor, Marconi, whose wireless radio had just been invented.

The rig's sails were relatively tall, and had peaked tops, or *heads*. Because the tops of these sails looked and functioned like the peaked heads of the familiar jib, they were also referred to as *jib-headed* sails.

Regardless of the terminology, the new rig worked splendidly as it was a more effective aerodynamic package, providing better windward ability, and greatly simplifying a boat's rigging.

Most of the design work leading to the jib-headed marconi rig took place after the great age of sail, and after most commercial sail had given way to power on the world's developed coasts.

It was the yachtsman, then, who developed the modern sailing boat. It took the amateur to put the finishing touches on the machine's rig.

## THE HULL

The design of the sailing boat hull has taken many and varied twists and turns, especially of late.

Because sails could be changed easily, and rigs could be fashioned in a number of ways and configurations for a given hull, early designers had more practice, at less expense, in rig design. Hulls were expensive and, once built, hard to modify.

Today, the art and science of yacht design has progressed to the point where a naval architect draws his hull on a computer, builds a scale model, tows it in a specially designed model tank, has it analyzed by more computers, and can have a complete and detailed picture of how it will perform in the real world long before it is actually built.

Unfortunately, early designers had no such luck. They learned from long, hard-earned experience; and as a result, hull design progressed slowly.

The yachts of Charles II were heavy, broad, shallow boats derived from Dutch workboats. Because they were shallow, there was little below the water to resist the side-slip to which a boat is prone when under a press of sail in a wind that is perpendicular to its direction of travel. These boats needed deeper *keels* to resist this side-slip.

The Dutch developed heavy, oblong boards attached to the sides of their broad, flat-bottomed coastal workboats to limit this side-slip or *leeway*. These *leeboards* pivoted downward and projected deep into the water, while the breadth of the hulls imparted stability.

Later British yacht designers also learned the value of deep projections below the

13

*The 1983 America's Cup winner Australia II (**left**) and a replica of the schooner America (1851) (**below left**) after which the Cup was named. Although separated by 153 years, these two yachts present a striking illustration of the evolution of yacht design.*

waterline, but rather than build leeboards attached to fat hulls, they designed underbodies that were themselves quite deep and very narrow. They filled these deep hulls with ballast material (rock, and later poured mortar) to counteract the vessel's tendency to blow over.

The contrast between the broad, shallow design and the deep keel was the central point in a centuries-long argument. Which is better, a ballasted keel on a narrow hull, or a light board on a wide hull?

The ultimate showdown occurred during the early days of the challenge between America and Britain, the America's Cup.

### SKIMMING DISH VS LEAD MINE

British yacht design of the 19th century had focused on the extremely deep, narrow "cutter-type" for speed and windward ability. Sails and hull worked closely together, it was thought, to drive the boat powerfully on an extremely acute angle to the wind. These boats were laden with tons of ballast to keep their narrow hulls upright.

Yankee boats, by contrast, were relatively shallow-bodied and light, relying for their stability on width at the waterline, some ballast, and often deep boards pivoting down into the water out of huge *trunks* on the centerline. These *centerboards* were exactly like those on today's sailing dinghies.

When the American "skimming dish" met the British "lead mine", the action was furious, but when the dust settled, no single design aspect was vindicated or proven inferior. Rather, a blending of the good aspects of both came about, and yacht design prospered from the competition.

The synthesis was so effective, in fact, that the America's Cup has finally been won back by the Australians, with a lightweight, shallow-bodied, deep-keeled (in this case *winged*) sailing yacht called *Australia II*.

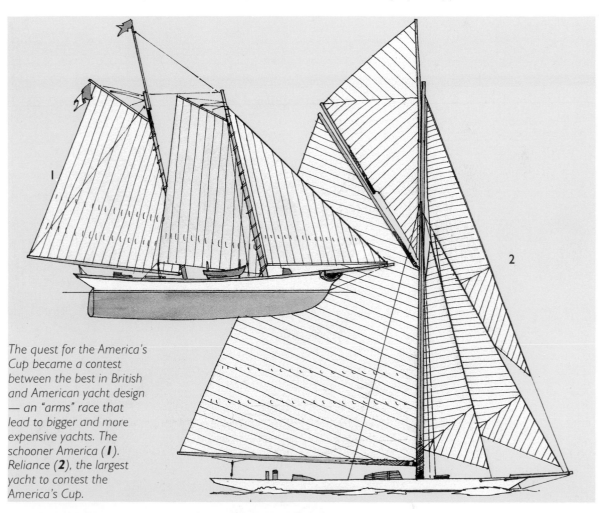

*The quest for the America's Cup became a contest between the best in British and American yacht design — an "arms" race that lead to bigger and more expensive yachts. The schooner America (**1**). Reliance (**2**), the largest yacht to contest the America's Cup.*

15

The modern sailing hull is a perfect blend of the good aspects of the British/American design synthesis. Modern racing yachts, the most efficient of their breed, have broad, flat-bottomed hulls whose design concept belongs to the Dutch and American tradition; but deep, heavily ballasted keels reach well down below the waterline to stabilize the boats against the pressure of the wind in the sails and resist leeway, the unmistakable British legacy.

The modern yacht, therefore, is a far cry from the primitive hide coracle with woven or beaten sail attached to primitive spars. Today's boats are built of fiberglass or a combination of fiberglass and other materials, with extruded aluminum spars and synthetic sails. Smaller centerboard-equipped dinghies are light and have flat bottoms and efficient underwater shapes that enable them to skim over the surface under sail.

Modern ocean racers have extremely strong rigs with tall masts and knifelike sails

that have extraordinary windward efficiency. While the earliest sailing vessels were lucky to make headway within 80–90 degrees of the wind's eye, today's sailing yacht is easily capable of sailing to within 50, 40, or even 35 degrees of the wind's true direction.

This high degree of performance is the fruit of a long and diligent development process. Technology and technique have been the twin forces in shaping this most perfect machine.

*Continued research and development has produced a breed of yacht like the mighty Condor (**left**) and offshore racer (**below**) whose ancestry is based on the British/ American design synthesis — broad flat- bottomed hulls allied to deep keels. The Flying Dutchman (**below**) — a lightweight, high performance planing dinghy.*

# DINGHY SAILING

# 3 | SAILING THEORY

Sailing at the very highest level — the Olympics; Jo Richards and Peter Allam (**below**), Flying Dutchman bronze medallists at Los Angeles, 1984.

A fleet of single-handed Topper dinghies (**bottom**) club racing on inland waters.

**B**ecause sailing is such a complicated, high-level sport, requiring many tools and much mechanical participation, a good understanding of the physical principles behind the motion of the sailing boat is needed. The best type of boat in which to learn these principles is a dinghy.

While the larger boat may bring more and greater forces to bear, a dinghy with a single sail and lightweight centerboard hull beautifully illustrates the fundamentals. A dinghy will show you what the sport is about before moving on to something grander and more powerful.

In this chapter you will discover how the modern sailboat responds to wind and water. The next chapter deals with the basic equipment associated with the dinghy and its rigging. Upon completing both, you should be ready to climb into a boat and begin sailing.

But take careful note: absorb the basic lessons now, particularly the theory, as ultimate ability will be based on it. Each time you make a maneuver, whether your boat is 10ft or 50ft, you will need to refer to some fundamental principle of sailing theory, and the better and more instinctive your insight, the more effective the maneuver will be.

## THE SAILBOAT

We have already discussed the wonderful

perfection of the sailboat. But let's go back a moment and look at the raw materials.

The boat is not just a dish or tub fashioned solely to keep the water on the outside. It has a shape that works with the wind and sea to produce motion. The body of the boat, or *hull*, is designed to cleave the water, its *bow* penetrating the seas while throwing water down and away from the crew. The *deck* is designed to provide a footing and keep water out. The underwater portion (the *underbody*) is also designed to penetrate the water, but is shaped to create as little resistance to forward motion as possible. The boat has a *keel* or *centerboard* underwater to provide lateral resistance as the pressure of the wind tries to push the boat sideways. The boat also has a *rudder*, usually hung on a set of hinged fittings somewhere at the boat's *stern*, for steering control.

Topside, the sailboat's rig is what provides the propulsion. It is composed of a

*The fine bow form and smooth hull of the Laser dinghy (**above right**) are designed to minimize resistance to forward motion.*

*The stern sections (**right**) have a flatter profile to carry crew weight and promote lift. Note the centerboard slot and the rudder (shown here raised) hung on the transom.*

The loose-footed Laser mainsail (**right**) is stretched along the boom until the right fullness is achieved for the strength of wind. The boom is controlled by the mainsheet attached to its outer end.

The sail is sleeved over the mast (**below**). The boom pivots on the gooseneck — a kind of universal joint — and is kept from lifting by the vang which is attached from the boom to the base of the mast.

wood or alloy spar called the *mast*, the sails hoisted on the mast, the wire *standing rigging* providing support for the mast, and the rope *running rigging* providing control for the sails.

Overall, the machine's purpose is to catch the wind and produce motion, but the modern sailboat has several ways of harnessing the wind, and that is the crux of this chapter.

### THE DINGHY AT WORK

On a modern boat like the Laser sailing dinghy, there is only one sail, the *mainsail*. It is laced or otherwise connected along one vertical side to the boat's mast, and along its bottom edge to the boat's *boom*, a spar that swings or pivots where it joins the mast. Its purpose is to give the sailor control over the rotation of the sail around the mast's axis.

The most basic way a modern boat uses the wind is the way the most primitive sailor must have used it; to be pushed along more or less in the same direction — to sail *downwind*. For this, the sailor simply lets the sail rotate out to the side and capture the breeze. The mast, which is securely mounted (or *stepped*) in the boat, and the boom, which is harnessed by its own running rigging (called the *mainsheet*), take the energy the sail captures from the wind and transmit it to the hull.

As the boat is steered from this downwind course toward any direction closer to the wind, the shape of the sail and the configuration of the boat's underbody become very important. It's not just a simple action/reaction system anymore.

Let's look at what the major components of a dinghy actually do when the boat is steered from its downwind direction ever closer to the wind's eye.

**Downwind** The hull is level; the wind is acting directly along the boat's centerline; there is no sideways component of wind thrust because the sail is rotated so as to catch the wind almost perpendicularly — so there is no need for a centerboard. The boat is simply being pushed along.

**Across the wind** Here the wind is more or less perpendicular to the direction in which the boat is headed. At this angle, the sail is rotated by the mainsheet closer to the boat — closer *inboard*. Now the centerboard

The aluminum mast is mounted in a hole in the foredeck (**right**) without any standing rigging to support it. The boat is fitted with a deck compass to allow the helmsman to gauge any changes in wind direction — a vital facility when racing.

When sailing downwind (**below, below right**) the wind simply pushes the boat along, so the sails are spread wide, to catch the maximum amount of wind while the centerboard is partially or completely raised to reduce any unnecessary underwater resistance.

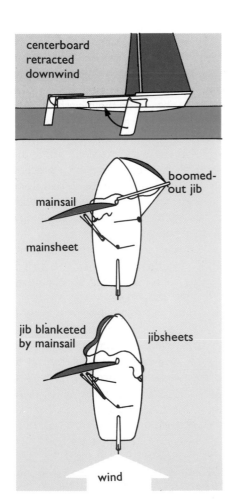

centerboard
retracted
downwind

mainsail

mainsheet

boomed-out jib

jib blanketed by mainsail

jibsheets

wind

becomes important in resisting the push of the wind. It digs in and prevents the wind from forcing the boat to slide sideways. The rudder not only keeps the boat heading across the wind, but also assists the centerboard in providing resistance to sideslip. The sail no longer simply catches the wind and pushes the boat; it now catches the wind and partially re-directs its vector with the help of the hull and centerboard. The force of the wind the sail is unable to re-direct acts to tip the boat away from the wind (to *leeward*). This tipping is called *heeling*. The sail also begins to take the shape of a wing, acting somewhat like an airfoil in building "lift" along its leading edge.

**Upwind** As the boat begins to head upwind, so that the breeze is taken at an angle close on the boat's bow, aerodynamics take over almost completely. The sail becomes a true airfoil as it is hauled very close inboard. The wind's force acts most vigorously to heel the boat. The hull, centerboard and rudder included, produces an action against the water that also creates a

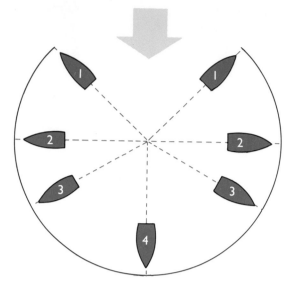

*The standard "points of sailing" (**above**) are: (**1**) close-hauled; (**2**) beam reach; (**3**) broad reach; and (**4**) run. Note how the boat cannot sail directly into the wind.*

*When sailing across the wind, the sail starts to act like an airfoil, and the boat is pushed both sideways and forward: this sideways force produces a heeling action which needs to be counterbalanced by the weight of the crew.*

wind pressure

forward component

centerboard

water pressure

kind of lift. These forces act together to make the typical dinghy sail to within about 45 degrees of the wind's direction.

It is easy to see how a boat sails downwind by being pushed, but performance across the wind and to windward is often most baffling to the beginner. To illustrate how a rig is able to produce motion, the *wind's force* acting on the hull's *lateral resistance* must be examined in more detail.

### TO WINDWARD

Picture a kite. If a kite had no special attributes, it would simply blow along the ground and away in the wind, like so much

*To sail to windward (ie close-hauled), the sails must be sheeted in, crew weight must be right out on the side deck and the centerboard must be fully extended.*

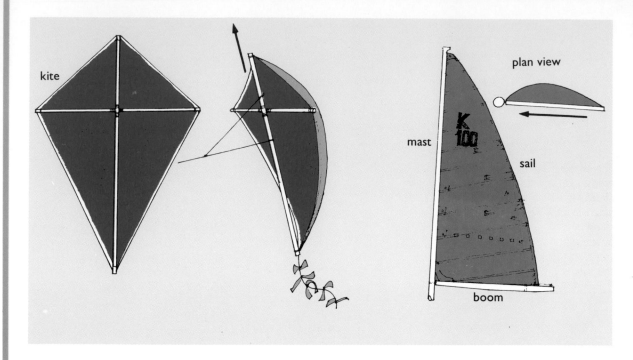

*The dynamics of a kite bear a close resemblance to those of a sailboat and are a useful way of illustrating how forward motion is created. A kite's aerodynamic shape creates lift, and when this lifting force is opposed by the pull of the string (the equivalent of the centerboard) it becomes airborne.*

rubbish in a spring storm. But a kite possesses two things. Firstly, a kite has a special shape. It is "aerodynamic". Its surface bellies slightly in the wind, and it has a way of capturing the *force* of the breeze within its structure. Secondly, a kite has a string. The string tethers it to the grounded kitesman who provides the *lateral resistance* needed to make it fly.

When you put the kite (with its special shape and its earthbound kitesman) together with a healthy wind, the kite with its top angled forward into the wind jumps aloft and climbs into the sky, starting perpendicular to the wind, but eventually angling itself toward the wind. Note that it does not flutter or fall when angled sharply into the wind, and could probably keep going on this angle to windward given enough scope of string and space for the kitesman to walk along the ground.

The shape of the kite helps it climb and allows it to capture the wind; the strength of the string and firmness of the kitesman's grip provide the "bite" or resistance the kite needs to fight the wind.

Now to the sailboat. The sail does the same thing as the kite's wing, catching the wind on an acute angle (one as acute as its design is capable of); and the boat's keel does the same thing as the kite's string and string-holder, stopping the wind blowing it away.

The major difference between sailboat and kite is that the kite will always run out of string, and the kitesman will always run out of walking room. The sailboat has the "string" built-in in the form of the keel or centerboard, and the only limit of travel is the surface of the sea. The sailboat can keep "climbing" to windward until it runs out of room.

### LIFT AND RESISTANCE

The similarities between sailboat and kite are fine for illustrating the basics, but they really don't show exactly what happens to rig and hull when a boat is sailing across the wind or to windward.

Because the boat has a centerboard or keel, the force of the wind in the sails is transformed into one component vector that heels the boat to leeward, and another that drives the boat forward. But the hull itself is also at work. As the boat tries to sideslip away from the direction of the wind, and as its keel or centerboard digs in and resists that slide, masses of water pile up on the side away from the wind — on the side upon which the water resistance is acting most powerfully.

But, because water is a liquid its piling up makes it tend to escape from around the lateral planes of the boat's underbody (the centerboard, rudder and immersed hull

This sequence (**right**) illustrates the way in which the fullness of the sail relates to the forward motion. With the sail let out (**1**), the wind blows ineffectually past and causes the sail to shake or luff. As the sail is sheeted (pulled) in (**2**), the wind begins to fill it and causes the heeling action and lateral motion which is resisted by the centerboard and hull. The more the sail is sheeted in (**3**) the greater these resultant forces become and the greater the acceleration.

The simplest sailing mode is downwind (**below**), where the dinghy is moved along by the airstream and can travel no faster than the wind.

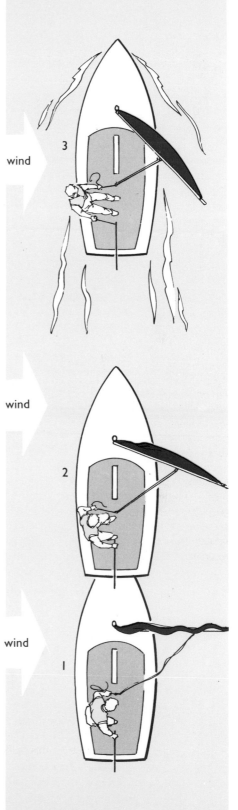

wind

wind

wind

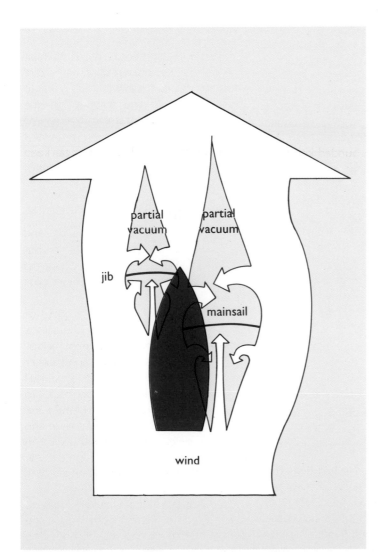

partial vacuum    partial vacuum

jib

mainsail

wind

sides). Due to the way these planes and surfaces are shaped, the motion of the water as it sloughs off the hull is rearward, toward the stern. A kind of "squeezing" of the boat's underbody occurs, then, which acts to force the boat forward.

On some designs with more modern foil-shaped keels or centerboards, there is an extra driving force at work. On the side of the keel or centerboard opposite the one with the water piling up, there is always a low-pressure area. In a foil shape, that area is especially pronounced on the forward edge.

*Airfoils (like the wing of an aeroplane) are designed to produce lift. As wind passes over an airfoil, the windward (under) side experiences a high-pressure build-up, while the leeward (top) side experiences a drop in pressure. This pressure differential is then translated into a push–and–pull force in a forward direction.*

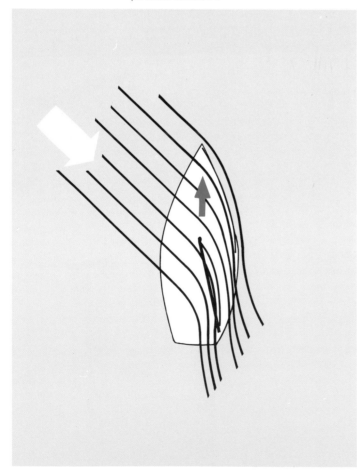

The lift that's generated on that forward surface helps not only pull the boat forward, but creates a component of force to windward as well.

A sail does a version of the same thing. Air piles up on the sail's windward side, and slides off in such a way as to re-direct its energy to create a forward push on the boat's rig. A low-pressure area is also created on the forward surface of the foil, and again, like a plane's wing, the sail develops lift which pulls the boat along.

## SYMMETRY

The rig of a modern sailboat has one more advantage over a simple child's kite: its ability to perform equally well with the wind on either side. There is longitudinal symmetry to a sailboat.

When you reach a point where you are running out of sea room, regardless of the angle of your boat to the wind, you can always change course, swing the boat's boom over to the opposite side, and continue on.

The process of *tacking*, which will be discussed shortly, involves this longitudinal symmetry. A dinghy can progress toward a destination directly into the wind — by tacking, or zig-zagging side-to-side, with sails hauled close inboard.

## CONTROL

Obviously, the most important difference between kite and dinghy is the presence of a skipper aboard the latter.

The skipper must learn to use his knowledge of the principles of sail to translate his wishes and commands to performance.

As the parts of a simple dinghy are explored, we will concentrate not only on nomenclature, but also on what each part does in the scheme of things.

But even as you become immersed in the minutiae of the technology, do not forget the basic driving forces. Without this groundwork, you will never be a fully realized sailor. And you will never be in complete control of your boat.

## WEATHER HELM

The interaction of sail and hull causes one other phenomenon and it affects the

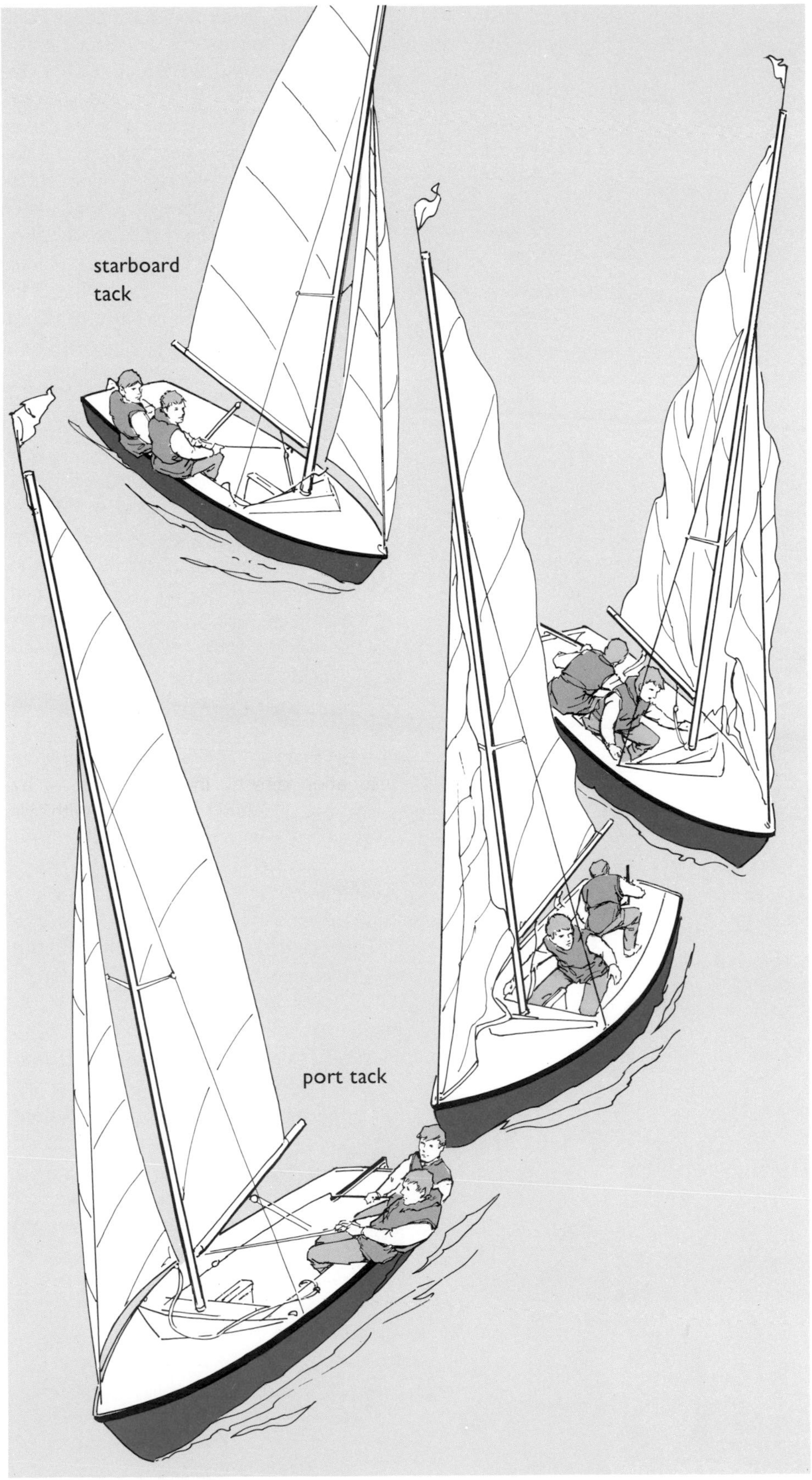

starboard
tack

port tack

Because a sailboat
cannot sail directly
into the wind, it can
only make progress
to windward by
zigzagging from one
tack to another.
Tacking consists of
turning the boat's
bow through the eye
of the wind.

29

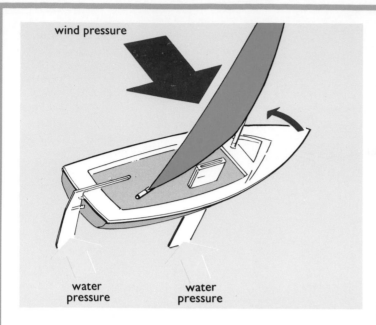

wind pressure

water pressure

water pressure

center of effort (CE)

center of lateral resistance (CLR)

steering of the boat in virtually any wind condition. It is the tendency of a boat to try to turn into the wind while under sail. The name of the phenomenon is *weather helm*.

The reason for it is simple. The force on a boat's sail can be assumed to act at a single point, the center of effort. Similarly, all the force of lateral resistance on a boat's hull (underbody, rudder, and keel) can be taken as acting at a single point, the center of lateral resistance. Because the center of effort (CE) and the center of lateral resistance (CLR) rarely line up, but are always offset from each other in a properly designed boat, their forces together form a "couple" which serves to twist the boat.

A simple example is when the sail is swung all the way out to the side as the boat is sailing downwind. The center of effort of the sail is far outboard, while the center of resistance is at the boat, below the waterline (where it always is). The result of this couple is that the boat wants to turn *away* from the side its sail is on. In other words, the force on the sail creates a twisting moment around the resisting force of the boat in the water.

A more complex example is seen when the boat is sailing perpendicular to the wind. The CLR is below the CE and aft of (behind) it. The forces involved between these two points, along with added moments created as the boat heels, try to twist the boat, pushing the stern away from the wind, and the bow up toward the wind.

To counteract these forces, the helmsman must apply some rudder angle and actually steer the boat against its tendency to sail up into the wind. Because he must pull the tiller to windward, and because the windward side of a boat is also called the "weather" side, the term *weather helm* is applied.

*There are essentially two forces (**above left**) acting on a small sailboat — wind pressure on the sails (aerodynamic) and water pressure on the under surfaces (hydrodynamic). It is the rudder's function to keep these two forces in balance.*

*The center of effort (CE) and the center of lateral resistance (CLR) rarely line up (**left**). This "misalignment" produces a twisting force.*

weather helm

lee helm

The effect of any imbalance due to incorrect sail trim, crew or centerboard position will be to cause the boat to screw round into the wind or "round up" (**below**). This imbalance will be transmitted to the rudder where it must be resisted by applying "weather helm" (**left**). However, in some badly designed boats it is sometimes necessary to apply the opposite force, ie "lee helm".

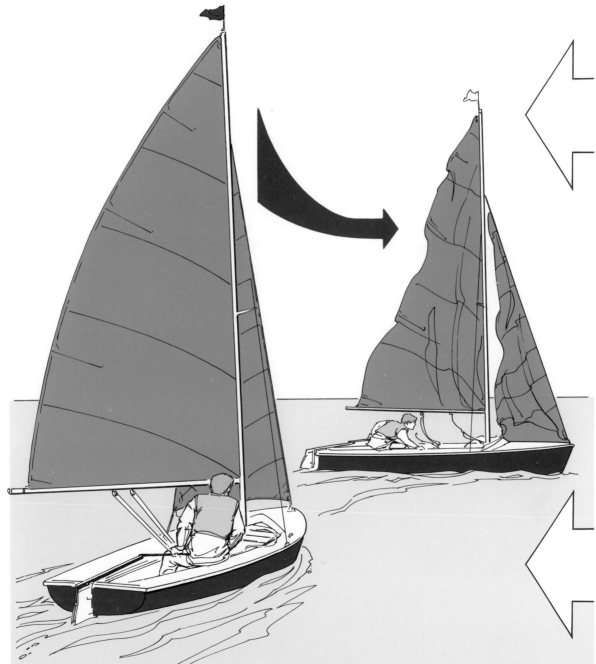

# 4 | THE SAILING DINGHY

*Dinghy sailing, and in particular racing, is the proving ground worldwide for all successful sailors.*

The sailing dinghy is the raw material of which sailors are built. Almost all successful skippers serve their time in dinghies of various descriptions.

There are many reasons why the dinghy is such a valuable learning tool and they include the speed and accuracy with which it responds to steering input and weight shift; the simplicity of its rig; its durability; its portability; and its low cost.

Of all these, the first is by far the most important in the long run. Learn how to manage a small sailing dinghy in a strong breeze and a bit of a sea, and you'll be able to handle almost anything. Things happen fast in a dinghy; mistakes are proven immediately, yet at the same time are easily and quickly corrected given the proper curative action.

If a mistake turns out to be incurable, the consequence is often mild in a dinghy. You may get wet, but you will recover and come back.

There are many types of sailing dinghies, some of which have more complex rigs than others. The best type for the beginner is the single-masted dinghy. This rig has one sail — the mainsail — attached to the mast and boom. Its running rigging (the cordage that manipulates the sail) is simple; and it may have no standing rigging (wire supporting the mast) at all.

## THE HULL

The hull of a modern sailing dinghy is usually built of several layers of fiberglass cloth laminated and encapsulated in hardened resin. A fiberglass boat like this is usually built using a mold, in which the hull is allowed to cure before it is removed and fitted with its other components.

Framing to add strength and stiffness may be bonded to the inside of the hull during the molding process, while other stiffening members — like wood trim — might be added later.

The principal dimensions of the hull are described in nautical terms as follows:
— Width is called *beam*.
— Depth of the hull below the waterline is called *draft*.
— Height of the hull above the waterline is called *freeboard*.
— The boat's length is simply that — length — but is measured in two places, and designed LWL, or length at the waterline, and LOA, or length overall.
— The boat's weight is called its *displacement*. Displacement is the weight of the water the hull actually displaces under Archimedes' Principle of Buoyancy — which states that a body will displace a weight of water equivalent to its own weight. Because salt water is denser than fresh water, less of it is required to float a hull, and your boat (and anything else, for that matter) will float higher in the sea than on a lake or river.

The typical sailing dinghy hull will have a LOA of roughly 8 — 10ft; a LWL of about 6 — 9ft; a beam of about 3½ — 5ft; a draft of perhaps 5in with the centerboard all the way up, and several feet with the board down; and a freeboard of 1 — 2ft. A dinghy might weigh a mere 75lb without any of its gear aboard, or it might weigh several hundred with mast, centerboard, rudder, paddles and gear aboard.

The hull form of a dinghy depends on its intended performance characteristics. A fast hull has *rounded bilges* — that is with the bottom radiused at the *chines* (the chines being the lower "cheeks" of the hull along the side at the waterline). A stable load-carrying hull has *hard chines* — that is, with hard angles at the lower cheeks. Rounded bilges promote smooth waterflow along the boat's hull, reducing resistance. Hard chines,

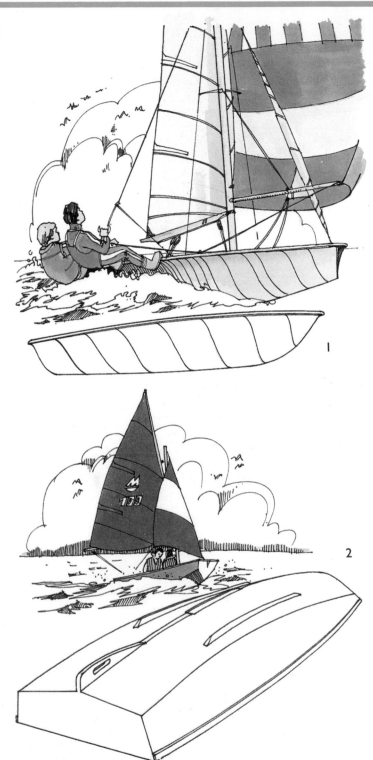

*Round bilge hull shapes are often, but not always, used for high performance racing dinghies. The simpler hard-chine designs are ideal for amateur boat-building. Round bilge (1). Hard-chine (2).*

when immersed, alter flow and produce resistance, but add a measure of initial transverse stability to the hull. (Note that the term *"bilge"* is also used to describe that portion of the hull that is at the lowest point. Water in the hull collects in the bilge.)

Some dinghies are built of materials other than fiberglass — most notably wood or aluminum. Wood often produces a heavier hull than fiberglass of equivalent strength, but some new types of wood construction, using state-of-the-art resins and extremely dry softwood stock, can produce surprisingly lightweight hulls.

## CENTERBOARDS, DAGGERBOARDS

Almost all sailing dinghies have centerboards. These are relatively large

These three GP14 dinghies (**left**) (seen here in close combat) offer a perfect demonstration of the three main points of sailing — (from left to right) close-hauled, reaching and running.

The two-man 470 racing dinghy (**right**) is a sophisticated Olympic class boat, requiring a high degree of agility and balance.

There are basically two types of centerboard — the pivoting centerboard (**right**) or the retractable daggerboard. The pivoting centerboard has the advantage of being easier to use when underway. A fairly complex arrangement, it needs to be well maintained.

panels that are specially shaped and slide within enclosures built in to the hull along the bottom's longitudinal axis, or *centerline*. The enclosure for a centerboard is called a *trunk* or *box*.

There are two types of centerboard. One is the pivoting type with fully enclosed trunk, while the other, often called a *daggerboard*, slides vertically within its trunk and can be lifted completely out of the open top. The first type has the advantage of its enclosed trunk, but suffers from the complexity of its own pivoting mechanism, which consists of a stout pin and a lanyard or lever mechanism to raise and lower the board. By contrast the daggerboard is light, simple and easily maintained — but it is harder to manipulate than a standard centerboard.

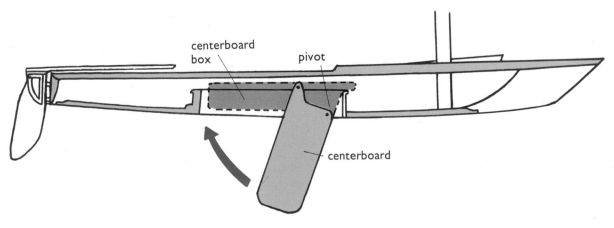

centerboard box

pivot

centerboard

As we've seen, the centerboard acts to provide lateral resistance as the wind tries to push the boat sideways under a press of sail. But the best thing about a centerboard, especially when it is applied to a sailing dinghy, is that it carries little or no weight (it is *unballasted*), it stores easily, and it can be raised for shallow-water operations.

In addition, a centerboard can be partially raised or lowered as conditions permit. When sailing downwind, the board does little good, and can be raised to reduce underwater friction. When sailing across the wind, or even upwind under certain conditions, a board can be raised partially to alter the sailing balance of the boat. This is a point we will discuss in detail when we begin to practice sailing.

Centerboards can also be airfoil-shaped for best hydrodynamic effect. Foil-section boards are very common on racing craft, although most dinghies have simple, flat-sectioned boards. This is because most builders find that mass-production dictates simplicity, and that the marginal improvement in performance offered by slick foil-sectioned boards is not worth the effort and cost.

However, things are different with rudders.

## THE RUDDER

The rudder on a dinghy is another simple mechanism, and like the centerboard is designed to operate in a variety of modes.

The dinghy rudder is normally detachable and is mounted on pairs of hinge mechanisms that can be uncoupled. These *gudgeons* (the "female" part of the hinge) and *pintles* (the male part) are stainless steel or bronze components. The gudgeons are mounted one above the other at the aftermost part of the hull (called the *transom*). The pintles are mounted on the rudder itself in corresponding fashion, so that the pairs mate when fitted together. Note that some dinghies use variants of the gudgeon/pintle arrangement, but rudders are almost always detachable.

The rudder has two principal parts: the *blade* (its lower extremity) and the *stock* (the upper portion, on which the mounting

*This Laser dinghy has a simple foil-sectioned daggerboard which fits neatly into the slot on the foredeck and is raised or lowered by hand.*

mechanisms are fastened). Some dinghies have rudder blades that pivot, allowing them to be raised and lowered for shallow-water work. This is usually accomplished by way of a short lanyard attached to the trailing edge of the blade.

A good dinghy will also have a rudder blade shaped like an airfoil for optimum effect. A well-shaped rudder produces minimum drag, and helps control turbulence that can slow a boat. Shaping a rudder properly is something a manufacturer can do easily and cost-

effectively. The benefits of reduced turbulence and improved performance are more than worth it.

The rudder hangs on the transom and pivots right-to-left (*port* to *starboard*), but it is controlled by the sailor with a short wood or aluminum stick known as a *tiller*. The tiller is mounted on top of the rudder and protrudes over the transom and into the boat a short distance. There may be an extension mounted at the tiller's inboard end so that the sailor can move about in the boat while still controlling the rudder.

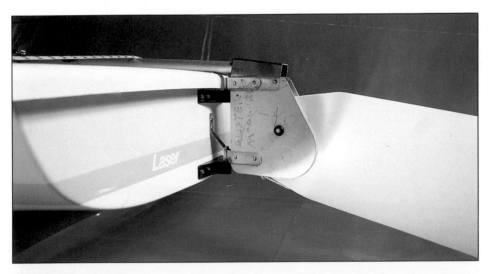

*The rudder is hung on pintles and gudgeons. Some types can be raised for beaching or shallow-water work. Note the retaining clip to stop the rudder lifting off its hangings.*

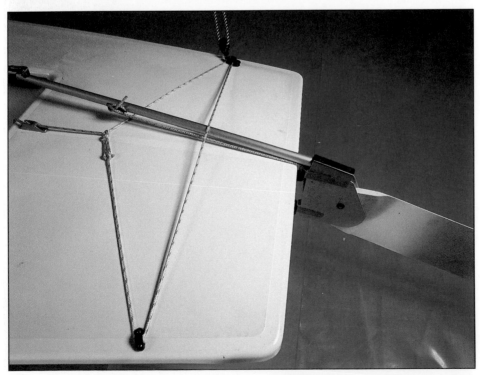

*The tiller fits into the rudder head and is retained by a pin. The line running to the blade is used for lowering and raising the rudder.*

## INSIDE

A dinghy may or may not have seats for its crew. Most multi-purpose dinghies have *thwarts*, or transverse seats. Thwarts are usually suspended from the outer edges of the boat's hull, the *gunwales*. The center thwart is the one on which the oarsman sits when rowing the dinghy, and is usually attached to the centerboard trunk as an added stiffening member. On some dinghies, that's all there will be; others may have forward and after thwarts as well.

Larger dinghies often have longitudinal seats port and starboard, and still others may have full sidedecks and small *cockpits*, in which the crew has a measure of security.

Seats or thwarts will often carry enclosed flotation material on their undersides, and boats with wide sidedecks will often have their flotation built-in under the deck area. This flotation, usually closed-cell foam material, should be capable of keeping the boat, its crew, and all gear afloat even when completely swamped. Needless to say, the flotation material should be securely fastened to the boat.

At or near the dinghy's transom, there should be a self-bailing device. Normally a small "trap-door" built into the boat's bottom near the stern, this device is designed to be opened when the boat becomes uncomfortably full of water. The motion of the boat is usually enough to suck out the water from inside. Note that the boat must have enough speed so that no water is able to run back in. On some dinghies, the self-bailer is at the bottom edge of the transom, but the principle is the same. Obviously, the self-bailer plug should be left open when the boat is out of the water on its trailer to allow any rainwater to drain.

All dinghies have some device for mounting the boat's mast. Called a *mast step*, this is simply a socket in the forward part of the boat's bottom, on the centerline, designed to accept the *butt* of the mast. On most dinghies, there is another mast support above the step, through which the mast passes. This is called the *mast partner*. On open dinghies, the partner is usually the forward thwart. On others, the forward deck (*foredeck*) provides partner support.

*This view of the cockpit well shows the mainsheet block and the hiking straps which allow the crew to lean or hike out of the boat to counterbalance any heeling. The sidedecks contain closed-cell buoyancy bags.*

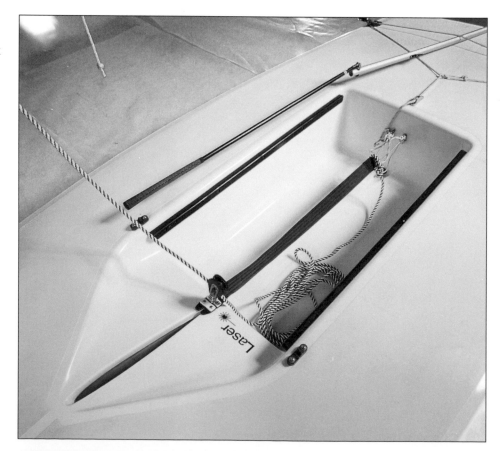

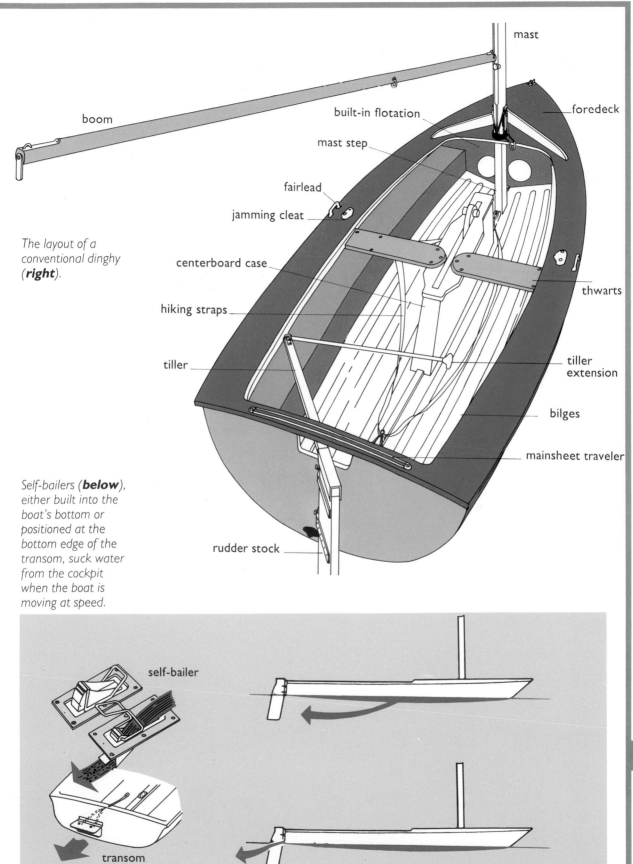

boom

mast

built-in flotation

foredeck

mast step

fairlead

jamming cleat

The layout of a conventional dinghy (**right**).

centerboard case

thwarts

hiking straps

tiller

tiller extension

bilges

mainsheet traveler

Self-bailers (**below**), either built into the boat's bottom or positioned at the bottom edge of the transom, suck water from the cockpit when the boat is moving at speed.

rudder stock

self-bailer

transom flaps

This comparison of the Laser I and Laser II dinghies illustrates the difference between a simple unstayed mast and a more complicated fully stayed mast. The Laser I is a single-handed dinghy, while the Laser II is a fairly sophisticated two-man dinghy.

## THE SPARS

The mast is the principal *spar* of any sailboat. On some dinghies, the mast can be broken down into two parts for stowage purpose. Most performance dinghies, however, have one-piece masts.

A mast need not always be built of wood. Hollow aluminum extrusions are becoming more common as dinghies become increasingly adapted to high performance. Aluminum is lighter and, in some cases, stronger than wood — and therefore has the advantage in portability and keeps weight low in the boat.

The *boom* is the other major spar and it attaches to the mast via a hinged device known as the *gooseneck*. The boom's purpose is to provide control for the lower edge, or *foot*, of the sail. The boom pivots on its gooseneck, allowing it to swing through an arc of approximately 180 degrees.

## STANDING RIGGING

There are two types of rigging: *standing rigging* and *running rigging*. Standing rigging is usually stainless steel cable that attaches to the upper points of a mast and leads to various points on the hull or deck for support. These "guy wires" are seen on larger dinghies and on cruising boats, but rarely have any purpose on small learner's dinghies. If your first dinghy has any standing rigging, it will most likely consist of a single forestay or cable extending from the head of the mast to the boat's prow. This single stay helps resist the bending forces produced by the tensions of the boat's single sail when sailing to windward. As boats get larger, they are also more likely to need a *backstay* which runs from masthead to transom.

All pieces of standing rigging supporting the mast in a fore-and-aft direction are known as *stays*. All pieces supporting in a transverse direction are called *shrouds*. Port and starboard *shrouds* run from the masthead, or additionally from points below that, to the sides of the hull adjacent ot the mast. These obviously help resist side-to-side bending forces.

Shrouds and stays usually attach to the mast via metal straps called *tangs*. Lower terminals of shrouds and stays are often adjustable via lashings or pieces of hardware called *turnbuckles* with opposite-threaded

fittings for tensioning the wire. Turnbuckles are attached to the boat's hull via strapping called *chainplates*.

As mentioned, small dinghies do not usually need standing rigging, as mast loads are minimal due to the small sail area and relatively high strength of the materials used in the rig. However, a larger boat with tall mast and much more sail needs stays and shrouds to help support its rig. The size of boat where standing rigging becomes practical and important is about 13–14ft.

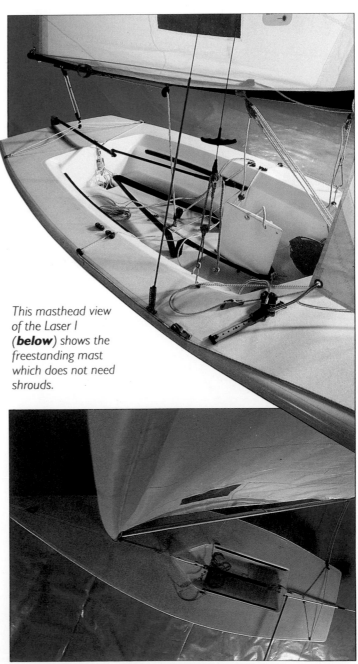

*The cockpit layout of the Laser II dinghy (**below**) has a typical degree of complexity, and features shrouds to provide lateral support to the mast.*

*This masthead view of the Laser I (**below**) shows the freestanding mast which does not need shrouds.*

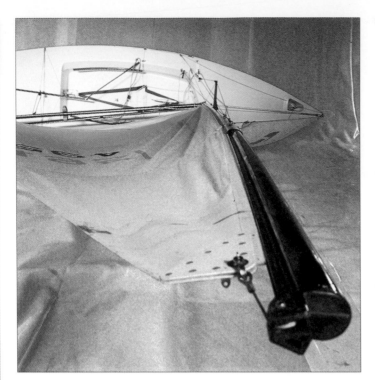

## RUNNING RIGGING

Running rigging provides sail control. It is composed of lines and cordage that attach to points on the boat's sail or sails and are hauled or slacked to manipulate them against the wind.

The two major types of running rigging are *halyards* and *sheets*. A halyard attaches to the top of a sail and is taken through a *halyard* block or *halyard sheave* at the masthead (a pulley or pulley wheel built into the mast itself) and down to the deck. A crewman simply hauls on the halyard to raise the sail.

A sheet is a length of cordage attached to the lower edge of a sail and used to *trim* that sail — that is, to haul the sail close for windward work, or to let it slack away for sailing off the wind. Sheets can attach to the boat's boom, or may attach to the loose foot of a sail without a boom. They are often led

*The mainsail on the Laser II (**above**) is hoisted by a halyard which runs over a sheave at the top of the mast.*

*This view of the two-man Laser II cockpit (**right**) shows the multitude of sail controls including the mainsheet, jib sheets and spinnaker sheets. The spinnaker itself is hoisted from a tube that runs from the fore end of the cockpit to an opening on the bow.*

through a set of blocks (pulleys) to gain proper positioning within the boat and some mechanical advantage.

The sheet that controls a boat's *mainsail* is called the *mainsheet*. The one that controls the *jib* (if any) is the *jibsheet*. Similarly, the halyards are named after the sails they hoist: *main halyard*, *jib halyard* and so on.

There is often a piece of cordage or wire rope across a dinghy's transom on which the mainsheet block slides port to starboard. This is called the *main traveler*. On more sophisticated boats, the mainsheet may have a complex "block-and-tackle" system which terminates on the boat in a track mounted to the deck or thwart. This track may be semicircular or straight, but will always run across the boat, or *athwartships*. This track serves the same purpose as the mainsheet traveler.

*The foredeck and jib sheeting on a two-man dinghy (**above**), showing the athwartships tracks which allow the crew to make precise adjustments to the jib trim.*

*The additional running rigging on a two-man dinghy requires close cooperation between helmsman and crew (**left**). While the helmsman steers and controls the mainsheet, the crew watches the set of the jib and responds to his partner's commands while feeding back information about boats ahead and wind changes.*

43

There will be a line attached to the rear corner of the mainsail at the outboard end of the boom. This line, which tensions the sail along the boom, is called the *outhaul*.

A similar line will be attached to the lower forward corner of the mainsail, and this will serve to tension the sail (once the main halyard has been set) by pulling down along the mast. This line is called the *downhaul*.

Note that there are numerous places for sheets, halyards and other pieces of running rigging to be fastened, or "made fast" aboard a boat. Twin-horned *cleats* are the normal fastening points for most running rigging. Halyards usually fasten to cleats positioned on the lower part of the mast. Sheets are usually wrapped around cleats inboard, near the center thwart.

The difference between sheets and halyards is that sheets should never be *belayed* on a cleat, while halyards should

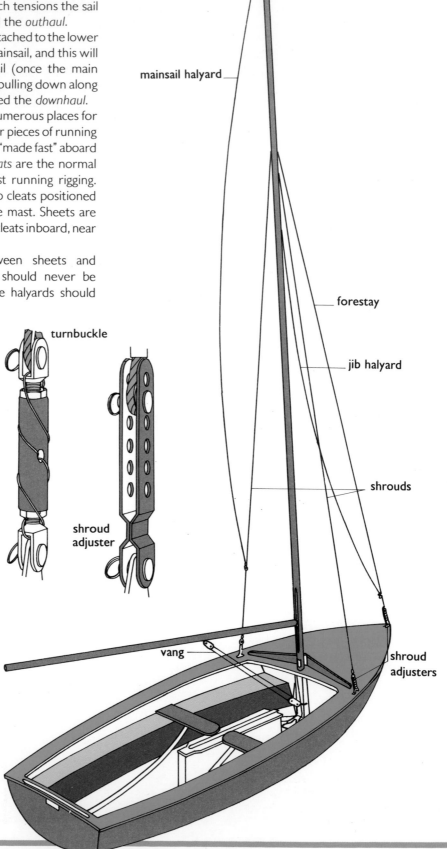

turnbuckle

mainsheet jammer

block

shroud adjuster

mainsail halyard

forestay

jib halyard

shrouds

vang

shroud adjusters

*The component parts of the dinghy rig set up and ready for sail hoisting.*

always be belayed. Belaying is the act of securely wrapping a line on a cleat, and then throwing a single half-hitch to secure it. A sheet should simply be wrapped around a cleat, with no hitch to belay it. This is because a crewman might want to free the sheet quickly, and a hitch on the cleat could slow that process.

On some mainsheet arrangements, a *cam–cleat* belays the line. This is a system using twin spring-loaded "cams" through which the sheet passes. The cams have saw-toothed edges which grip the line, allowing it to be hauled in but not released. When the skipper or crew wishes to release the sheet quickly, he need only grab it and flip it upwards and out of the grip of the cam–cleat.

One last piece of running rigging is the *topping lift*. This is a line run from the boom's outboard end to the masthead. It is used to carry the weight of the boom in the absence of the mainsail when the mainsail is lowered. It keeps the boom up and out of the boat, making it easy for the crew to secure sail and gear aboard. The topping lift can be run through a block at the masthead and down to the base of the mast, and operated like a halyard; or it may run from the masthead and down through a block at the end of the boom, where it can be manipulated by a crewman aft.

## SAILS

Most sailing dinghies only need one sail — the mainsail. However, some have a small sail forward of the mast, called the *jib*. A dinghy with a jib is said to be "sloop-rigged", while a single–sailed boat is a "catboat".

The mainsail has three corners; the top corner is the *head*; the forward lower corner is the *tack*; and the after lower corner is the *clew*. There are grommets or cringles at each corner, named after their location. The head grommet takes the fitting for the main halyard; the tack grommet takes the downhaul's fitting; and the clew grommet takes the end of the outhaul.

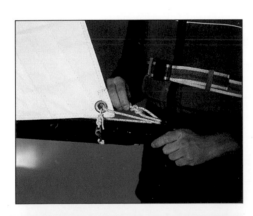

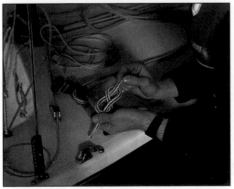

*The outhaul (**top**) is used to tension the sail along the boom. A figure-of-eight knot (**above**) is used to prevent sheets slipping back through blocks and fairleads.*

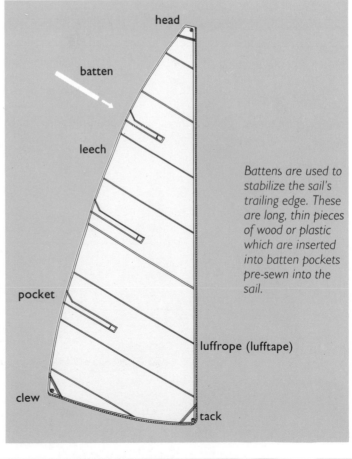

*Battens are used to stabilize the sail's trailing edge. These are long, thin pieces of wood or plastic which are inserted into batten pockets pre-sewn into the sail.*

The edge of the sail between the tack and head is called the *luff*. This is the leading edge of the sail, the edge that most often meets the wind. The edge between the tack and clew is called the *foot*. This is the edge that is attached to, or stretches along, the boom. The edge between head and clew is called the *leech*. This is the trailing edge of the sail.

The sail is made of *panels*, sewn together and shaped to maximize its aerodynamic qualities. In order to maintain the stability of the sail's trailing edge (leech), there may be several *batten pockets* sewn in. These receive long, thin pieces of wood or plastic that help stiffen the sail and create an arc along the trailing edge. This arc is called the *roach*. A full-roached sail is one with a pronounced arc along the leech and requires long and stiff battens; a shallow-roached sail has a slight arc and requires small (if any) battens.

To add stability at the luff and foot, rope or tape is often sewn-in to the edge of the sail. This provides good resistance to stretching as the sail is tensioned along those two axes. This rope is named after its sail-part: *luffrope*, *footrope* or *lufftape*, *foottape*.

On some larger dinghies, there may be a set of *reef points*. These allow the sail to be reduced in size in heavy conditions. First the topping lift is tensioned so that the mainsail halyard may be lowered without dumping the boom into the boat. Then the sail is lowered until the row of reefpoints aligns with the boom. The points are tied-off around the foot of the sail, bundling the sail together along the boom. Tension is taken on the main halyard, and the sail is again usable, though much smaller and capable of handling high winds comfortably.

On a sloop-rigged boat, the nomenclature for parts of the jib is similar to that of the mainsail. Its lower forward corner is called the *tack*; its top is its *head*; and its lower aft corner is its *clew*. Most jibs are "loose-footed", meaning that they have no boom to stabilize their lower edges. Rather, a jib's sheet is hanked to its clew, and tension is applied rearward to trim the sail.

Most sails are made of synthetic cloth, which makes them resistant to weathering easy to clean, and impervious to the effects of salt water. They are not, however, invulnerable and must be protected against the harmful effects of ultra-violet radiation. Dinghy sails must be hung up to dry.

*Simple reefing on a dinghy consists of either rolling the sail round the boom or lacing it down at the appropriate reef points to reduce sail to a more manageable area.*

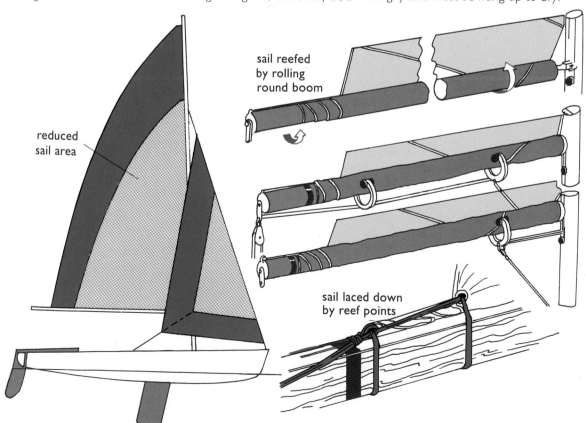

reduced sail area

sail reefed by rolling round boom

sail laced down by reef points

## BASIC SAFETY GEAR

Your dinghy will be equipped with all the gear necessary to handle it, but you will have to provide some extras.

It is wise to equip your boat with a set of oars and *oarlocks* (the fittings on which the oars bear and pivot) — or at the least a paddle or two. These can be stowed aboard, under the thwarts.

Life-saving gear is important. A dinghy should have flotation cushions aboard for both comfort and emergency buoyancy, and every member of crew should be required to wear a personal lifejacket at all times whether he swims or not.

A substantial length of light line should be attached to one of the flotation cushions, just in case someone falls overboard while underway. The cushion can be thrown to the man overboard, and the line hauled to bring him closer to the boat.

A strong waterproof flashlight capable of considerable range should also be included in any emergency kit. If you should get caught out after dark, the light should be shone periodically to signal your presence to other craft.

A small noise–making device — either a hand whistle or gas-propelled horn — should also be carried to attract the attention of other boatmen who may not notice you in crowded anchorages or in reduced visibility.

The boat should also have a hand-bailer and a sponge aboard, even though she may be equipped with a self-bailing device. Keeping the boat dry keeps you dry and more comfortable.

The U.S. Coast Guard lists the safety items required on a small boat. The list may be obtained from your nearest Coast Guard facility or from Coast Guard district headquarters.

## ADVANCED SAFETY GEAR

Flares and/or a hand-held radio–telephone are two other items you might want to add to your on-board kit.

In some areas, and on boats of a certain size, flare equipment is required. Marine hardware stores sell flare packages consisting of stick flares and a small gun for rockets. The gear is packed in a waterproof container and can be stowed almost anywhere.

A hand-held radio–telephone can be a life saver but is generally unnecessary in areas of high traffic. A bright-colored flag or shape for hand-signalling would certainly be less expensive, and might serve the purpose as well. At night, a stick flare could be used to attract attention in an emergency.

Remember that too much gear can be a hindrance aboard a small boat. Make sure you have the space to stow securely the equipment you bring along, and make sure you bring those things you'll really need before you start loading up with extras.

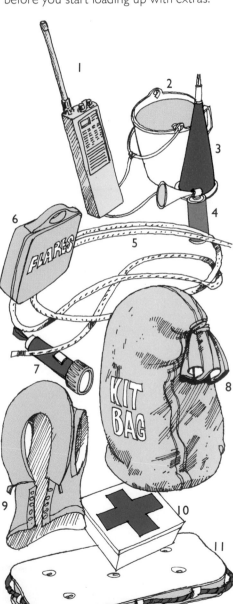

*Essential safety equipment should include: radio (**1**), bailing bucket (**2**), bullhorn (**3**), gas-propelled horn (**4**), spare line (**5**), flares (**6**), waterproof flashlight (**7**), waterproof kitbag (**8**), life jacket (**9**), first-aid kit (**10**), flotation cushion (**11**).*

# 5 | SMALL BOAT SAILING THEORY

*The ability to cope with ever-changing sea conditions is the key to successful dinghy sailing.*

**B**efore you start sailing, you need to know some general things about your boat and how she responds to the wind and water. The important basics are:
— The wind and how to understand and use it.
— The classic points of sail and what they mean.
— The several basic maneuvers.

The most basic of all is understanding the character of the wind you use. A sailor must be aware of the wind's direction, strength and how it affects his boat at all times. At first this takes much concentration but it soon becomes almost second nature.

## SEEING THE WIND

The wind, of course, is invisible. It is simply the air in motion, but how it affects the water can reflect its direction and strength. In fact, the water is a better wind indicator than almost anything else.

Waves are created by the wind, but only certain waves are indicative of the wind in your immediate surroundings.

**Swells** Swells are large, long-period waves that travel great distances. Although swells are first caused by wind — a storm at sea — they can orginate far away and can travel against "local" current and wind. Swells that travel inshore from a great distance are often called *ground swells* when they fetch up

in the shallow coastal banks. They usually do not reflect immediate weather conditions.

**Wind waves** Although wind waves are caused by local wind, they can grow into storm swells if acted upon by a large weather pattern in deep water. The wind waves you'll find will be those caused by the wind inshore. Sometimes, wind waves can ride on top of ground swells and act against the direction of a swell, causing a confused sea. Usually, wind waves are the biggest waves you'll be dealing with. Note that wind waves *always* travel in the overall direction of the local wind. They're the ones that break on top and create those foamy crests called *whitecaps*.

**Ripples** Ripples are the smallest of wind waves, and always show the latest trend in the wind's direction and strength. Groups of ripples may appear on the water's surface as dark patches, called "cat's paws". By the movement of these dark patches, you can tell where small, localized gusts are forming and in what direction they are moving. Sometimes cat's paws group to form whole sheets of ripples which show as huge dark blotches on the surface and indicate strong gusts.

It is important to learn to see the smallest ripples on the water's surface, even if that surface is lumpy with larger wind waves. Sometimes, the larger waves will reflect what the wind's direction was one or two hours ago, while the small ripples will show the current trend.

Probably the best way to understand the nature of the wind is to observe it as it affects the water. Note the progress of cat's paws on a windy day, and learn to use your senses to detect the wind. Feel the wind on your face, and listen to its rush in your ears. When you get out on your boat, you will find your increased sensitivity a great help in mastering the conditions.

## WIND SHIFTS

The wind can behave erratically, and the most common reason for shifts, lulls and puffs can be the local topography. Land masses can re-direct the wind, funnel it, and effectively block it as well.

Headlands can cause the wind to eddy and change direction. Sailing too close to a downwind headland can put a boat in a split

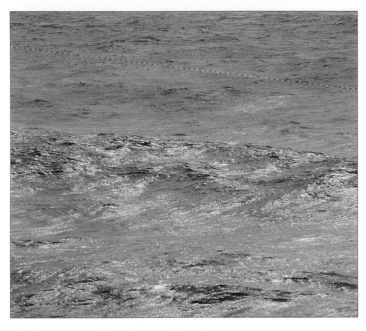

*Swells are caused by wind conditions far out at sea (**above**) which often bear no relation to local weather patterns.*

*Originating far offshore, a swell traveling inshore becomes a ground swell which will break fiercely by the time it reaches the beach (**above**).*

current of wind or even a reverse flow or "echo" off the land. Sailing around a windward headland can put you in a lull, only to expose you to a blast as you get around the end.

Two headlands separated by a low beach can create a funnel that actually "squeezes" the wind and boosts its speed. The same thing can happen at the mouth of a harbor or within a narrow channel between two islands.

There are also thermal phenomena created to a certain extent by topography. Local wind conditions often vary according to the time of day because of the uneven heating and cooling of the land. Because of this, daily shifts in wind occur. The process is best illustrated by a typical summer day in a temperate region.

**Morning** Land and water are at thermal equilibrium as the sun warms the air. There can be no convection, the flow of air from cool to hot, so there is no wind.

**Midday** The land is warming rapidly, the water is staying at its normal summer temperature. As the air over the land warms, it starts to rise. The air over the water, being cooler, moves in to displace the rising land-air, and a convection begins. This is the start of the sea breeze or onshore breeze.

**Afternoon** The convection is in full swing, and the sea breeze is getting stronger. This is the warmest part of the day in many seaside locations, and therefore the wind's potential is greatest now.

**Late Afternoon** With the sun low on the horizon, the trend is back toward thermal equilibrium. The afternoon breeze begins dying.

**Evening** Thermal equilibrium is again achieved. No wind.

**Late Night** Sometimes an offshore or "land" breeze can develop if the night is clear enough and the atmosphere allows enough heat to radiate from the land. Because the water holds heat better, a thermal imbalance can develop and a convection can begin, though seldom as vigorous as the daytime version.

Obviously, large weather systems can also cause extreme wind shifts. However, these are usually associated with periods of extreme weather and are irrelevant for the

*Land masses bend and modify wind direction and force, causing funneling between high cliffs or more extreme effects due to blanketing (i.e., blocking the wind).*

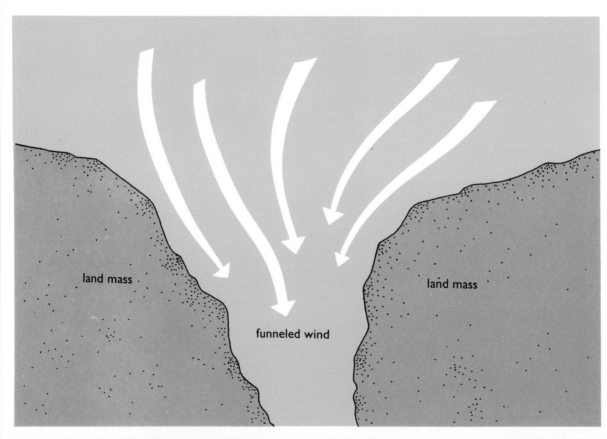

land mass

land mass

funneled wind

novice, who should not venture out during such periods.

## TELLTALES

Flags are the most basic form of wind indicator. But a flag on a pole ashore will indicate only how the wind is blowing atop its staff; it will not tell you the nature of the wind in your location.

For that you need a wind indicator aboard. On larger cruising boats, ribbons tied to the shrouds are the simplest form of wind indicator. As many small dinghies do not have shrouds, however, a masthead windvane is necessary. Regardless of the type of boat, a skipper needs more than just his own wind sense to monitor the exact direction of the wind.

One thing to keep in mind about wind indicators is that they show only *apparent wind*. As a boat moves through the water under any propulsive force — be it sail, oars or outboard — it creates its own wind. And the vector (the force and direction) of that motion-created wind (always straight ahead) combines with the vector of the natural or "true" wind to modify its direction.

If there is no natural breeze, the apparent wind will be straight ahead. If the true wind is straight ahead, the apparent wind will also be straight ahead, but stronger for the

*Flags, either onshore (**above left**) or out on a buoy (**above**), provide easy clues to wind direction.*

*Tell tales, burgees or windvanes (**below**) provide visible evidence of the apparent wind and*

*help the sailor to trim sail accordingly.*

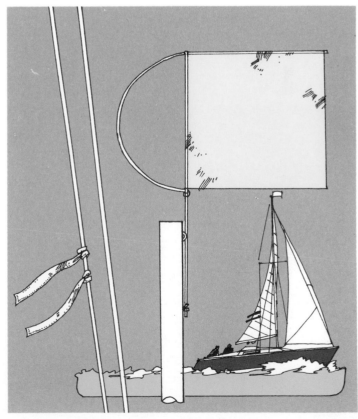

**1**

**2**

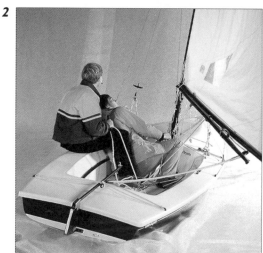

**3**

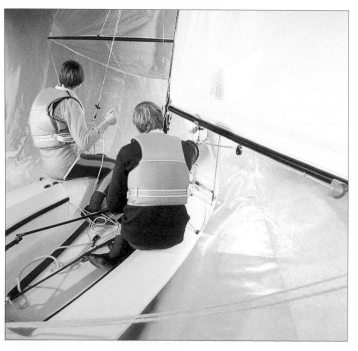

The three basic points of sailing are close-hauled (**1**), reaching (**2**) and running (**3**), and each requires different responses from the crew both in terms of sail trim and balance. When running downwind, the spinnaker provides an enormous amount of extra sail area, although interestingly the fastest point of sailing is the reach, when the apparent wind is high and the sails act as airfoils.

motion of the boat. If the natural wind is right behind, the apparent wind will reduce or even nullify its effect — or be reduced itself, depending on which is greater, the speed of the boat or the strength of the following wind.

And if the natural wind is perpendicular to the boat's direction of travel, or at any other angle, the motion of the boat will add a vector and tend to swing the true wind toward the direction of its travel.

None of this really matters while sailing, as the wind a sailor deals with is always the apparent wind. Therefore, his own sense and his own on-board wind indicators are the most appropriate sources of information on the wind.

### THE CLASSIC POINTS OF SAIL

There are three basic angles — or points on the compass relative to the wind's apparent direction — on which a boat may sail. These angles are described with specific terms.

**The reach** When the wind is said to be "on the beam" and the boat is sailing along a course perpendicular to the wind's apparent direction. Here, the sail is acting rather like a wing, developing lift and spilling the breeze astern to create propulsion. A reach is normally the fastest, most efficient point of sail.

**Close-hauled** When the boat is sailing at an acute angle to the apparent wind, with sails hauled in as far as possible. Here the sail is a true wing, developing lift at its leading edge due to the way it is set relative to the wind.

**The run** Where the wind is astern, and the boat is traveling in the same direction as the wind is moving. Here, the sail is not a wing at all, but rather a "pocket" which simply catches the wind for propulsion.

Of course, there are points in between:

*The close reach* The point or points between the reach and close-hauled. The sail acts like a wing on these points.

*The broad reach* The point or points between the reach and the run. Here again, the sail acts most like a "pocket" in catching the force of the wind.

### SAIL TRIM

Achieving the points of sail involves more than simply steering the boat with the tiller. Sail trim is very important, as boat

performance depends more on it than anything else.

On a reach, the sail must be trimmed so that just enough wind is captured, and some is allowed to spill away astern. The best way to achieve this trim is to slack the mainsheet away until the sail begins to ripple along its luff. Then trim the sheet until the fluttering is just eliminated. This is called *trimming to the point of draw*, or trimming until the sail just begins to "draw" the breeze effectively.

On a close reach and when close-hauled, the angle of trim will be tighter inboard, but the same principle applies. The sail is a wing.

Note that the reach, close reach, and close-hauled (windward) points of sail are those that display the true aerodynamic lift of the modern rig. And it is on these points that effective trimming can mean the difference between sailing poorly or sailing well.

When sailing on a broad reach or run, however, the sail is just a pocket to create "push" for the boat along with the wind. Therefore, angle of trim is not as critical. On these points of sail, the sailor must learn to watch his on-board telltales and gauge the angles at which the wind is striking the sail.

*Perfectly balanced and set up on a close reach, the crew concentrate on keeping the boat level and the sails drawing and trimmed for maximum power.*

### THE MANEUVERS

There are several basic maneuvers involved in handling a boat between all the major points of sail:

*Heading up* When a sailor wants to change course toward the direction of the wind, he heads up. For example, let's say he's on a reach and wishes to come up to a close reach, toward the wind. He steers toward the wind's direction and trims his sails accordingly. To go from a close reach to close-hauled, he heads up further.

*Falling off* This is the opposite to heading up; steering away from the wind. As the boat falls off from the close-hauled direction, for example, sail is slacked off for a close reach . . . and so on.

*Rounding up* This is the process of coming directly up into the wind so as to allow the wind to pass around both sides of a close-hauled sail. It is used to slow the boat and take wind pressure off the rig.

In addition to these general maneuvers, there are the two specific turning maneuvers: coming about and jibing.

*A boat is said to be on starboard tack when it is sailing with the wind coming over the starboard side. Likewise, a boat is on port tack when the wind comes over the port side.*

**Coming About** This maneuver is designed to turn the boat *through* the eye of the wind. When a boat is sailing with the wind coming over the starboard side, it is said to be on the *starboard tack*, no matter what point of sail it is on. Coming about swings the boat's bow through the eye of the wind, so that the wind blows over the opposite (port) side. The boat is then said to be on the *port tack*.

For example, let's say a boat is on the starboard tack, on a reach. To come about, the skipper must head up, trimming his sail through the close reach and to the close-hauled condition. He then pushes the tiller over and swings the boat through the eye of the wind. The sail flutters as the bow swings through, and then the boat begins to fall off away from the wind. If the skipper wants to return to a reach, on the port tack, he falls off through a close-hauled port tack, through a close reach, and trims for a port-tack reach.

**Jibing** This maneuver also gets the wind around to the other side of the boat, but involves a turn *downwind*, away from the

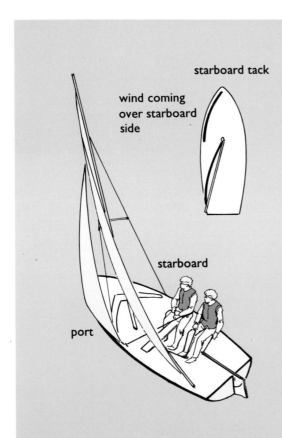

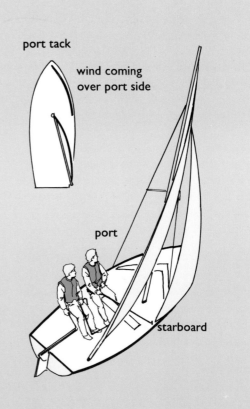

starboard tack

wind coming over starboard side

port tack

wind coming over port side

starboard

port

port

starboard

wind's direction. The process entails falling off until the wind is directly astern, and the boat is on a run. Sail is then trimmed in until the wind is just about ready to catch the leech and swing the boom over. The boat is then turned so that its stern passes through the wind's eye and the sail snaps over to the desired side.

Jibing is a maneuver to be mastered slowly and carefully. In light winds, it can be easy, but in heavy going, the wind can take the boom around quickly and sometimes out of control.

When a boat is sailing at a point of sail between a reach and close-hauled, it is always wise to come about when a change of direction is called for. Only when a boat is sailing well off the wind, on a very broad reach or a dead run, is it wise or proper to execute a jibe, and even then it should be attempted with extreme care.

There is one more maneuver which will come in handy during the first phase of the learning process.

*Luffing* This is the practice of heading up without trimming sail. The wind is purposely allowed to get around the leading edge of the sail and spill off to leeward, fluttering the luff of the sail. This process dumps wind and slows the boat, taking pressure off the rig. Luffing can be used when things get slightly hectic, or when the wind gets too strong for the rig to handle. The sail can be luffed to whatever extent a skipper desires, depending on the strength of the wind.

## WHAT'S NEXT

A basic understanding of the maneuvers and points of sail provides the theory behind the art of sailing. But performing the maneuvers and understanding the dynamics of sail trim at each point are other matters entirely.

The next step is to get aboard and learn the moves within the context of the sailing dinghy. If you take aboard with you a good understanding of the aerodynamics of the rig and the function of the basic components of the boat, plus a familiarity with the terms of sailing, you'll be ready to master the process in real life.

*A sailboat can sail in every direction except dead into the wind. To sail any course between the major points of sail, it is necessary to come about (tack) or jibe.*

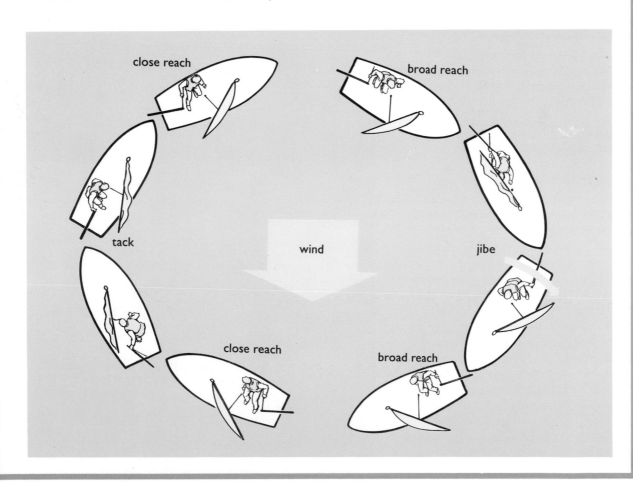

# **6** | **GETTING UNDERWAY**

*The dinghy launching area, a scene of colorful activity as crews prepare to go afloat.*

You have now explored the basic theories of sailing; it's time to put some of it into practice.

The important thing to remember is that each principle is interrelated to all the others, and all combine to form the maneuvers and basic points of sail discussed. No single maneuver can be performed without understanding all the basics. If you are unsure about any of the theories and techniques so far explained, review them now *before* you embark on the practical instruction in this section.

### MAN (OR WOMAN) POWER

Assume you've bought or acquired a small open sailing dinghy with dismountable cat rig. Before you assemble your boat and try to sail her away, you should get more familiar with her. Because the boat is so small, she will react rapidly to shifts in weight, changes in wind strength, steering input and other outside forces. This could surprise you if you do not get used to her motion and reactions.

After launching, but before putting the rig together, climb aboard. Sit on the middle thwart, or crouch near the middle of the boat if there is no thwart. Shift your weight side-to-side slowly; feel the way the boat heels to your weight shift, and make a mental note of what your changes in position do to the angle of heel. Now go forward, and aft. Get a feel for the boat's attitude changes. The attitude a boat takes in the water relative to her designed waterline is called her *trim*.

Now stand up — making sure to do it right amidships and on the boat's centerline. Step side-to-side slowly, keeping aware of the effect your weight shift has on the boat. Again, shift fore-and-aft. Your weight will affect the boat's equilibrium more drastically when you are standing up because your own center of gravity actually raises the boat's, and makes her less stable. Of course, when moving around aboard, it's best to keep your weight as low as possible; and when stepping aboard, it is wise to crouch down as soon as possible.

Now have a friend or family member climb aboard. Try the movements you've just done again, with one person seated motionless and the other shifting weight. Watch how this affects the boat's attitude in the water. Note that while one person moves about, the other can often counter the weight shifts with his or her own weight. This is the most basic method of controlling a small boat's trim.

Again, before rigging the boat for sail, it's important to learn other means of propulsion. If your boat is an open sailing dinghy, she probably has oars and a set of oarlocks. Learn to use them properly. See what reaction the boat produces to the various basic oar strokes. Learn how to mount and dismount the oarlocks easily and quickly, and decide on the safest and best method to stow (the sailor's term for "store") the oars and oarlocks aboard.

If your boat does not have oars and oarlocks, she should have at least one paddle. Learn how to use it, and if there are two paddles, practice with your crew. Either oars or a paddle will have to be used eventually, and each boat has its own way of responding to manual propulsion.

There is one more way of moving by muscle-power: sculling. This consists of working the boat's tiller back and forth, side-to-side. The resultant oscillation of the rudder underwater creates thrust which moves the boat. Sculling is handy for short distances, and especially when you want to turn your boat in close quarters or help with a maneuver under sail in light winds. Practice

sculling, especially to turn your boat, as it can be more convenient than rowing or paddling in certain situations, but note that it is no substitute for either.

By pushing your boat along with oars or paddles — or by sculling her — you will find out how easily or not she moves through the water, and the kind of momentum she has once underway. By trying to move her against the wind, across the wind, with the wind and into a choppy sea, you will also understand how she'll behave in various adverse conditions should you ever need to row or paddle in an emergency on open water.

*The best way to get to know your boat is to step aboard and feel how she reacts to your weight.*

*Sculling (**1**), paddling (**2**) and rowing (**3**) are all essential skills.*

*Most rudders have a simple retaining clip (**below**) to stop them from riding up (**below right**) when underway.*

## RIGGING THE DINGHY

Getting the sailing dinghy ready to sail is actually quite simple, made so by the relatively few pieces of gear that make up the whole. There are the components attached to the hull to facilitate steering and lateral stability, and the components of the rig itself. Let's take them one at a time, in order of typical installation.

**Rudder** Installed on the hull via its mating gudgeons and pintles. The pintles are normally on the rudder itself, with the gudgeons on the boat's transom. This is sometimes reversed, but the principle remains the same. Make sure to fasten whatever system is provided with any hold-down hardware included, so the rudder is prevented from floating up and off its mounts while underway.

**Centerboard or daggerboard** A centerboard need only be lowered within its trunk and secured. A daggerboard, on the other hand, must be inserted into its trunk. Many daggerboards have pins that must be inserted to prevent them from riding up and out of their slots. A daggerboard is often

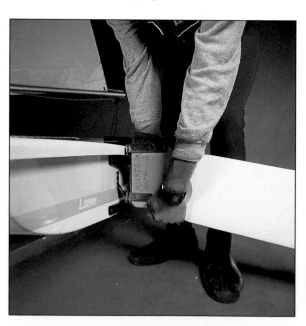

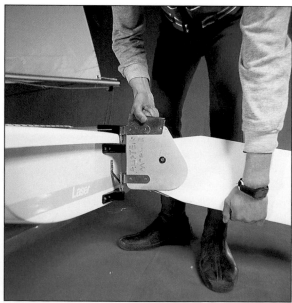

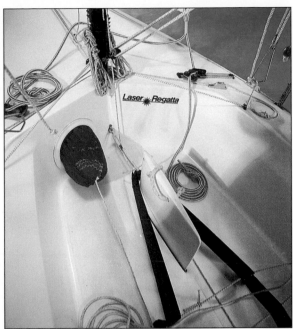

fashioned with one longer edge, and this edge should face forward.

**Mast** Raise the mast vertically over its step, and lower it slowly so that it fits firmly into its socket. Make sure the side designed to take the luff of the mainsail is facing aft. Fasten any standing rigging as necessary, and follow manufacturer's guidelines on rigging tension.

The next two steps can often be interchanged, depending on how the dinghy's boom is joined to its mainsail.

**Boom** The gooseneck is attached to the mast. The boom end often rests in the boat while the end of the mainsheet is attached to the main traveler, and its hauling end is taken through the necessary order of blocks (pulleys). The hauling end is then coiled and stowed on the dinghy's floorboards or thwart. The boom end then can be cradled in its own *boom crutch*, or supported by its topping lift, or simply left resting in the boat, while the next step is taken.

**Mainsail** Sometimes, the mainsail may be hoisted on the mast before the boom is rigged. But often it is done in this order.

*Daggerboards are installed by sliding them into their trunk (**above left**) with the longer or fatter edge facing forward (**above**).*

*Cleating off the jib halyard (**below left**) and fitting the battens into their pockets (**below**).*

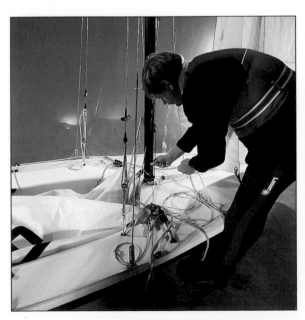

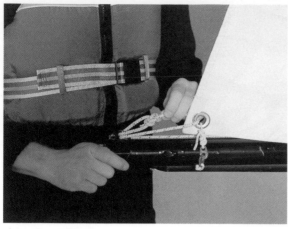

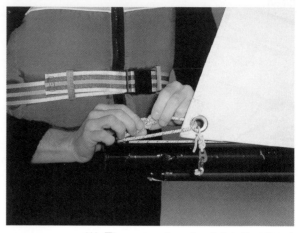

*A bowline (**above right**) is the most useful knot afloat; here the crew uses it to attach the outhaul to the boom (**above**).*
*This mainsail is fitted with a downhaul or cunningham (**right**).*
*The boom is attached to the mast via the gooseneck (**below**).*
*The vang (**below right**) is then tensioned to prevent the boom rising and to give extra control over sail shape.*

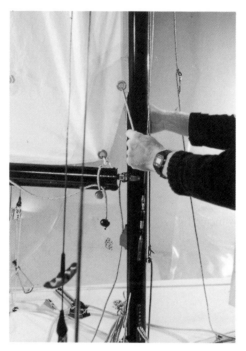

*(1)* The mainsail, or "main", is first fitted to the boom, via a set of slides on the sail which attach to a track on the boom; or a groove in the boom might accept the sail's footrope; or the sail may not attach at all along its foot, but simply be stretched along the boom between its tack and its clew. (This last is a type of *loose-footed* mainsail.)

*(2)* The sail is then attached to the mast via a set of slides on the sail and a mast-mounted track, or a groove on the mast and a corresponding luffrope on the sail.

*(3)* The outhaul is made fast to the clew of the mainsail, and the tack fitting is secured to the tack of the sail at the gooseneck. The sail is then stretched (not too tightly) along the boom.

*(4)* The main halyard is attached to the head of the mainsail, and the sail is hoisted. Make sure the slides or luffrope moves smoothly along track or groove while

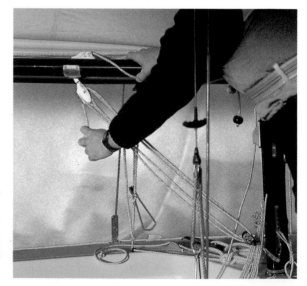

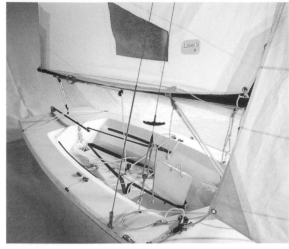

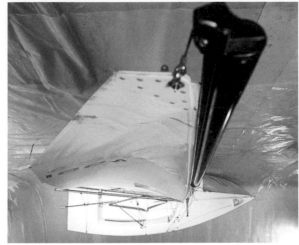

hoisting the sail. The skipper should take care to see that the mainsheet is running free, that the boat is pointed to windward so that the sail will dump all its wind (keeping the boom from swinging away from the boat), and that all other gear is stowed aboard in a proper fashion. The main halyard is belayed firmly at its cleat so that the luff of the sail is in modest tension — enough to take the wrinkles out of the luffrope and adjacent sail panels.

**Other gear** Now is the time to stow personal gear aboard, as well as the necessary safety gear, keeping weight as low as possible. If the dinghy is decked wear a buoyancy aid or a lifejacket. Oars and paddles should be aboard, as should the basic safety kit with its signalling gear. There also should be at least two 20ft lengths of synthetic line (³⁄₁₆in will do) aboard to use as docklines or towlines should the need arise.

## SAILING OFF

At this point, you are close to being able to run out and go sailing. But just close, not there yet — because there are some critical maneuvers to be learned before all the parts fit together. First you must learn something about the problems of leaving dry land — preferably before trying it in practice.

**Leaving a dock** For your first sail, try to choose a dock for your departure point. When sailing away from a dock, it is sometimes tricky to get your boat to point directly to windward for hoisting sail. Try to get her to the face of the dock that's closest to being aligned with the wind, then allow enough slack to your sheet to let the boom swing and the sail vane into the wind. Watch the boom so that it doesn't hit the dock or

any of its fittings.

Once sail is hoisted, you can push your boat's bow off and trim for a point of sail that will take you away from the face of the dock and into the clear.

If it is impossible to find a face of the dock more or less aligned with the wind, you'd be better off to paddle or scull away from the dock, to windward, and hoist sail there.

In any casting-off maneuver, make sure you know exactly what point of sail you'll be on and how you will want your sail to be trimmed before you actually sail away. Have your route into the clear planned in advance — including where you'll be coming about and how you'll execute the turns and various angles of sail trim — and be aware of traffic and wind gusts just the moment before casting off.

**Letting go a mooring** A mooring is a large anchor set permanently on the bottom, with a large-diameter line or chain securing it to a float. A mooring is prone to tide and current, and a skipper must provide a way to shuttle between his boat and the shore. It is still best to practice from a dock first, but the art of casting off and picking up a mooring is a good one to know, and therefore bears covering in this section.

The procedure is quite simple. In most cases, a boat will already be riding into the wind as she sits on her mooring. And, as we've seen, hoisting sail is made easy when the boat is pointed to windward.

When sail is hoisted, make sure to take note of the wind's direction, as it will dictate the point of sail on which you will start off.

Cast off the mooring then pull the mainsail over *toward the side of your planned first tack.* If you want to start on the

*Basic sail shape (**above, above left**) depends on the correct tensioning of outhaul, cunningham, and main halyard.*

## LETTING GO A MOORING

**4** trim sails

**3** fall off

wind

**2** back jib

**1** let go mooring

## LEAVING A DOCK

**4** trim sails

**2 & 3** back jib

**1** cast off

wind

**1** cast off

**4** trim sails

**3** fall off

**2** back jib

**2 & 3** trim sails

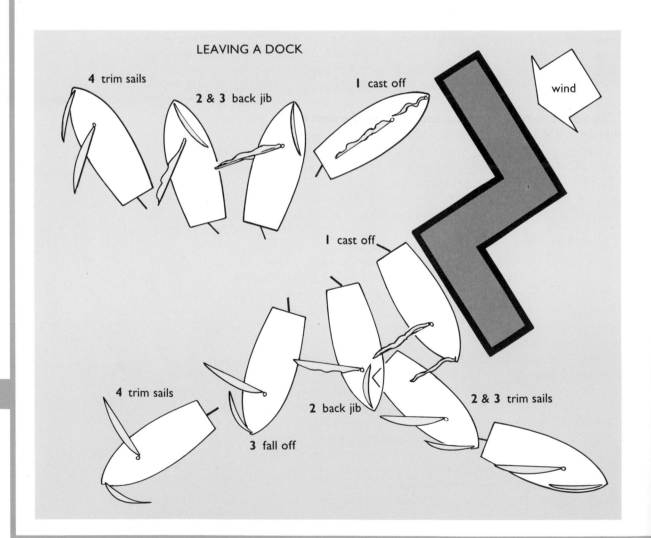

starboard tack, pull the sail over to starboard, catching some wind. If need be, push the boom outboard and to starboard against the force of the wind. This procedure is called *backing* the mainsail and is effective in pushing your boat's bow off the wind.

Your boat's bow should fall away to port using the above method. Once fallen off enough to trim for the starboard tack, let your sail back aboard, let it fill normally, haul your rudder amidships for control, and trim for whatever point of sail you wish to use to get clear of your mooring. Obviously, to fall away on the port tack, backwind your sail to port, fall away, trim, and sail off on the port tack.

**Sailing from a beach** This is one of the most awkward maneuvers in sailing, and it should be avoided during the beginning phase. However, it is sometimes necessary to launch from a beach or boat ramp.

A beginner should then rig his boat, but he may have to keep the rudder (unless it is retractable) in the boat and the centerboard raised until he gets to deeper water where there is no danger of accidental grounding and he can then attempt to attach the rudder.

Should the wind be blowing strongly offshore — that is, from the direction of the beach itself — sail should not be hoisted at all until the boat is paddled or rowed some distance offshore, because initial maneuvers could become uncontrollable and some damage to the gooseneck fitting or the sail could result from the boom's swinging too far offwind. The boat should be rowed out, turned toward the wind, and sail raised only then.

If the wind is blowing along the beach allowing the boom to swing out to one side or other and swing free without damaging the gooseneck fitting or sail, then sail could be hoisted and the boat paddled slowly offshore.

Note that the main thing is to get to water sufficiently deep in which the centerboard (or daggerboard) and rudder can be rigged for sailing. If your boat is shallow enough so that you can walk her into water deep enough, fine, but most people prefer to stay dry and row or paddle off a beach. Once clear, all you need do is point the bow to windward, fit rudder (not easy) and centerboard, hoist sail (if you haven't already) and backwind toward the side you'd like the wind on (as in sailing from a mooring). Once the boat is positioned to sail, trim the sheet for whatever point of sail you want, and you're off.

wind

I launch with rudder raised

4 trim sails

3 mainsail trimmed, crew aboard

2 helmsman aboard

**SAILING FROM A BEACH**

# 7 | MASTERING THE MANEUVERS

*A fleet of Lasers rounding a mark in close company — a time for split-second timing and perfect boat control.*

You now know exactly how to start sailing — and no more. You have perhaps gained a vague sense of the maneuvers and points of sail, but until the techniques involved are actually attempted, your knowledge will be incomplete.

What follows is a study of the *activity* of sailing — how the crew and boat work together, what movements are required to accomplish the basic maneuvers, and what to expect from the boat when certain commands are executed.

### SOME REVIEW

A boat can sail in a direction exactly perpendicular to the wind by capturing the breeze in its sails and re-directing its thrust to move forward, with the keel preventing sideslip and helping the boat move as well.

A boat can also sail all the points in between (see p.24).

The smallest angle at which a boat may sail effectively to windward is the *close-hauled* point of sail, and that angle is usually between 40 and 50 degrees.

A boat may take the wind over either side, port or starboard, simply by changing direction of travel relative to that of the wind. When a boat changes direction so as to pass her bow through the wind and take her sails around to the opposite side, she is said to be *coming about*. If the wind is coming over the starboard side, filling the sails to port, she is on the *starboard tack*. When she's taking the wind over the port side, she is on the *port tack*. Note again that this term applies to all points of sail relative to the wind's direction.

When a boat widens her angle to the wind, she is said to be *falling off*. When she falls off enough to take the wind at about 90 degrees of her direction of travel, she is said to be *reaching*. Between the beat and the reach is a point of sail known as a *close reach*. To achieve this point of sail from a beat, the boat is allowed to fall off slightly. To achieve it from a reach, the boat *heads up* on the wind. Any of these points of sail can be achieved on either the port or starboard tack.

By falling off from a reach, you achieve a *broad reach*, and by falling off so that the wind is coming from directly astern, you achieve a *run*.

All these are simply the terms of sailing. Now to the maneuvers.

## SETTING UP THE REACH

Let's examine the most efficient, fastest, easiest point of sail — the reach. To illustrate the fine points, picture a boat out on an open body of water in a good breeze.

You are sailing out on the bay, and the wind is perpendicular to the direction of travel and coming over the starboard side. The boom, then, is carried by the sail over to port. You are on the *starboard tack*.

If the sail is trimmed in tight, flattening it against the wind's force, the dinghy just lies over and wallows, moving poorly and simply laboring under an over-trimmed press of sail. The cure is to slack or "ease" the sheet, to *pay it out* until some of the wind spills off its leech.

When this is done, the boat jumps ahead and comes alive. If you continue to pay out the sheet slowly, you will soon see some wind beginning to flutter around the luff. If the sheet is paid out farther, the boom will trail off to leeward and the sail will begin to flutter like a flag. The boat will also slow to a stop.

When the sail begins that first faint flutter as the wind tries to get around the luff, the sheet is hauled in just enough to stop it. This is *trimming to the point of draw*, and it

**Reaching** *Start with the sail trimmed in tight and the boat heading up into the wind (**1**).* *Now bear away and sheet out so that the sail fills (**2**). With the boat smoothly* *accelerating and the sail trimmed to the point of draw, sit out to counterbalance the heel (**3**) and watch the luff for any sign of fluttering.*

applies to more than half the sailing you'll do. It is, in other words, a factor in *reaching*, *close-reaching*, and in beating, ie, the *close-hauled* condition.

As you begin to master the reach in a moderate breeze, take care to position your weight properly in the boat. Note that the wind pressure heels the boat over to

The purpose of hiking out (**above**) is to limit the degree of heel, and judging just how far you should hike out takes some practice. The secret is to always be on the lookout for gusts and lulls and to move your weight in or out (**below**) as necessary, all the time watching the luff of the jib.

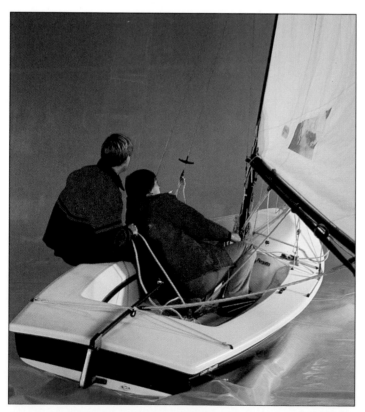

leeward, and that the pressure must be balanced with a shift of weight to the windward side. If you are alone, the wind's strength may be too much for your weight, even if you're sitting as far outboard as possible.

Now is the time for some acrobatics. First get your weight up and onto the edge of the boat's gunwale or deck. Plant your feet in the cockpit and hang on to the boat's rail with your free hand (snug the mainsheet into a cam-cleat or take a quick turn on a standard cleat). Some boats have straps designed to secure your feet in the cockpit while you are positioned out on deck. With these straps, you can lever your body over the side and far outboard — a practice called *hiking*, from which the straps get their name, *hiking straps*.

On some dinghies, the tiller will have an extension called a *hiking stick*, which is designed to allow the skipper to steer while seated far out on the boat's rail or even while leaning far out over the water. All these tools — stick and straps, and such — are fine for the performance sailor or the daysailor who has mastered the basics, but for now, do not attempt to hike outboard too far. Keep your weight safely inboard, and use some other method to keep an even keel in a breeze.

You must also be aware continually of the balance between your weight and the wind's pressure. Be prepared to get back inboard in lulls, and hike out further in the puffs.

There comes a time when comfort or just plain physics dictate that your weight is no longer enough to counteract the wind's force. Then you must *luff up* into the breeze or pay out the sheet so that the sail luffs slightly.

Let's say you're on a reach and the wind begins to overpower you, even though you are hiked out to the limits of your ability.

There are two ways of luffing the sail and "dumping" wind. The first is simply to let the natural tug of weather helm head the boat upwind. Once the boat is relieved of the pressure of wind in her sails, but before all the wind is dumped, stop her heading-up by hauling the tiller amidships again. The sail is now luffing, but not completely. Some of it is still catching wind, and it's enough to keep you moving under control. This is *luffing up*.

The other way to luff your sail is to pay out sheet until the wind is dumped. You can let the sail luff without changing the boat's direction, slow down, and get back under control. Should you want to continue your reaching perpendicularly across the wind, this is the method to use, because it involves no change in direction.

Mastering a boat on a reach in a good breeze is not easy. It is the basis for all future skills. Knowing how to balance the boat in gusts and lulls and against all wind strengths, and knowing how to ease the pressure of the wind in the sail by luffing are techniques vital to all other points of sail.

## COMING ABOUT

*(1)* The boat is on a reach, on the starboard tack. You now want to go back in the opposite direction, so you change tacks, or come about. Coming about — or changing tacks, or in today's vernacular, "tacking" — is simply the act of turning the boat's bow through the eye of the wind so that the sails take the wind on the side opposite that which it was on when the maneuver began.

Head up to windward at the beginning of the maneuver *(2)*, hauling on the sheet to get set for the moment at which you are on a close reach, starboard tack. Keep heading up *(3)*, hauling even more to get her set close-hauled. It is then that you swing her right through the wind's eye *(4)*.

As you come through the eye, the wind flutters the sail briefly, before she begins to fall off on the other tack . . . the port tack *(5)*. At first, the boat is close-hauled on port tack, but as she falls off further, she begins a close reach, port tack *(6)*. As this happens, pay out the sheet so as to maintain the proper sail trim. Finally, after falling off and paying out sheet gradually, you are on a reach again, this time with the wind over the port rail — the port tack reach *(7)*.

*Coming about or tacking from reach to reach involves precise sail trimming at each stage of the maneuver, and is essential practice for the novice. You should aim for a smooth transition with minimal loss of speed.*

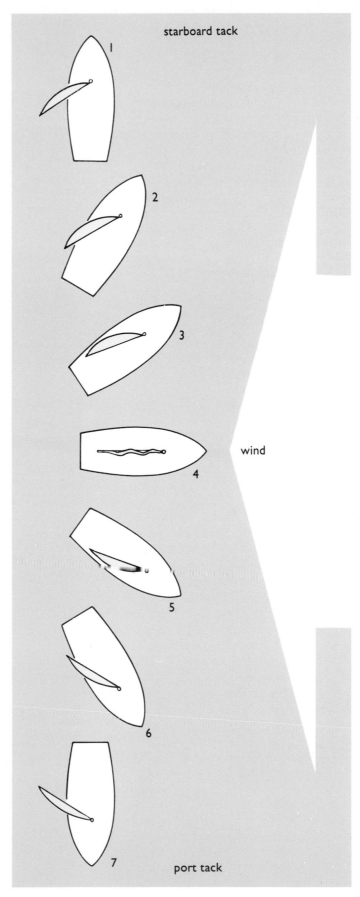

starboard tack

wind

port tack

67

## JIBING

Jibing is a maneuver designed to move the boat from one tack to another by passing its *stern* through the eye of the wind and letting the wind swing the leach of the sail across from one side to the other. Jibing is relatively hazardous, to be practiced in light winds at first, until the beginner has mastered all the steps in sail-handling and weight-shifting.

Again, an example. The boat is on a reach on the starboard tack *(1)*. Fall off slowly and deliberately so that the boat is broad-reaching on the starboard tack, being pushed along by a brisk breeze *(2)*. You will have shifted your weight slightly inboard now, because the force of the wind in the sails is not as intent on heeling the boat as it is on pushing it along.

Now fall off still farther until the wind is directly astern, and the sheet is paid out so the boom is straight off to the port side *(3)*. You are now on a run, your weight more directly on the centerline of the boat, and amidships. At this point, you need only counterbalance the weight of the boom as it hangs suspended off to the port side.

Pay particular attention now because you could get into serious trouble. The wind could get around behind the sail if you turn too much to port (toward the side the boom's on), or if the breeze shifts a few points clockwise. If the wind got around behind the sail, you would hear a loud slap as the sail suddenly filled from the other side and came around hard, carrying the boom violently and uncontrollably across the boat.

This is the accidental jibe, and is something you should not allow. When running offwind, pay constant attention to the wind direction and your sail's position.

In a controlled jibe, begin to haul in the sheet before you steer through the eye of the wind *(4)*. You do this as you bear off directly downwind. Then, as you steer the boat's stern through the eye of the wind, toward the side your boom is on, trim the sheet in even more, until the wind gets around behind the sail and takes it across *(5)*. Duck your head to keep clear of the boom, and let the sail take some sheet out of your hand as it fills away on the opposite tack after jibing. Pay out the sheet until you are sailing on a run *(6)*, with the boom to starboard.

Note that you should not have to do too

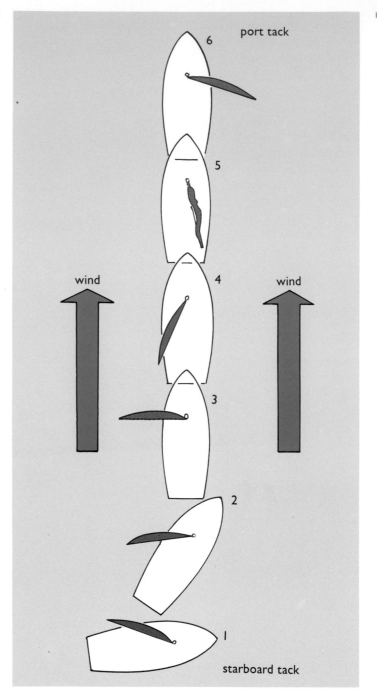

*Jibing involves swinging the stern of the boat through the eye of the wind, and the maneuver requires careful control of the boom to prevent it swinging across too violently in strong winds. Practice the technique in light winds and remember to duck as the boom swings across.*

*No matter how strong the wind, the boat should be kept at a uniform angle by the movement of crew weight. As the wind strengthens it may be necessary to use a trapeze (**top**) so that weight can be shifted right out (**above**) and dramatically increase the leverage.*

much weight shifting during all this, at least while you are aimed downwind. Should you wish to head up to a reach in a good breeze, you would then use your weight to balance the heeling effect. But offwind, the force is not directed so much toward heeling the boat as to pushing it along, so your weight can stay centered. At first, try to concentrate on sheet manipulation and timing the jibe. The sooner you learn your boat's behavior in a jibe, the easier the maneuver will be.

## THE WINDWARD BEAT

Assume you want to get the boat back on a reach again. Also assume that you now want to get to a point directly upwind — a buoy on a racecourse, the launching ramp, a sandy beach, whatever.

The first step is to head up so that the boat is close-hauled on the port tack. The sail is trimmed to the point of draw, with a slight flutter at the luff, and the boat is not being crowded so close to the wind that she begins to slow to a stall.

No matter how hard you try, you cannot make the boat sail directly into the wind. On your present course, you will sail wide of the target. You must go through a series of tacking maneuvers and carve a zig-zag course to windward. This is the *windward beat.*

The process is relatively easy, because the main sheet can be kept close-hauled and the boat tacked back and forth between port and starboard, shifting your weight as necessary. In light air the sheet can be fastened by taking a couple of wraps around a cleat or a pass through the cam cleat. The traveler will provide the consistency of trim automatically as you tack.

Push the tiller to starboard (off wind) and let the boat come up and through the wind's eye. As the sail flutters, shift your weight amidships, keeping the tiller over to starboard. She comes around quickly, and the sail fills away to port as the wind comes full over the starboard side. Get your weight to starboard to balance the wind force in the sails, and straighten the tiller to get the boat tracking along, close-hauled and on the starboard tack. Keep her from stalling by not sailing too close to the wind's direction, and watch the trim of the sail. If the luff is quivering slightly, it's probably alright but if you steer her off the wind too much and eliminate all luff action, the boat might not be sailing in her most efficient close-hauled condition. She may be "over-trimmed", which robs the sail of its aerodynamic efficiency.

Notice that the sheet has not been touched at all during this maneuver. The boat has been trimmed for close-hauled sailing only and has passed through no other points of sail from beat to beat, port to starboard.

### OFFWIND SAIL TRIM

All that remains of the basic maneuvers is the art of offwind sail trim that is, trimming for a broad reach or run.

On any offwind point of sail, the wind strikes the sail straight-on. The sail captures the wind, rather than acting like an airfoil.

On a broad reach, this capturing of the wind creates an athwartships vector of force which would push the boat sideways were it not for the centerboard. With the board digging in, however, the boat simply heels slightly. Trimming for a broad reach simply involves setting the boom so that the apparent wind meets the sail at right angles.

A look at the masthead windvane, a glance at the water, or a good feel for the wind (or all of the above) will enable you to trim properly.

On a run, the sail is similarly set to catch the wind, but on many boats it is impossible to swing the boom so that it is exactly at right angles to the boat's centerline. What is important is that the sail's average surface is presented at right angles to the wind. Note that because the wind's vector is acting along with the boat's centerline, there is no component vector pushing the boat sideways, nor is there any heeling moment. In a perfect downwind run, the centerboard can be raised to reduce frictional resistance and speed the boat.

### GETTING HOME

You are now aware of the major maneuvers, how to trim sail effectively on all points of sail, and how to handle a few special situations. Now it's time to learn how to return to your home base.

**Mooring** As you approach your mooring, check on the wind direction in relation to the positions of the buoy and any nearby obstacles. Be aware of wind direction all the time, and trim properly for whatever point of sail you are on as you approach the mooring area.

The basic maneuver is to get downwind of the mooring buoy while keeping some speed on the boat, and then as you reach a point directly downwind of the buoy, round up quickly and coast directly upwind, sails luffing until you can reach out and take the buoy and make it fast. See left for an overview of this method.

Some things to keep in mind: when rounding up your boat you must be going slowly enough not to pass the mooring. Practice timing your rounding up.

One way to kill speed is to let the sheet pay out and luff the sail, even as you approach your rounding-up point. Another speed-killer is the rounding-up maneuver itself. The more drastic it is, the more speed it takes off.

If you round up and find that you cannot quite coast to the mooring, but are slowing to a stop a bit short, you can try sculling up to the buoy vigorously pushing the tiller from side to side.

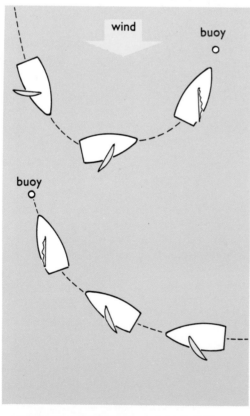

*Always approach a mooring from downwind, even if it means sailing down to it and then rounding up. Slow the boat by luffing and try to judge your approach so that you have enough momentum to reach the buoy. Approaching from a run is not to be recommended since it allows you no chance to slow down.*

In time, after some practice, you will learn how much room you need to perform this maneuver, and how to handle your boat as you approach on different points of sail and different wind conditions. But at first, if there's enough space, try to perform the maneuver from a reach. You will be able to see your path better, and your turning angles will be simplest.

Don't worry if you feel uncomfortable at first sailing to a mooring. Take all sail down in the clear and row or paddle to the mooring under control.

**Docking** As a beginner, you would be ill-advised to try docking in a busy harbor under sail. Some of the more crowded harbors and rivers have rules against maneuvering under sail in tight commercial areas.

You would be wise to approach under oars or paddle. If you must sail, use the training gained in rounding up to a mooring. Pick the point on the dock that's farthest downwind, and think of it as a mooring

buoy. If the front face of the dock is entirely downwind, you are lucky — its entire length can be rounded-up to, and the wind will hold your boat off the dock and cushion her.

But what happens if the wind is exactly the opposite and blowing you towards the dock? Round up at a point several yards to windward of the dock, and take down your sail. The wind will blow you to the dock, and you can fend off as you make contact. This will prevent your boom from crashing into the dock to leeward as your sail flutters wildly.

If the dock has a rear side, you could try to get around to it and use it as a windward point toward which to round up. Again, think of some point of the dock as the mooring buoy, and round up to it. You can always work the boat around to a better spot when you are secure.

**Beaching** As you approach a beach, prepare to do two things: get the centerboard or daggerboard up, and get the rudder's blade up. A centerboard will

*The correct way to approach a dock, depending on wind direction. If in doubt, drop all sail and row or paddle in.*

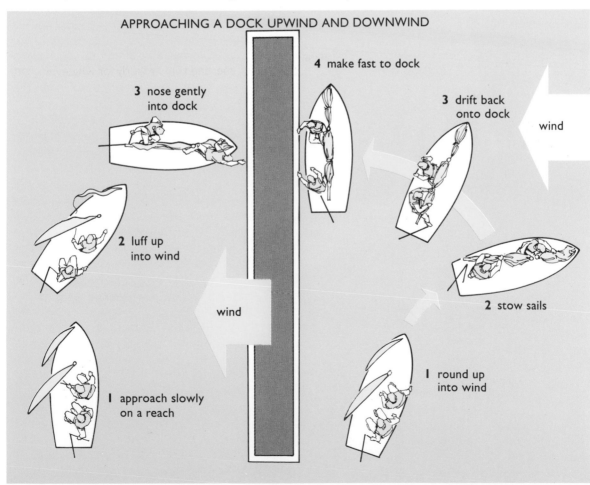

APPROACHING A DOCK UPWIND AND DOWNWIND

**4** make fast to dock

**3** nose gently into dock

**3** drift back onto dock

wind

**2** luff up into wind

**2** stow sails

wind

**1** approach slowly on a reach

**1** round up into wind

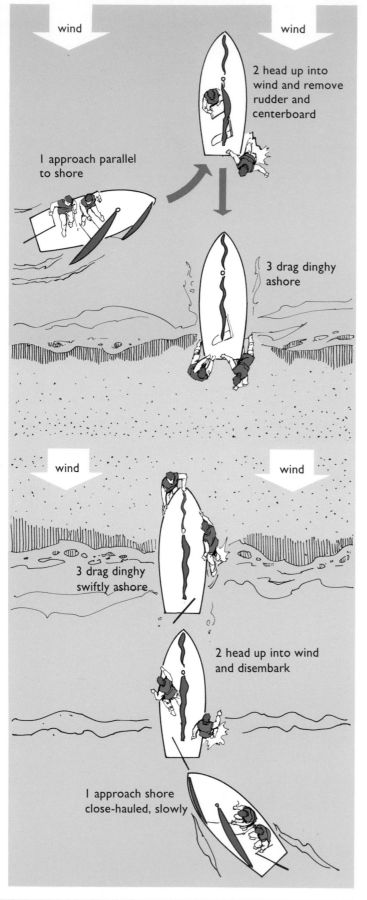

wind

wind

1 approach parallel
to shore

2 head up into
wind and remove
rudder and
centerboard

3 drag dinghy
ashore

wind

wind

3 drag dinghy
swiftly ashore

2 head up into wind
and disembark

1 approach shore
close-hauled, slowly

normally ride up by itself when it strikes the bottom, making it a fine tool for sounding the depth as you're sailing in toward your beach (although this is inadvisable with a rocky bottom, which could damage the board). Raising a daggerboard is trickier.

With a daggerboard, raise it in stages. As the water shallows, pull it halfway out of its trunk. Then, as you feel bottom, lift it right out and stow it in the boat.

Once you're feeling the bottom, either with daggerboard or centerboard, let the sails luff, allowing the sheet to run free to spill the wind completely out of the sail, and step gently out of the boat. Get around astern and dismount (or *unship*) the rudder and position the boat directly into the wind if she isn't pointed that way.

There are two general types of beach landings. The first is the upwind landing, made on a windward shore. The boat is run toward the beach close-hauled. At the last moment, the boat is steered directly into the wind and allowed to luff in a stall. The boat's speed decreases, and the centerboard begins to feel bottom and is pulled up. The sail is allowed to continue to luff as the skipper steps out and secures his rudder. The boat may then be hauled up on the beach, where the sail can be taken down and the gear secured.

The second type of beaching should never be attempted in anything but light winds. It is the down-wind landing. The boat approaches the beach on a broad reach or a run. As the water shallows the boat is rounded up right into the wind. The skipper pulls his board and rudder, then steps over the side and wades the boat toward the shore — stern first. If the boat is light enough, the rudder should be unshipped and the boat dragged a short distance up the beach transom-first before the sail is taken down. If the boat is heavy and unmanageable, the sail should be taken down while the boat is still in the shallows, and the boat then swung around and

*Beaching on a lee shore (**above left**) involves rounding up into the wind, removing centerboard and rudder and dragging the boat back up onto the beach. Weather shore approaches (**left**) are more straightforward, and there is inevitably less chance of damage from breaking waves.*

beached bow-first.

If the wind is strong and the waves too big, do not attempt to beach on any but a windward shore. Wave action creates breakers on lee shores and on shores that run parallel to the wind's direction. Breakers can sweep a boat out of control and cause damage/or injury in extreme cases. A downwind or cross-wind beaching in anything but light conditions can be extremely tricky and should not be attempted until you have gained much experience.

Always try to pick a windward shore for a beaching, as the land shields the water from the wind, keeping wave-action to a minimum. Any waves present will be running towards an approaching boat, away from the shoreline — and will be far easier to handle than big breaking waves pushing a small boat toward a lee shore.

## IN THE GROOVE

On any point of sail between the reach and close hauled — when the sail is literally acting like a wing — the boat should be kept on the "cutting edge" of the wind. To keep the boat sailing "in the groove", the skipper must be continually aware of wind direction and sail trim.

This is one of the finer points of sailing to windward. Learn to keep the boat from stalling by steering off the wind just enough to keep the sail full and drawing properly. Keep easing her upwind slightly now and then to check the luff for proper draw.

Try to develop a sense of boatspeed. It will serve you well throughout your sailing career. Learn to sense the sounds of speed: the gurgle, swish, or swoosh of water at the bow; the rattle of the sail's luff and the pop of the leech; the hum of tiller and daggerboard. Learn the feel of speed: the angle of heel; the tug of the tiller as the helm starts to fight you; the force of the wind on your cheek; learn to watch your dinghy's wake as it builds under her transom. The faster she goes the bigger

*The key to planing (**below**) is the correct distribution of weight so that the heel angle is kept as near to zero as possible.*

**Planing** *A boat will only plane if she is trimmed nearly level. Once she begins to lift the crew will have their work cut out keeping her on that critical path through adjustments to sails and movement of weight. In a strong wind that may well mean using a trapeze. Once on a plane the rudder becomes extremely touchy, with the slightest movement producing a dramatic change in the boat's behavior, and the helmsman and crew must work in close, almost telepathic harmony.*

**Handling the spinnaker** *Hoisting and controlling a spinnaker calls for a considerable degree of coordination between helmsman and crew. The maneuver starts by heading the boat offwind (**1**), while the crew cleats the jib sheet before clipping the spinnaker guy into the pole end fitting (**2**) and then attaching the inboard end to the mast fitting (**3**). The helmsman then hoists the spinnaker halyard (**4**) and the sail emerges from the bow chute. As soon as the sail has emerged the crew begins to trim it (**5**), adjusting sheet and guy (**6**) to keep the sail filled and the two clews more or less level (**7**). It looks simple, but out in a Force 4 among big waves it is a very highly skilled maneuver.*

1

4

5

the wave form becomes until either the boat will not go any faster, or until she actually gets up and planes like a speedboat.

These senses of speed, direction and efficiency will allow you to get the most out of your boat no matter what point of sail. The windward beat, however, when the boat is on that fine cutting edge, in the groove, is one of the most rewarding aspects of sailing.

Of course, on a reach — with the wind right abeam — a boat attains its maximum speed potential in any given conditions. It is on the reach that your first experiences with high performance will take place.

### PLANING

A performance dinghy like a Laser or 470 will have a tiller extension or hiking stick. It will also have toe or hiking straps, and, almost certainly, the design of the boat's board and rudder will be extremely efficient. The hull will be shaped to *plane* over the waves in ideal conditions.

It is thrilling to get a boat planing in a breeze; and it is something to work up to by degrees. Don't think that just because your boat was designed with performance in mind, she will be easy to get on plane. Learn to trim sail properly and smartly, in response and anticipation to gusts and wind shifts (by reading the water to windward). Then learn how to shift your weight smartly and automatically. Then master the art of hiking, and learn your boat's limits.

A boat will plane only if she is trimmed nearly level. In a good breeze, a crew who use their weight to keep heel angle to zero and hold a gust long enough for boatspeed to rise beyond the critical point, will get their boat to plane. (Planing usually occurs at a speed equivalent to twice the square-root of the boat's length on the waterline.) A boat can be kept on the plane by shifting weight slightly aft, taking care to keep the boat absolutely level.

Most centerboarders can plane under ideal conditions, but it takes a true performance boat to do it on command, and a true performance sailor to make it happen.

Whether you wish to become a performance sailor or not, learning to get the most from your boat is as important as learning the basic maneuvers. Even a cruising sailor needs speed under certain conditions, and knowing how to keep her moving at her best — whether that simply means "in the groove", or "on plane" — is a fine art.

### CAPSIZE

If you react properly to gusts of wind, and avoid jibing accidentally, and are able to shift your weight appropriately when the time comes, you might not capsize, but there will come a time when you are caught unawares and the wind overpowers your small boat. In the event it pays to be prepared.

Most good sailing courses insist you purposely capsize under supervised and controlled conditions. However, if you are not fortunate enough to go on such a course you should take note of the methods of recovery illustrated here, as they may help you understand the process should you need it.

First, and once your boat is completely swamped, grab hold of the boat and make sure you and your crew are OK. Don't leave the boat; that is the first rule in a capsize.

The boat will be lying on her side, most probably with the bow pointed upwind. Uncleat the main and jib sheets.

Swim around to the boat's bottom side, and grab the centerboard or daggerboard, keeping the boat pointed directly upwind. Use your weight to push down on the board, but not too close to the top, and make the boat wallow upright. Be careful not to push too much, as the boat might roll right over and capsize again, toward you.

Once you get her upright, the sail will be streaming unrestricted. If there is too much wind, you may have to uncleat the halyards and wrestle the sails off before righting. In most cases, however, you'll be able to leave sail up.

One of the crew now climbs aboard and starts bailing. Have your crew steady the boat and counterbalance as you climb over the side. If you're alone, you might want to climb aboard over the transom. On a dinghy, there should be a bucket or cutaway plastic scoop. Try to get as much water bailed out as quickly as possible, trying not to capsize the boat with your weight.

If your boat is so heavily swamped that bailing will not get the water out faster than

1

2

3

*The first rule in a capsize is "don't leave the boat." Swim round to the bottom side (having uncleated main and jibsheets) and clamber on to the centerboard (**1**), taking care not to stand too near the top. Use this extra leverage to ease the boat upright (**2**), pulling on a jibsheet if necessary. As soon as the boat is upright, and with your crew steadying the boat, clamber aboard (**3**) and start bailing.*

it comes back in over the rail, then try going to the transom and pushing the boat ahead in bursts, letting the water slosh rapidly back over the transom. As your push ends, the water inside the boat sloshes forward and often picks the transom up and out again. After a few of these pushes, you should be able to bail with the scoop and then climb aboard.

Finish bailing, and get the loose gear stowed. Keep your sail streaming aft and sheets free. If the boat starts to point off downwind, try to scull her to windward. If your hands are too full for that, at least make sure you keep the sail dumping wind and the boat on an even keel as you finish your recovery.

One more check on stowage and proper rigging, and you're off again.

The most important thing to remember is that you will be able to recover if you take the time to think things through. Don't panic. And if you feel concerned about capsizing at the early stages of your education, don't get too far from a friendly boat. It's nice to have help handy.

MASTERING THE MANEUVERS

77

# 8 | GENERAL SAFETY

All the skill in the world is no substitute for experience and the "sense" a sailor develops for the sea, the sky, and his shipmates. Plenty of logic goes into building that sense, and that logic breeds caution. The best sailor is *careful*.

## THE SKY

Whenever you sail on a small boat, keep an eye on the developments in the sky. The area to watch is directly to windward, but it pays to look all around.

In the earth's temperate zones, weather usually arrives from the west, and heads off east into the sunrise. In tropical regions, weather patterns can be quite local, depending on terrain, local wind, and a number of other factors.

You must, therefore, learn the general trends of weather in your area. Television or newspaper weather maps display the overall motion of the various systems. Satellite photography has improved the forecaster's art immensely, helping the viewer see the speed and direction of approaching weather.

## SQUALLS

In summer, the most frequent danger is the afternoon squall or thunderstorm, usually accompanied by strong wind and heavy rain. These squalls can catch you unawares.

*The brute force of the sea demands a healthy respect from all who venture out on it.*

Luckily, squalls signal their presence long before they arrive. Everyone has seen the dark clouds that rise high into the troposphere, capped by huge blown-out tops that often resemble an anvil. Cumulonimbus are a sure sign of squalls.

When a squall gets close enough for you to start worrying about it, you will see the details of its substructure. Often, a well-developed squall will have feathery clouds rolling out from its base, patches of dark shadow well underneath, and will emit a rumbling indicative of electrostatic activity. All these things can be sensed some time before the arrival of the storm.

Action to avoid a squall should be taken early. If you find yourself watching pretty swatches of gray cloud break away from the squall's bottom as lightning shoots down through prominent rain showers, you've left it too late.

As a general rule, when you can clearly hear the thunder of a squall, and if the center of the cloud structure is bearing down on your position, it's time to tuck into shelter.

A fine afternoon breeze will die just before a squall, a sure signal of its impending arrival. When the breeze begins to riffle the water and blow *toward* the heart of the storm, you've only got a few minutes to react. This is usually when the roll clouds become obvious at the squall's base.

If you find yourself out on a broad expanse of water on a steamy afternoon, and your examination of the horizon shows several squall-like formations around, don't panic. The ones to windward (to "weather") are the most likely to cause trouble. If you're surrounded by large and prominent land masses, the squalls may be building over land and never venture over water. On the other hand, they could build enough strength and slide over the bay or sound, so you must continue to *track* the storms.

Watch them in relation to landmarks, or get an idea of their direction from you relative to your own course (their *relative bearing*, in seaman's language). Their course

*The changing face of the sky gives a clear indication of any impending weather changes. Common sense dictates that you should learn to "read" the sky and react in good time.*

Thunder clouds forming indicate the risk of squalls (**right**). The wisest course of action is to seek the closest upwind shelter.

Always head for the closest upwind shelter when a severe squall threatens (**below**). Getting trapped on a lee shore can prove disastrous.

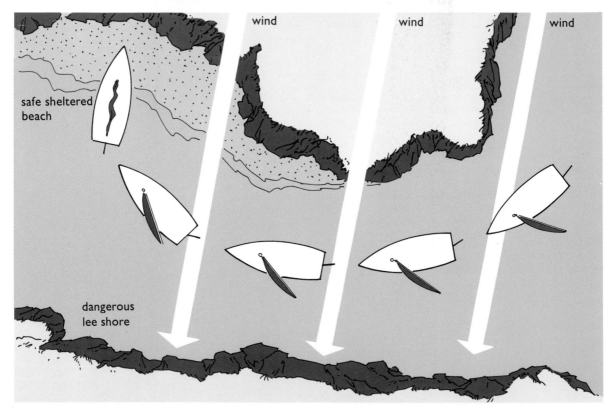

safe sheltered beach

wind

wind

wind

dangerous lee shore

will more than likely be in the general direction of the overall weather pattern — west-to-east, for example. Watch out if that big storm directly to the west holds its bearing, and begins to loom over you, its top blowing out above. Note that even if the center of a big squall blows past to one side of your position, its arms — in the form of roll clouds — can race out and hit you a blow just as sure as if the whole storm had run you down. Always respect a squall, even if it looks like it will pass you by.

If a squall is approaching, and you are convinced it will arrive before you can get to refuge, always head for *the closest upwind shelter.* Upwind means in the direction from which the storm is approaching, as the wind will utlimately blow its hardest *out* of a squall. Do not, under any circumstances, get caught off a lee shore, downwind or out in the open bay. Getting into the lee of an upwind shore is better than facing the fury of a blow in the open. Beaching upwind is much safer.

Pull your boat up on the beach, dismantle the rig, and secure the boat with a line to a tree, or an anchor, then get yourself and your crew to shelter. You may even find you'll get best shelter by staying beneath your overturned dinghy until the storm passes.

## THE CREW

Sailing with friends can be among the most rewarding experiences afloat, but there is a fine art to handling friendship aboard a small sailboat. Here are a few pointers:

(1) Ask only those friends who have the "right stuff" for sailing — willingness to learn, respect for the water, a love of the outdoors, and willingness to respect your control of your vessel even though you are yourself a beginner.

(2) Be wary of asking extremely experienced sailors to crew for you. You may want to invite a good skipper along to captain your boat during your early days, but avoid asking him back as crew until you have refined your skills considerably.

(3) Make it clear to your crew what your day's goals are before setting out, where you want to go, what you're going to do, and the things to expect out on the water. If it is windy, make sure everyone understands the moves required to counterbalance the wind's force in a small boat.

(4) Before setting out, explain the commands you will use to signal the major maneuvers. We'll learn these commands in the next section.

(5) Finally, use control in the exercise of your power. Remember that these are your friends, not your navy. No matter how stupid they may seem, you will seem more so if you lose your temper.

## SIGNALS AND COMMANDS

The basic commands for guiding a small boat through the cardinal maneuvers are:
**Coming about**

*Ready about* Prepare to come about. Crew should get ready for their respective duties. On a small boat, most important will be weight-shifting. On a boat with a jib, one crewman will prepare to handle the jibsheet.

*Hard alee* The skipper puts the tiller down to the leeward side, steering the boat into the wind. The crew shifts weight to the centerline, then to the opposite side as the tack is completed.
**Jibing**

*Prepare to jibe* Again, prepare for the maneuver, but this time with the extra caution to watch for a premature or accidental jibe. Prepare weight-shift, jib-handling.

*Jibe-ho* Helm is put to windward, and boat is steered so that the stern passes through the eye of the wind. Crew keeps low in the boat to clear the rapid passage of the boom overhead. Weight shift must be relatively swift, precise. Practice is important here.
**General**

*Head up* or *Heading up* The statement that the boat should be steered, or is being steered, more to windward. This is used on a beat when the skipper wishes to inform the crew that he wants to trim the sheet slightly to sail more closely-hauled.

*Luff up* or *Luffing up* The statement that the boat should be steered, or is being steered, to windward and the sails luffed in a gust of wind to ease her through the gust safely.

*Fall off* or *Falling off* The statement that the boat should be steered, or is being steered away from the wind, as from a close reach to a beam reach, or from a beam reach to a broad reach, etc.

*Trim* The request to a crewman to haul slowly on a sheet (main, jib, etc) until asked to stop.

*Ease* The request to a crewman to slack away on a sheet (main, jib, etc) until asked to stop.

One more point: brief your crew on the language you will be using. If your crew hasn't learned the language, keep your commands simple and phrase them in plain language.

## BASIC PILOTAGE

"Pilotage" is the art of finding your way about on the water. Nobody expects you to be a Hornblower immediately, especially in a sailing dinghy, but a little common sense can go a long way toward making your early experiences rewarding and safe.

*(1)* Try to make your average course trend an *upwind* one for most of your day. It's far better to be upwind of your starting point should you have trouble, than to be downwind with a long row or paddle home. If you cannot sail upwind from your starting point, then try to stay close to home base and that friendly windward shore.

*(2)* Watch the state of the tide. Getting down-tide of your destination is almost as bad as being downwind. Tidal streams can sweep you far off course. Watch stationary objects on shore to get an idea of how the current is affecting your intended course. Buoys anchored to the bottom can be used as references, and you often can see the tide sweep past a buoy. Always keep in mind that a fair tide now can be a foul tide in a few hours. Carry a tide table for your locality and know how to use it.

*(3)* Learn what angle to the wind your boat will tack through on a close-hauled beat to windward. Knowing this will help you estimate what point of land or reference you will be able to make whenever you come about. Looking to windward at approximately a right angle, or "abeam to windward" will provide a good estimate of the course you'll be able to make good when you change tacks.

*(4)* Carry a pocket compass and learn how to use it. When you are on a large body of water, keep an occasional check on your course, and check the directions ("compass headings") to your home base, and to various points ashore or places of refuge.

*Try to keep upwind and up-tide of your destination; heading for the mark may not be enough if the tide is sweeping you down toward danger. The effect of the tide on buoys (**inset**) is self evident.*

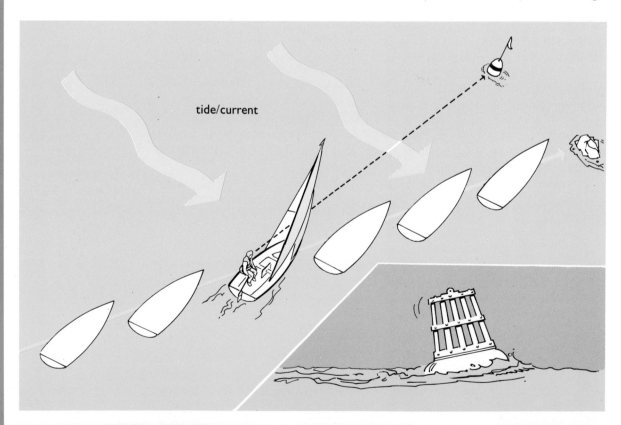

tide/current

This is especially important if you expect squalls or see heavy rain or fog approaching. While you've got the visibility, get your bearings, write down your course heading, plan where you'd steer if things got thick, and estimate how far you'd have to sail to refuge. These things, though approximate, are better than no information at all.

A small compass will give you reciprocals. Check your course as you sail out from home base, then find its reciprocal and practice sailing back where you came from. It's a good exercise, and one you'll need to build on for future navigation projects.

## PRUDENCE

In your early sailing, you will have enough to worry about without having to study the orthodoxy of the Rules Of The Road. But there will be traffic out there, and you will need some awareness of the basic principles of avoiding collisions. So, here are the things you must keep in mind when sailing in areas also used by other vessels:

*(1)* Take care to ensure the safety of your own vessel and her crew. It is your first responsibility to protect your own safety without endangering other vessels. Stay clear of traffic when any doubt about right of way exists.

*(2)* Powerboats must give right of way to sailboats — that is a rule everyone knows, but sailboats are powerboats when they augment their driving sails with engine power. Both sail and power boats should stay clear of paddle- or oar-driven boats.

*(3)* When two sailboats have the wind on a different side, the boat with the wind on the port side shall keep out of the way of the other.

*(4)* When two sailboats have the wind on the same side, the boat to windward shall keep out of the way of the boat to leeward.

*(5)* If a sailboat with the wind on the port side sees a boat to windward but cannot tell with certainty whether the other boat has the wind on the port or starboard side, she shall keep out of the way of the other.

*(6)* An overtaking vessel must yield to the overtaken vessel, regardless of what their respective means of propulsion.

*(7)* Finally, keep clear of all commercial

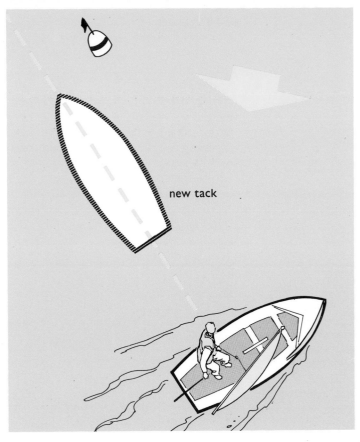

new tack

*To find the approximate direction of the next tack (**above**), look over your shoulder to windward at right angles, but remember to allow for any tide.*

*Back bearings taken with a hand bearing compass when leaving harbor (**below**) provide a valuable check on position and tidal influences.*

vessels. Dredgers, tugs, ships, fishermen, and so on — all can pose a threat to safety, as all have limited maneuverability when compared to a yacht or small boat. Don't push your luck.

The next major section of this book will discuss the larger and more complex boat. It will explore the basic types of rig, the increasing sophistication as you move up from your sailing dinghy, and the theory of big-boat sailing.

But for now, enjoy your small boat. Practice your maneuvers, learn the language, develop your awareness of the world around you. Learn the weather, and know your locality. There is no better platform for this kind of study than a small boat. It brings you closer to the elements and helps you see clearly the connections between wind and wave, land and sea.

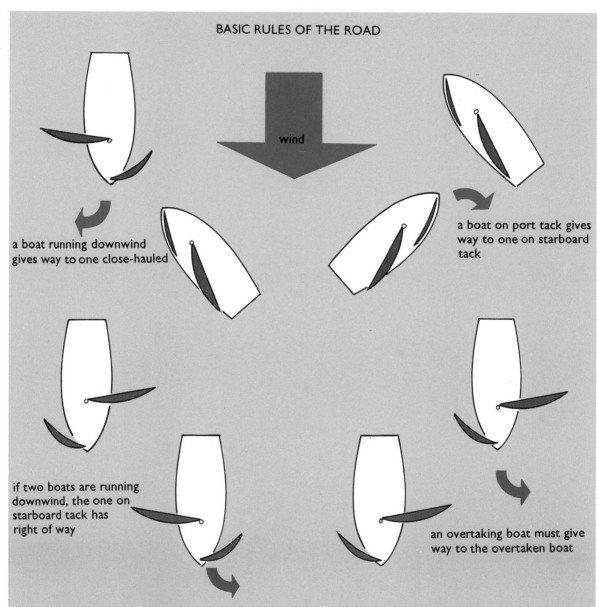

## BASIC RULES OF THE ROAD

wind

a boat running downwind gives way to one close-hauled

a boat on port tack gives way to one on starboard tack

if two boats are running downwind, the one on starboard tack has right of way

an overtaking boat must give way to the overtaken boat

*Common sense dictates that a sailboat should keep clear of all commercial vessels, especially large ships with limited maneuverability.*

## ROUTINE SAIL CARE

While most new sails are Dacron synthetic fiber, they still need some attendance if they are to serve you well as propulsion devices.

Here are some tips:

*(1)* Let your sails dry as much as possible before bagging or covering them. Even synthetics are prone to mildew.

*(2)* Do not fold sails the same way each time. If you must fold them on the boom or at dockside, take care not to crease them.

*(3)* Sails may have *battens*. These are strips of wood or plastic that fit into pockets built into the sail's leech, and which help stabilize the sail's shape. When storing or bagging sail, remove the battens.

*(4)* Never use battens that are improperly sized for the pockets on your sail. They can cause wear.

## BAGGING SAIL

Ideally sails should be folded, but in any case when bagging a sail for the week, push it loosely into the bag. Have a bag that's large enough so that you can pack it without forcing sail in. Pack the sail in so that the last part packed is the first part to come out when *bending-on* sail again. If you're bagging the main, pack it clew-first, tack second, then stuff it down so that the luff and leech stay parallel and the head goes in last.

Remember, no battens.

When bagging a jib, pack the clew first, working up the leech toward the head, then down the luff toward the tack, which goes in last. That way, when making the jib ready to hoist, the tack can be made fast, then the luff clips can be attached to the stay, and finally the clew can be attached to the sheets in a neat and logical order.

## FURLING SAIL

Furling sail is the practice of securing it with short pieces of line, usually called *sail ties*, to the boom. When furling, you simply "roll" the sail in on itself and pack it loosely until it is against the boom. The ties are then passed around and knotted with simple slipknots. Some ties are actually lengths of elastic cord with loops and chocks that eliminate the need for knotting.

One more sail-care tip: if you are leaving your boat for several days or more, do not leave your sail furled on its boom without covering it. Ultra-violet light from the sun, even if not direct sunlight, can weaken the synthetic fibers of the cloth. Too much exposure can drastically shorten the life of a sail, which can be as long as 10 to 15 years with proper care.

# CRUISER
# SAILING

# 2

# 9 | THE BIGGER BOAT

*A cruising boat relies on keel weight rather than crew weight for stability.*

When most people move up from a dinghy or small centerboarder, they buy a keelboat; a heavier, deeper, more stoutly fashioned boat with a fixed, ballasted keel. The boat will usually carry more crew and have rudimentary accommodation belowdecks.

The larger boat will have more complex rigging. She may have two masts, for instance; or she may have a *bowsprit* (a spar that effectively extends the length of the boat forward); or she may have a number of extra sails for use in varying winds; or she may have more sophisticated sail handling and trimming devices.

She is likely to have an engine, with a fuel tank and electrical system and a water system and lavatory facilities (a *head*).

She will certainly be heavier and more sluggish to maneuver, yet far more able in a big wind on open water.

## EXTRA WEIGHT

Because a keel carries weight in the form of *fixed ballast* a keelboat is much heavier than a dinghy. The ballast in a keel, attached by strong bolts or encapsulated into the hull itself, does the same thing your crew's weight does in a dinghy — provides stability. The lateral surface below the waterline that a keel comprises also resists sideslip or leeway and helps a boat sail just as a

centerboard does.

The combined effects of a keel become obvious when you sail a bigger boat. Because of the extra weight, the momentum of a boat is greater. It takes more effort to stop her, but at the same time maneuvers are slower. Instead of snapping through a tack like a small centerboarder, a keelboat takes much longer, but tends to keep moving through the course change.

There are two general rules to remember in keelboat design: (1) The amount a boat displaces compared to her overall length will have a direct bearing on

her maneuverability. (2) The longer a boat's sailing waterline, the higher will be her ultimate top speed.

The first rule simply means that a heavy boat will tend to be more sluggish than a light one of the same size. It will develop more momentum (not always a disadvantage) and will be that much harder to turn.

Displacement is not just weight, remember, but actually has a volumetric equivalent — the amount of water a boat displaces when floated. A boat with relatively little ballast, but a large and heavy

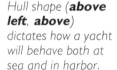

*Hull shape (**above left**, **above**) dictates how a yacht will behave both at sea and in harbor.*

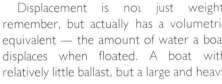

*Wide, beamy hulls (**far left**) allow plenty of room for accommodation, while traditional long keels (**left**) offer the best performance in tough conditions.*

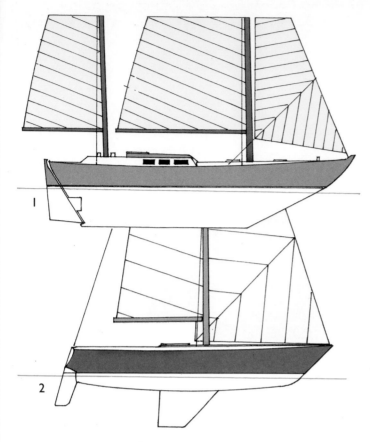

*Traditional cruising boats (**1**) have long keels which are part of the underbody. Racing yachts (**2**) have separate keels*

*attached to shallow underbodies.*

*A modern, light–weight ocean*

*racer (**below**) is really no more than a big dinghy, with all considerations of comfort sacrificed for speed.*

hull with long, deep keel, could very well displace quite a bit. Its long keel helps its directional stability (its ability to maintain a straight course) while providing a huge surface to resist leeway. Such a boat would have to rely on its width and underbody shape to resist heeling forces, as its ballast might not be enough to do it alone.

A modern racing keelboat's keel tends to be quite deep and quite short. It also can carry much weight in ballast. Combine all that with a very light hull and a rudder separated from the keel itself for improved effect, and you've got a quick, performance-oriented machine with relatively unstable directional qualities but a high degree of resistance to heeling and very effective underwater surfaces designed to resist leeway and produce superior lift and sensitive steering.

On a heavy-displacement boat, performance is sacrificed to provide steering stability (helped by a rudder mounted directly on the long keel), interior volume, and comfortable motion. Such a boat consequently makes a better cruiser than racer. On a light-displacement boat, the opposite is true.

General Rule No 2 relates to waterline length. There is a hard-and-fast axiom designers use to express the maximum speed a hull is capable of. That speed is called "hull speed" and is simply the point at which a displacement hull begins to resist any more power applied to make it go faster. It is that point when the stern wave builds up under a boat's transom, when the boat is "digging a hole" in the water and consequently will not go any faster.

The formula for determining hull speed is dependent largely on the length of the boat on its waterline: Hull Speed = square root of waterline length (in feet) multiplied by a fixed ratio of between 1.34 and 1.40 depending on the type of hull.

The fixed ratio for a boat skimming over the top of the water, or "planing", is 2.0. However, a keelboat is usually incapable of planing, and obeys the more stringent rules of the displacement hull. A centerboarder, because of its light weight, shallow underbody shape, and shiftable ballast (in the form of its crew), can lift out of the "hole" to plane on the surface.

## SLOOPS AND CUTTERS

Both sloop and cutter have one mast. The mast could be either aluminum or wood, and would normally be hollow in cross-section. The sloop's mast is stepped (mounted in the boat) at a point slightly forward of amidships. The cutter's mast is normally stepped exactly amidships.

The typical sloop has a *headstay*, a piece of wire standing rigging extending from the masthead (or close to it) right to the *stem head* or extreme end of the boat's bow. The sloop also has a *backstay*, or piece of wire standing rigging from the masthead to the transom. Both these stays support the mast and take rigging loads in a longitudinal (fore/aft) direction.

The sloop also has a set of *shrouds*, port and starboard. These shrouds are pieces of wire standing rigging that support the mast in a transverse (port/starboard) direction. It is common to see a pair of lower shrouds and a single upper shroud on each side to take rigging loads produced by the boat's few large sails.

The sloop's upper shrouds usually pass over the set of *spreaders*, which are struts attached to the mast port and starboard. The spreaders provide a favorable angle of tension for the upper shrouds.

The modern sloop rig usually has its headstay attached right at the masthead; the reason for the descriptive term, *masthead rig*. However, there are some rigs that have the headstay attachment at a point $\frac{7}{8}$ths of the way up the mast, or others that have it $\frac{13}{16}$ths of the way up. These are called *fractional rigs* and are seen on older yachts and increasingly on some state-of-the-art racing yachts. To support the masthead on fractional rigs, a set of *jumper stays* passes over small spreader-like struts called *jumper struts* which provide a favorable angle of tension for these short lengths of standing wire rigging.

See page 92 for a look at the sloop's standing rigging, both masthead and fractional.

Because the tall mast on a modern sloop (or cutter, for that matter) looks rather like a radio antenna, and because the first such masts appeared on boats built during the beginnings of the era of radio technology, the rig used to be called *the marconi rig*, after

*This little fractional-rigged sloop (**above**) has swept spreaders and, unusually, no backstay.*

*The headstay is attached some way below the masthead on this Waarschip 570 (**left**).*

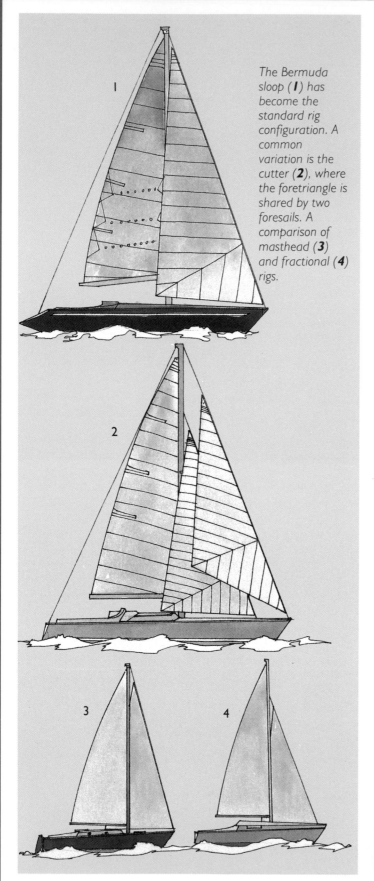

*The Bermuda sloop (1) has become the standard rig configuration. A common variation is the cutter (2), where the foretriangle is shared by two foresails. A comparison of masthead (3) and fractional (4) rigs.*

the inventor of the radio/telegraph transmitter. The term is now no longer widely used.

A sloop has two standard sails, or *working sails*: a mainsail and a jib. Both are triangular. There are other sails that can add flexibility and speed, but the "main" and the jib are the heart of the rig's function.

There are a number of different sizes and designs of jib. The most basic cut is the *working jib*. The working jib is triangular, and fits more or less within the area described by the sloop's headstay, mast, and foredeck — the boat's *foretriangle*.

Other jibs overlap the mainsail aft and are called *genoas*. A number one genoa laps back almost to the leech of the main; a number two laps about half way back; and a number three laps only slightly past the mast. Genoas, or "gennies" all are cut so that the foot runs more or less parallel to the boat's deckline.

Other jibs may also overlap the main, but may not be proper genoas. The *yankee* jib overlaps the main slightly, but has its foot cut high and its clew quite a distance off the deck. This sail can be better than the genoa in some instances when visibility below the

The large overlapping, deck-sweeping genoa (**left**).

These cruising yachts (**above**) are enjoying a little competition during a flotilla holiday in Turkey.

The design of this French cruising yacht (**below**), in particular the sloping reverse transom and wide hull, is clearly derived from the modern racing yacht.

sail to leeward is desirable.

There are also *roller-furling* jibs of all descriptions — sails popular on cruising boats because they need not be taken down and bagged. These sails roll up on their own swivel-mounted headstay at the pull of a lanyard led to the cockpit. Because roller-furling rigs are considered inefficient, however, and do not allow the skipper to tailor precisely his rig to prevailing conditions, they are not used by serious racing sailors.

The cutter rig uses all the sails described for the sloop rig, but the cutter has some subtle advantages. Because the cutter's mast is farther aft than the sloop's, her foretriangle is larger, and because the foretriangle is larger, more sail can be put there. The space becomes more flexible.

Many cutters have a second stay forward of the mast, fastened on deck abaft the stemhead, and run to a point on the mast below the masthead terminus of the boat's headstay (cutters always have masthead headstays). This is the *forestay*.

The forestay can carry another, smaller jib-like sail called a *forestaysail*, or, simply a *staysail*. The staysail can be used with a small,

high-cut jib on a cutter to completely fill a foretriangle yet the sail, being divided, can easily be handled by a small crew. Instead of taking down or hoisting one large foresail, two small ones are there to work with. When the wind howls and it's time to get some sail off her, simply dropping the jib does the trick without upsetting the balance required to make her sail.

Two smaller overlapping sails can also be more efficient, as explained later.

## MULTI-MASTED RIGS

Now for the schooner, the ketch, the yawl. There was a time, perhaps 25 years ago, when designers built schooners, ketches, and yawls just for the sake of offering two masts to the buying public. Efficiency and simplicity be damned, the buyers seemed to think that two masts meant seaworthiness or speed or power.

In fact, there is no efficiency gained by adding masts to a boat. Masts are big poles that create disturbances in the smooth flow of air over sails.

Some sailors, however, — especially cruising people — swear by multi-masted rigs, and there are some good reasons why.

*This little ketch has a roller furling jib (**right**) which contrasts with the more traditional jib hanks attaching sail to forestay (**far right**).*

This clipper-bowed ketch with bowsprit (**above**) has an easily managed sail plan divided up into a number of small sails, unlike the sloop configuration.

The roller furling jib on this ketch (**below**) also makes for easier sail handling.

The staysail schooner (**below**), although less efficient than the sloop, is easier to sail as the sail area is divided into more manageable units.

On a really large hull, one that must carry an enormous amount of sail to move well, a single mast is impractical, as each sail is so large that it would require a crew of 50 to handle. Therefore, large hulls often carry ketch or schooner rigs to spread their huge sail area over more than one mast.

Another good reason for dividing sail between two masts is the ease with which sail can be reduced when the wind begins to blow really hard. This is especially true of a ketch rig, where the sail carried by the shorter, aftermost mast (the *mizzen mast*, which carries the *mizzen*) normally has about the same total area as the sail carried forward of the mainmast, in the foretriangle. So, when the wind begins to howl, you drop the mainsail and carry on in perfect balance under jib and mizzen.

Of all the multi-masted rigs, the ketch remains the most popular. This is probably because of the inherent balance between mizzen and foresails described above. The ketch's sails are also all of modest size, even on a quite large hull, making hoisting and dousing sail easy by a small crew. This makes the ketch especially attractive to the cruising family.

The ketch's mainmast is stepped slightly forward of amidships, more so than a sloop's. The mizzen mast is stepped *forward of the rudder post*, and is approximately two-thirds the height of the mainmast above the deck.

The opposite of the ketch (almost literally) is the schooner. The schooner rig has its mainmast, the taller of its two, stepped aft — perhaps a third of the way forward from the boat's transom, depending on the design. Stepped at a point well forward of amidships is the *foremast*. The mainmast carries the mainsail; the foremast carries the *foresail*. Forward of the foremast is the boat's foretriangle, which can carry as many as four or five combinations of jib, staysail, *jib topsail*, *flying jib*, and so on.

The schooner's foretriangle is often extended with the addition of a *bowsprit*. The bowsprit is a spar that extends out over the water forward. It carries at its very tip the boat's headstay, and is tensioned from below with one or more pieces of wire standing rigging called *bobstays*. The bowsprit allows a schooner to set more sail area forward of the foremast, which serves to balance the large sails aft.

These large sails provide the main driving force on a schooner. The mainsail is usually the largest sail aboard. The foresail is somewhat smaller. On the typical schooner, the mainsail is shaped as a triangle, while the foresail is shaped as a rectangle. On older schooner designs, the mainsail may also be rectangular. These rectangular sails have at their top a spar called a *gaff*.

On some schooners, the space between the foremast and mainmast is filled with a number of sails. One sail rides on a stay run from the mainmast's head forward to a position on deck just abaft the foremast. This is the staysail. Above that often rides a *fisherman's staysail*, positioned on a halyard, stretched taut between foremast and mainmast, and controlled by two sheets and one downhaul. On this *staysail schooner*, other staysails and fishermen sails can be positioned between the boat's two masts — so many that the rig is said to be the most complex short of a true square-rigger.

The schooner, regardless of type, is often said to be the least efficient of rigs. This may be true, but there are few sailing designs that are capable of the power of a schooner on a reach in a good breeze. Unfortunately, both the complexity and aerodynamic inefficency of the rig when going to windward has given the schooner a bad name in this modern era — an era that puts great stock in a boat's upwind ability.

The last multi-masted rig we'll discuss is the yawl. A yawl resembles a ketch in that there is a mizzen mast. A yawl's mizzen mast, however, is stepped *abaft the boat's rudder post*, and is usually much shorter than the ketch's — measuring up to about one third the height of the mainmast.

The yawl's popularity has faded drastically since its heyday in the 1950s and 1960s. In those days, racing handicap rules did not take into account the small mizzen and its accompanying sails. The yawl, being essentially a sloop with a tiny mizzen, got that unpenalized sail area, some more power, plus a place to hang even more sails in the form of mizzen staysails and such.

Like many of the multi-masted rigs, complexity — in the form of number of lines to pull on and number of spars to maintain

The most efficient rig is the Bermuda sloop, but the large sail areas require large crews, hence the considerable number of variations. Cutter (**1**). Sloop (**2**). Ketch (**3**). Yawl (**4**). Schooner (**5**).

*The Twelve Meter yacht (**below**) is probably the most efficient windward craft around, but it requires enormous skill to handle the big sails.*

and number of sails to mend and bend and trim — led to the slow decline of the yawl. Its tiny mizzen hardly contributed to the rig's power, and the extra sail only created aerodynamic drag. Finally, when the racing rules were adjusted to account for the yawl's perceived advantages, the rig all but vanished.

## HEADSAIL EFFICIENCY

The jib — or jib and staysail, or yankee and staysail, or staysail and flying jib and jib — is a main driving force in a big boat's rig. On a modern sloop rig, it's fair to say that the jib or genoa provides more drive than the mainsail. Main and jib form one of the most aerodynamic sail designs ever created.

A modern Twelve Meter racing yacht, for instance, is capable of developing enough horsepower out of a moderate breeze to move itself at more than eight knots on a dead beat to windward — within a 35 degree angle to the direction of the wind. Despite the constraints of the hull design, the boat's incredible windward ability comes from the design and construction of

*The slot effect (**right**) is based on the venturi principle — the narrower the slot the faster the airflow accelerates between the sails. Correct setting (**1**). Narrow for light airs (**2**). Choked (**3**).*

*The interaction between sails is clearly illustrated by this view of the "slot" effect in action (**below**) on a ketch.*

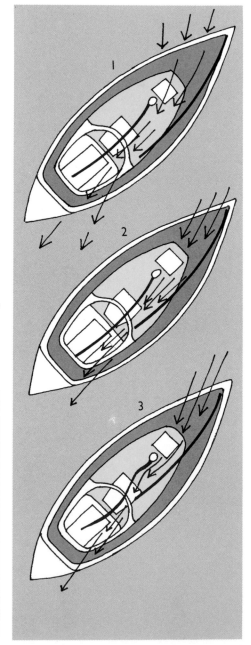

her two sails: main and genoa jib.

There is no question that headsails help a boat go to windward. They do so by providing a second airfoil, and therefore a "lifting" surface to help draw the boat forward in the water. In other words, two wings are better than one, but there's something else, too.

During the last century of headsail development, designers discovered an interesting thing. When a headsail was brought into a close relationship with either another headsail or the mainsail, and when the boat was trimmed in such a way that this proximity had both sails set perfectly for a windward beat, there was a perceivable increase in speed, beyond what could normally be expected as the simple sum of the two parts.

Many explanations have been offered for this phenomenon — often called the *slot* effect. Designers agree that it is the result of the overlapping of two or more sails. The overlap — like one formed between a genoa jib and a main, or between two headsails on a cutter — produces a "slot" through which air re-directed off the leading sail is channelled.

The slot is actually a venturi, or narrowing of space through which a fluid (air, in this case) flows. A quick look at fluid dynamics shows that when fluid flows through a venturi, its velocity increases while the pressure it exerts on the funneling channels decreases.

When the venturi is at the leading edge of the mainsail, and the pressure drops on the lifting side of the luff, even more lift is generated. You also get a bit of extra push out of the re-directed wind as it speeds through the slot.

Today's naval architects have taken full advantage of this slot principle by building boats with very tall masts and short main booms — in other words, tall, narrow sails. These *high aspect-ratio* rigs have more leading edge than other, older rigs — simply by virtue of the length of their headstays and masts. The longer the leading edge on the mainsail, the longer the slot or venturi. They can, therefore, develop much more lift when on a beat, especially when using genoa jibs with 150% or more overlap (or "number one" genoas) to enlarge the slot.

## HEADSAIL TRIM

The trimming of a jib or staysail presents an entirely new problem.

There are some important differences in geometry between jib and main. The first is that most jibs are *loose-footed*. That is, they have no boom along the foot or lower edge. Rather, their clew (their after, lower corner) flies loose in the breeze, free of any encumbrance. The jib has two sheets, therefore, attached to its clew leading back one on each side of the mast. These sheets serve to trim the jib's clew. When you want to haul in the jib for a beat, you trim the leeward sheet. When you want to reach or run, you pay out the leeward sheet. In coming about or jibing, when the wind comes around to the other side of the boat, you simply bring the jib around with its partner sheet.

*This masthead sloop powering to windward under main and genoa clearly illustrates how the two sails complement each other as foils.*

The jib's sheets run back along the deck, port and starboard, and through blocks (pulleys) fastened to fittings on deck. These blocks are *fairleads* — meaning that they lead the sheet in a fair line to its termination point — and by their positioning help provide proper shape for the jib.

Some jibs (or staysails) do have booms, and are usually termed *club-footed* headsails. The advantage of the club-footed headsail is that only one sheet need lead aft for controlling trim. The sheet will have one part attached to a traveler forward which will allow the sail to be manipulated from side to side when changing tacks or jibing. Like the mainsail, when a club-footed headsail is sheeted into position, you can come about without having to tend to the sail's trim.

While a club-footed sail is easier to trim, an advantage to the small crew, the boom on the headsail can diminish its effectiveness as a driving sail in partnership with the boat's main. It cannot overlap (the boom would never swing past the boat's mainmast), and also the boom itself adversely alters the sail's shape.

On a cutter, there is an added headsail-trimming problem: the forestay, upon which is hoisted the staysail, keeps any jib hoisted on the headstay from naturally switching sides during a tack. The jib just gets hung-up on the forestay unless it is walked around by hand.

Perhaps the best solution to this problem — a problem which would be found on any boat with a forestay/headstay combination in the foretriangle — would be a jib with roller-furling gear. With this system, a jib could be rolled on its stay, the boat changed

*Poor headsail halyard tension will impair windward ability. Long vertical creases — halyard too tight (1). Baggy luff — halyard too loose (2). Smooth airfoil — correct halyard tension (3)*

tacks from port to starboard or vice-versa, and the jib then unfurled again with its simple roller gear, all without fouling the forestay and its staysail.

Obviously, headsails produce complexity but sailors seem to thrive on it, and in fact have developed even more variants than those we've discussed thus far. Some racing boats have 20 or 30 bags of sails aboard, of which at least six are jibs alone.

## OTHER SAILS

For instance, you may add any number of special sails which can help your boat reach or run more effectively. A *spinnaker*, for instance, is a huge near-hemispherical sail made of lightweight nylon fabric which fills with the lightest breezes and helps push you on broad reaches and runs. You may also use a special spinnaker which has a flatter cut so

*This ocean racer (**left**) is heading downwind under spinnaker and blooper.*

*Heavily reinforced storm sails (**below**) — jib and trysail instead of mainsail — enable a yacht to keep sailing in all but the severest weather and claw off dangerous lee shores.*

*The bowsprit on an elderly Brixham trawler.*

*This gaff-rigged cutter sets flying jib and topsail as well as a more modern overlapping genoa in light airs.*

*Old and new . . . . a Thames barge passes under a yacht's spinnaker.*

as to be more effective on a reach.

There are more variants, such as the *reacher*, a sail designed to do what a genoa jib does, but on a close reach, or the *blooper*, a sail used in conjunction with a spinnaker for downwind work.

There are also sails designed for heavy weather — storm sails. A typical storm jib, for instance will be less than a third the size of a boat's working jib, and be made of material at least twice the weight. It will attach to the headstay (or forestay on a cutter) with oversized *hanks*, and have extra-heavy roping, sometimes all around its perimeter.

To replace the main in a storm, there is the storm trysail. This is a similarly heavy three-cornered sail with a relatively high-cut tack and a short clew. Its short luff is hoisted on the mainmast, its tack hauled down to the gooseneck, and its clew sheeted to a point slightly to leeward on deck. A trysail is probably less than one-fourth the mainsail's size.

For all these, remember, there are sheets, halyards, and more. A spinnaker, for example, even has its own spar — a *spinnaker pole* — to keep its windward clew raised, under control, and the sail drawing properly. All these are described in a later chapter.

## LESS COMMON RIGS AND VARIANTS

The gaff rig is derived from the days when the technology of metallurgy and the science of rig design did not permit tall masts and strong standing rigging. The gaff rig was a way of putting a vast amount of sail on a relatively short mast — one that could be fashioned from a single softwood tree.

The rig derives its name from the spar that carries the top or head of the sail. On a gaff-rigged sloop, for instance, the mainsail would have a gaff joined to the upper edge of the sail with a lacing line. The gaff itself may be joined to the mast with a gooseneck-like device attached to a "car" which would travel up and down the mast on a track for hoisting and dousing sail. Or the gaff may "straddle" the mast with a set of jaws similar to the simplest boom attachment on a small dinghy. The gaff would be raised up the mast with two distinct halyards — a *peak halyard* to hoist the outboard end or tip, and a *throat halyard* to hoist the end closest to the mast.

A gaff-headed sail might be attached to the mast via a set of oaken *mast hoops*, a light lacing line, or it might have a track and slides like a standard modern marconi rig.

A gaff-rigged boat would probably have a set of headsails not unlike those seen on more modern rigs. The gaff rig would probably have a pair of *running backstays*. These tension the mast rearward, but because the gaff sail is so broad, and because the gaff juts out abaft — and higher than — the mast, a single standing wire would interfere with the mainsail. So, the running backstays straddle the sail, and only one — the one to windward — is hauled tight at any one time.

Because the gaff rig is complex, and with its extra spar is heavier, its overall performance is not considered to be quite as good as that of the more modern rig.

### SIMPLER, OLDER

Early Chinese sailors enjoyed seagoing supremacy in their junks, which sported a type of *lug rig*. Chinese lug rigs have many thin full-length battens integral with their sails. These serve to stabilize the shape of the sail and control its efficiency on all points of sail.

The European lug rig, by contrast, had no full-length battens, but used only a single spar aloft to hold the sail's head. Trimming was accomplished with a single sheet attached to the sail's loose clew.

A variant of the simple lug rig is the *sprit rig*, still seen on Thames barges. A thin spar (the sprit) is fastened to the mast via a short pendant (a *snotter*) and diagonally supports the head of the nearly square sail.

The lateen rig is a type of lug rig where the sprit is a long spar rather like a yard which carries a triangular sail. The foot of the sail can be either loose or laced to a boom. On early lateen rigs, the sail was almost always loose-footed; on modern ones, such as the well-known Sunfish class of sailing boat, there is a boom.

Gaff and lug rigs are found today on replicas and restored classics.

### BRAND NEW

In recent years some builders have taken advantage of advances in technology and developed rigs that need no supporting standing rigging. Some of these have tall masts made of composite materials or special alloys of aluminum. Many have no headsails at all, but rather have one mast right forward, and another one of nearly equal height aft. These are "cat ketches" or "cat schooners", and have proved impressive in quite difficult conditions. Simplicity of rig and the efficiency of their sail design makes them interesting alternatives. to the status quo.

*The Freedom rig with unstayed masts and sailboard-like wishbone booms winged out to catch the wind.*

# 10 THE ANATOMY OF A KEELBOAT

*The enormous loads on this multiple spreader, 100ft maxi yacht mast need complex standing rigging.*

**E**fficient rig design had to wait until materials were discovered that could withstand the loads imposed by the several huge sails and tall, thin, aerodynamic spar sections. Needless to say, the latest developments, Mylar and Kevlar sails, carbon fiber topmasts, and some of the other futuristic gear seen on the big Twelve Meter yachts, have put the "ideal" boat quite out of the reach of the average yachtsman.

But even in the typical racing/cruising keelboat, rig strength and configuration are quite important.

### THE STRONG RIG

With the reduction in number of sails comes the increase in sail size and in the force they are able to exert. After all, a big, efficient sail is also a very powerful one able to put enormous loads on a rig. Add to that a further increase in the height of masts, and you've got a rigging stress problem to solve.

Designers have solved it in a number of ways, the most basic of which is seen on everyday cruising boats, and the most sophisticated seen on high-performance keelboats designed for competition.

The taller the rig, the more wire standing rigging is required. Some especially tall racing rigs require multiple sets of spreaders, with intermediate shrouds terminating at various intervals up the mast to assist in bracing against lateral forces. Just to complicate things, some boats have their shroud terminals on deck placed inboard so as to allow closer (and better) trimming of overlapping headsails. By losing several feet of advantageous width, the rig's wire standing rigging must be stronger and possibly more numerous.

Where stays and shrouds on most boats are still made of rigging wire, some performance rigs use solid stainless steel rods. The rods are set up in much the same fashion as rigging wire, and carry headsails just as the stainless wire does.

Rod rigging stretches far less than normal wire, can take more tension for its cross-sectional diameter, and is therefore ideal for boats with large rigging loads, tall masts and huge headsails.

Modern headsails put huge strains on racing rigs which must be able to sustain huge headstay and backstay loads. Many performance boats with fractional rigs have systems of increasing headstay tension for windward sailing, whether they're equipped with rod rigging or plain wire. The most common is a backstay tensioner — a large screw, tackle system, or hydraulic pump arrangement — at the backstay fitting on the transom which can be manipulated to bend the top of the mast aft, thereby stressing the headstay and altering mainsail shape in response to wind and sea conditions.

Boats with very tall masts will need *running backstays* to augment the fixed backstay seen on most conventional rigs. Running backstays attach to the mast and lead aft and down to the deck, port and starboard and outboard of the boat's cockpit and usually not completely clear of the boom's swinging arc. The upper portion of the running backstay is always wire, while the lower portion may be wire or fiber rope. The lower portion passes through a tackle arrangement which consists of at least one pulley aloft and a deck block. Whichever running backstay is on the weather side during a tack is tensioned via its tackle, while the leeward stay is slacked away to allow the boom to swing free.

Ketches and schooners, with tall mizzens and foremasts which can exert powerful forces of their own, need considerable standing-rigging support. They often have a

*The adjustable backstay and runners on this fractional-rigged ocean racer (**below**) allow precise control of mast bend and hence sail shape.*

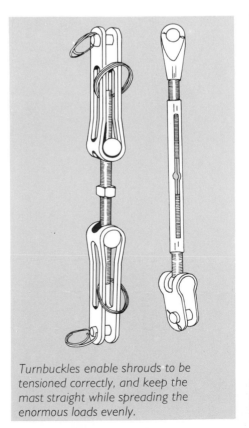

*Turnbuckles enable shrouds to be tensioned correctly, and keep the mast straight while spreading the enormous loads evenly.*

single stay connecting main- and foremast in a schooner, or main- and mizzen in a ketch, called a triatic stay. This stay simply serves to continue the load of the headstay to the aftermost mast's backstay. Both the schooner's foremast and a ketch's mainmast will often have either independent running backstays or, in the case of a ketch or yawl, sometimes a split fixed backstay.

### RUNNING RIGGING DETAILS

Every sail must have a set of running rigging — halyard, sheet or sheets, and sometimes a *topping lift*, which is simply a length of line taken over a block on the mast that serves to support the boom.

For all this running rigging, a boat must have *blocks* (or pulleys), *cleats* (or twin-horned metal or wooden parts for fastening line), and sometimes *winches* (large drumlike devices which, when cranked by hand or electric power, serve to pull on sheets and halyards).

These devices come in a number of variations. There are thousands of assorted sizes and designs. There are aluminum-faced blocks, wood-cheeked blocks, double-sheave blocks (a *sheave* is the wheel itself), tandem blocks, and so on.

*Sail controls cluster around the base of this mast. Note the piston on the hydraulic boom vang.*

The *snatchblock* is particularly useful especially in the manipulation of headsails. This block is built in such a way that one cheek can be unclipped and a line inserted directly, without having to run the line through from its bitter end. In seaman's terms, there is no need to *reeve* the line through the block. A snatchblock also has a swivel-and-shackle arrangement at its base with which it can be fastened to a sturdy track or perforated rail at the gunwale. Position the block wherever you want it along the track, according to the jib you're going to use.

A jibsheet is simply placed in the block, the block's cheek snapped shut, and the sail can be trimmed immediately. Should you wish to change jibs (to a smaller or larger one, for instance), the snatchblock is unlatched, the sheet yanked out and your first jib is removed. The new jib is attached, the new sail's sheet is put into the snatchblock and its cheek closed, and sail is hoisted. See opposite for a look at how a snatchblock works.

Some headsails, especially genoa jibs, are so large that they must be trimmed with winches mounted back along the cockpit's outboard railings or *coamings*. The sheet on

the lee side is passed around the drum of the winch several times and a handle is inserted into the slot at the top of the winch. One crew member holds onto the sheet under tension; he *tails* the sheet. Another crewman cranks on the winch, and the sheet is hauled in. To pay out a jibsheet around a winch, a crewman slacks the sheet while keeping a hand on the winch drum to control the rate at which the sheet pays out and to prevent the sheet from "over-riding" on the drum (right).

Winches are also used to hoist sails on larger boats. The halyard is simply taken around the winch drum, and the crank turned to take up tension.

On sophisticated racing rigs, there are often various means to control the shape, or *draft* of the sails. On racing sailboats, boom *vangs* — in addition to centrally located mainsheet traveler systems — assist in tensioning the boom, bending it down toward the deck and flattening the mainsail in the process, making it a more effective windward sail.

Sail shape may also be adjusted by various methods of bending the mast, such as backstay tensioners or by tensioning the mainsail's *outhaul* — the line that controls

*While one crewman grinds, another tails the end of the sheet (**above**). The grinder then reverts to trimming (**below**).*

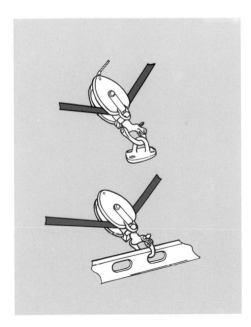

*Snatchblocks (**above**) enable sheets to be changed at will. They can be attached to any strong fitting to provide a fairlead.*

107

tension of the foot of the sail — or increasing luff tension via the main halyard, the downhaul, or a device called a *cunningham* (a length of line taken through a grommet on the main's luff and drawn tight).

Lastly, there will come a time on any big boat when sail must be reduced by *reefing*.

Modern boats usually have one of two types of reefing gear. The most common is called *jiffy reefing*. This setup uses a length of line, or *reefing pendant,* rove (the past tense of "reeve") through a block at the after end of the main boom and through a reefing grommet up on the sail's leech. At the same height as the leech grommet, but on the sail's luff, is another grommet or cringle with another pendant passing through it and down to the forward end of the boom, near the gooseneck. By hauling tightly on both these pendants while easing the main halyard and lowering the main slowly, you bring the lower "slab" of the main onto the boom and draw tension along a line between the two reefing grommets, creating a new "false foot" on the sail, thereby shortening it. Between the two reefing grommets are a number of *reef points* which may have short lines attached. These short lines are passed around the loose slab of sail along the boom to keep it lashed down and out the way. (See left for amplification of the *jiffy reefing* or *slab reefing* system.)

Another reefing system is called *roller reefing*. Instead of using pendants and reef points to shorten sail, the boom rotates along its axis, rolling the sail up like a window shade. Roller reefing is great in principle, but because it has a way of distorting the sail as it rolls it, it is less than ideal and not practical for large boats.

### THE HELM

Obviously, the helmsman in a large cruising/racing boat has far more space than the dinghy sailor. All the controls and

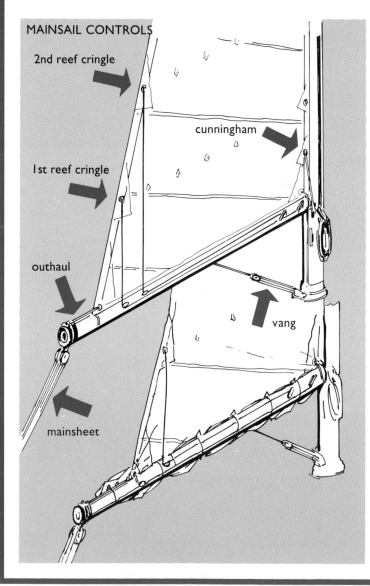

MAINSAIL CONTROLS

2nd reef cringle

cunningham

1st reef cringle

outhaul

vang

mainsheet

*Reefing pendants exiting from the gooseneck (**above left**) lead to cringles on the mainsail leech.*

sailhandling gear and navigation equipment surround him — and on a big racing boat, for example, that can mean considerable complexity.

On the typical mid-sized cruising sloop, however, simplicity can still be a virtue. Many cruisers and some racers still have tiller-steering, for instance. Some even eschew winches in favor of smaller headsails that can be manipulated without them.

A good cockpit layout on a typical mid-sized (30-foot) cruiser would look

*The cockpit of a yacht, whether tiller- or wheel-steered, should be designed around the helmsman and crew.*

something like this:

* Cockpit well (self-draining) about 7ft long, 3ft wide, 2½ft deep.

* Helmsman's position at aftermost corner of cockpit, steering either with tiller or wheel on a pedestal.

* Compass in a binnacle on steering pedestal or affixed to athwartships bulkhead adjacent helm position.

* Seating all around perimeter of cockpit with stowage compartments beneath seat hatches.

* Cockpit coaming around outboard edges of cockpit seating, high enough to provide a degree of protection from water on deck and to form comfortable seat-backs for crew.

* Winches (normally two large genoa winches) mounted on heavy bosses fastened to the coamings and deck port and starboard, symmetrically, with adjacent cleats.

* Winch-handle holders mounted on cockpit bulkheads, adjacent to appropriate winches.

* Halyards and any roller-furling control lines led aft to cabin coachroof at forward edge of cockpit for hoisting and dousing sail without climbing up on deck. Cleats positioned appropriately. Perhaps one small winch to take up halyard tension. If halyards

are not controlled from the cockpit, then they will terminate at the base of the mast, with halyard winches mounted on the mast itself.

* Engine controls placed either on helm pedestal or on cockpit bulkhead, with gauges adjacent to controls.

* Canvas *dodger* designed to fold up to partially protect forward end of cockpit.

### ON DECK

The deck layout of the mid-sized cruiser/racer would be similarly functional.

* Wide deck surfaces free of extraneous fittings, particularly along the sides of the cabin and forward.

* A surface textured to provide sufficient grip for soft-soled deck shoes. Un-finished or oiled teak planking is best, but textured fiberglass is suitable.

* Cabintop or coachroof with handrails port and starboard.

* A hatch serving the belowdecks spaces on the cabin coachroof.

* Anchor-handling equipment consisting of at least two deck cleats and anchorline fairleads. Anchor should be stowed either in a shallow self-draining well flush with the deckline, or mounted within strong chocks on deck.

* Decks surrounded by strong lifelines suspended from stout stainless steel

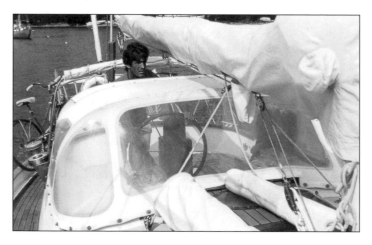

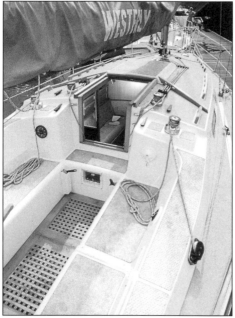

Canvas spray hoods, dodgers and non-slip deck surfaces all help when the going gets tough — comfort and safety are closely allied.

stanchions through-bolted to the deck just inboard of the rail. A bow pulpit should protect sailhandlers working on the foredeck.

* If a spinnaker pole is necessary, it should be chocked and lashed securely on deck or against the cabin sides.

* Toerail around deck's outboard perimeter (gunwale) with either a track securely bolted to it or a strong perforated rail to carry fairleads or other running-gear attachment points.

* Toerail with generous freeing ports to drain water off deck quickly.

If the deck and cockpit are the places where the ship's work is done, then the cabin is the place to rest from it.

## BELOW DECKS

Here the cruiser differs from the racer. The racing yacht's biggest enemy is weight, and interior amenities are heavy. There is much wood and fittings and gear involved in a cruising boat's interior that a racer doesn't need. That's why racing boats usually have canvas *berths* (sailors' beds), minimal *galley* equipment (stove, refrigeration, and such), and much space devoted to sails and navigation.

A true cruiser has much more in the way of equipment below. Here's what a good, modest cruising sailboat should look like below:

* The two main purposes of any cruiser's interior are sleeping and eating. Therefore, the most comfortable spaces aboard should be devoted to these. That means the midships section, because that's where the widest part of the boat is, and that's where the fulcrum of her motion at sea is, too. Being at the fulcrum of motion means the least motion will be felt when the going gets rough. So, our cruiser will have her main sleeping accommodations and galley close to amidships. The berths will double as settees, port and starboard, and a large table will fit

*The accommodation is split into a number of closely defined compartments based on the yacht's bulkhead structure. The galley is almost always situated near the widest point by the companionway.*

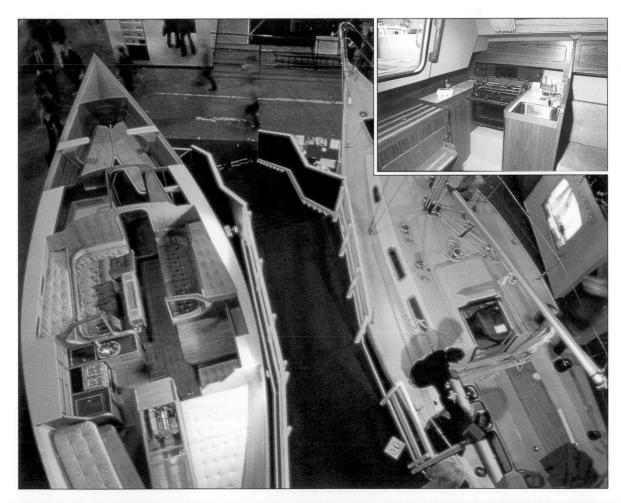

between the settees. The table's outboard leaves will hinge downward so that crew may pass alongside the table when they're not dining.

* The galley is usually found at the foot of the steps leading down into the cabin from the cockpit — the *companionway* steps. It will surround the cook, putting all tasks within easy reach. The sink will be deep so as to hold water even while heeled. All working surfaces and the stove's burners will have sea rails (*fiddles*) to keep utensils and food from sliding off. There will be plentiful utensil stowage in drawers and cabinetry within reach. The cook must also be able to secure him- or herself by bracing against a structural bulkhead or some other sturdy part while underway. Lastly, there must be ample ventilation for the cook, and a window or portlight close to eye level.

* The lavatory compartment — the *head* — will be located forward of the main dining/sleeping space, and usually will separate that space from the forward sleeping quarters. The head will have a toilet which either will pump sewage out through a hose and through a valved skin fitting and into the water, or into a holding-tank built into the boat's hull. The head should also have stowage enough for toiletries, and may have a small shower head connected to the ship's pressure water system.

* The forward sleeping quarters normally will have two separate berths arranged in a "V" configuration within the shape of the boat's bow. Forward of these will be the boat's *forepeak*, which normally contains a locker for anchor-line stowage, and other deck equipment. There will usually be a hatch directly over the forward sleeping space, leading up to the cabin coachroof.

* Sail stowage on a cruising boat is usually confined to one small space, either in the forepeak locker, or along one side or the other closer to amidships. On a cruiser,

*Saloon, head and navigation areas with plenty of handholds, pillars and fiddles are necessary to prevent items of gear slipping off surfaces when the boat is heeled over.*

thankfully, there are usually fewer sails to worry about, and the principle driving sails can be left rigged to their spars and under cover during the season. On a racer, however, one often sees piles of sailbags taking up the entire forward accommodations area, or cluttering the crew's day quarters.

* All good cruising boats need space below for navigation and piloting work. Many smaller boats make do with the cabin's dining table, others have special nooks with a small chart table and navigation tools nearby. It is important that the space is adequately ventilated and that dry stowage is provided for charts and plotting tools.

## POWER

Finally, the engine. The most important thing about a sailing boat's auxiliary engine is that it run. Never mind about the "purity" of sail, a good engine can be a friend in times of need, and a bad one can make things awkward.

Therefore, the most important thing about the ship's auxiliary is that it be easy to get to for routine checks and service. If the oil is difficult to change, chances are it will not be changed often, and that could lead to poor performance. The engine in a small cruiser is usually bedded beneath the cockpit, directly abaft the companionway steps. The steps should come away completely to offer access to the engine's oil filter, fuel lines and fuel filter, cooling-water intake (and its valve), cooling water strainer, and other maintenance items — all these should be close to hand.

Finally, the engine's compartment, when closed off from the rest of the boat, should be as sound-proof as possible to keep the rumble to a dull roar.

Some boats have diesel engines, others have gasoline engines. Gasoline is a more volatile fuel, requires care in handling, and its storage is often subject to stringent regulation. Diesel fuel, on the other hand, is akin to home heating oil and is quite safe and non-explosive.

However, gasoline engines have had lower selling prices — while diesels have always been rather expensive, though somewhat less so to operate than gasoline engines.

On some smaller cruisers, outboard power is the answer, with a small two-stroke gasoline outboard motor mounted near the transom. An outboard's fuel can be carried conventionally in a tank built-in to the boat's hull, or in a portable tank secured below the cockpit seating. Outboard fuel must be pre-mixed with a special lubricating oil, as a two-stroke powerplant gets its internal lubrication from its fuel.

*The engine compartment under the cockpit sole (**below left**) — insulated and yet accessible for routine servicing and hand-starting. The little 5hp outboard on the transom bracket of this sloop (**below**) provides ample power.*

# II | BASIC BIG BOAT HANDLING

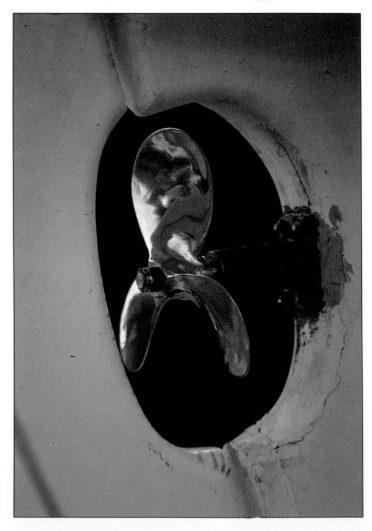

*Don't expect the propeller on a long-keeled cruiser to give precise handling, especially astern.*

The differences between handling a big boat and a small one lie in the speed with which the maneuvers can be undertaken, and the strength and range the big boat is capable of.

## UNDER POWER

Running a keelboat under power gives an overall sense of the boat. You find out how long it takes to turn her at speed, how much backing force it takes to slow her to a stop, and how much power it takes to keep her moving — even in a rough sea.

Practice your under-power maneuvers out on open water. It is there, in calm conditions, that you'll get the best lessons — *before* you really need the skills.

Here are the major principles of maneuvering underway:

* A marine auxiliary engine, whether outboard or inboard, has three gears — forward, neutral, reverse. Most engines are more powerful in forward gear than in reverse — because of propeller position, shape, and other factors.

* A major point to remember is that most inboard auxiliary engines, when in forward gear, turn their propellers in a clockwise direction when viewed from aft. These "right-hand" propellers turn the boat slightly when underway, and this action must be resisted by a sight offset on the

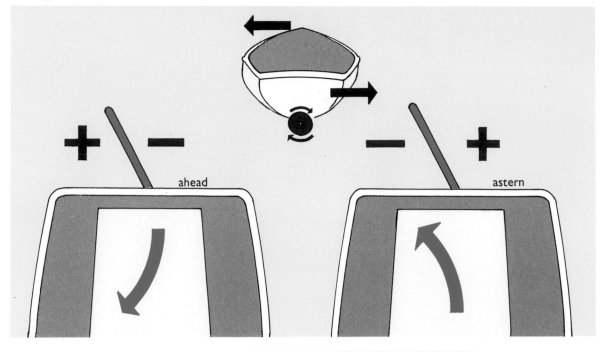

ahead                                                              astern

helm. Right-hand propellers turn a boat's bow to port when in forward gear, to starboard when backing. When backing from a stop, the bow of your boat will swing to starboard *before* you are able to offset that motion with the rudder, as the rudder needs water moving past it to produce control. So, allow room for that swing, and learn to compensate for it in your backing maneuvers.

* Steering will normally be more effective when in forward gear than in reverse. This is because the thrust of the propeller is usually directed across the surface of the rudder in forward, while in reverse that thrust is directed away from the rudder. Thus, in forward gear the propeller thrust may be re-directed by the angle of the rudder during a turn, helping the rudder do its work. Because of this, a boat is able to begin a forward turn from a standstill.

* An outboard motor hung on a transom bracket will be less effective in a rough sea than one in a motorwell, or an inboard engine. The wave action will pick up the lower unit of the outboard and lift its propeller clear of the water, while alternately threatening to immerse its powerhead. A motorwell inset from the boat's transom minimizes this problem, and an inboard engine's propeller is usually too deep to be affected.

## SAILING DIFFERENCES

The general principles of sailing apply equally as well to big boats as they do to small ones. Forces are larger, equipment is more complicated, but nature remains the same.

But there are some special characteristics that apply only to the larger keelboat:

* Because a cruising boat's ballast remains in its keel and cannot be shifted to compensate for gusts or lulls, sail control becomes more important. When a keelboat is suddenly overpowered by a strong gust, the prudent skipper slacks away some sheet, or heads up and luffs to avoid a *knockdown* — the near–capsize of a keelboat. If strong

*The paddlewheel effect of the propeller pushes the stern (**above**).*

*Keel weight keeps this cruiser on her feet (**below**), but the helmsman is ready to slack sheet if a gust hits her.*

gusts build and persist, it is wise to shorten sail or reef. If the wind begins to lull and die away, more sail must be added to keep a big boat sailing most effectively.

* Many keelboats sail most effectively at a modest angle of heel. This is not true of most modern centerboard designs, which tend to do better at flatter angles. A keelboat has an optimal angle of heel of about 12-15 degrees; any more will begin to burden the boat's performance. If the designed heel angle is exceeded by too much, sail should be taken down or reefed.

* Steering characteristics of keelboats make them move more deliberately. Whereas a centerboarder can be snapped through the wind while coming about, a keelboat must usually be "sailed" through the wind. When tacking, it is important to harden up on the wind and continue trimming sails right up to the moment of stall; the trimming helps steer the boat through the tack, and having the sails strapped tight as the boat swings off on the other tack helps her gain speed again. More on this later.

* Sail trimming is a more deliberate science aboard a keelboat. While a centerboarder shows immediate response to variances in sail trim, a larger keelboat will take time to show increases or decreases of speed or heel angle.

Obviously, there are more subtleties to observe, each type of keelboat will show different variations in performance. Suffice to say that experience will soon teach you

*Racing crews brave the rigors of the weather deck (**above**) to provide extra leverage.*

*The crew attaches the main halyard (**below**). Sail ties keep the mainsail neatly snugged on the boom until it's time to hoist.*

the finer points of how your big boat differs from your first dinghy.

Remember to do that practicing in open water; and let your big boat teach you how she likes to move.

## HOISTING SAIL

The best reason for an auxiliary engine in a larger keelboat is the over-crowdedness of harbors and marinas. In many of today's harbors, the sheer number of yachts on a typical summer weekend prevent any sailor from actually hoisting sail and maneuvering out of the anchorage or marina. Smaller, quicker centerboarders may find it easier to find their way amongst the crowd, but the more sluggish keelboat is wise to power into the clear before hoisting sail.

The typical exercise in hoisting sail on a cruising boat would go as follows:

* Find a stretch of water outside the confines of the harbor, and slow the engine so the boat has just enough headway to maintain effective steering — this is called *steerageway*. Make sure that you have enough room to continue on a course directly upwind for several minutes.

* Take all sail covers off the working sails to be hoisted, make sure the main topping lift is taut and secure, and lift the main boom out of any cradling or securing device (a *boom crutch* or *boom gallows*). The boom will now be suspended by the topping lift. Trim the mainsheet so that the main boom swings through only a minimal arc, well inboard and under control.

* Attach the main halyard to the mainsail, and keep a few loose turns on the main halyard winch. Bring the bag containing the jib up to the foredeck. Because you've packed the jib correctly, the tack will come out first and be hanked on to the jib-tack snap-fitting at the base of the headstay. The greater part of the jib should be left in the bag as the luff is removed and hanked on to the headstay. Attach the jib halyard to the head of the jib.

* Pull the bag off the rest of the jib, and rig the jibsheets so that they lead fair back to the cockpit. If it's a genoa or overlapping jib, make sure to run the sheets outboard of the shrouds, port and starboard. Your snatchblocks or jib fairleads should be set up

*The jib halyard is attached to the head of the sail (**left**). The luff is already hanked to the forestay. The rest of the sail lies stretched along the leeward side deck.*

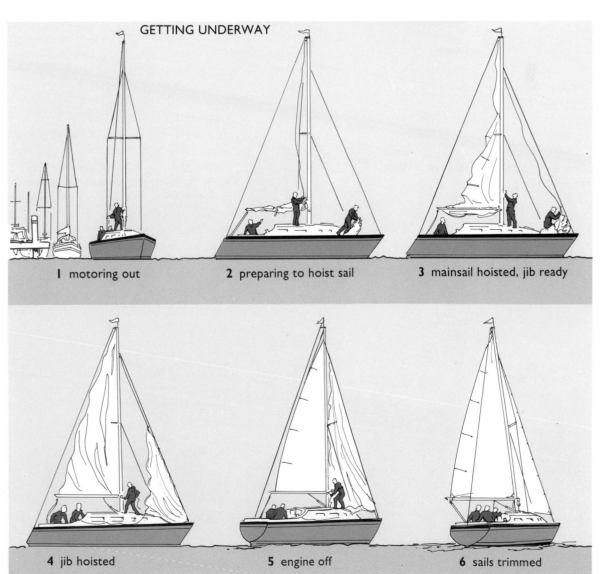

**GETTING UNDERWAY**

**I** motoring out

**2** preparing to hoist sail

**3** mainsail hoisted, jib ready

**4** jib hoisted

**5** engine off

**6** sails trimmed

*The self-tailing winch enables one man to grind without the help of a "tailer". The sheet is gripped in the jaws after passing over the "stripper" arm.*

*The main halyard (**below**) should be coiled neatly on its cleat.*

to take whatever jib you're using.

* Now remove all but one of the ties holding the main furled on the boom. The helmsman should make sure his course is directly into the wind, and that there are no loose lines trailing over the side to become fouled in the propeller.

* The command is "hoist away", and the mainsail is first. The halyard man frees the remaining sail tie, and hauls directly without the aid of the winch, until the sail is almost all the way up and the friction of the slides on the track makes it too hard. (On larger boats it may be necessary to haul the halyard by hand with one or two turns on the winch before using the winch handle.) The handle is then inserted, and the winch turned until a sufficient luff tension is drawn. The halyard is belayed, coiled neatly, and tucked behind itself just above the cleat. Lastly, if the topping lift is controlled from the mast, the halyard man will slack it away — but only slightly.

* If the jib is a genoa, it should be led toward the side on which it will be trimmed

when the boat is swung offwind and under sail. At the command "hoist away" the jib's halyard is hauled manually. When the sail is about half way up, the helmsman should begin a slow swing toward the direction of his first planned heading. The sail is pulled up taut with the aid of a winch, to get the proper luff tension, and allowed to stream off to leeward until the halyard man has finished securing forward. Again, he tucks the coiled halyard behind itself above the mast cleat. Then he brings the winch handles back to the cockpit (unless there is a pocket for the winch handle at the base of the mast). When everything is secure, sail can be trimmed.

* The helmsman has already trimmed the mainsheet properly for the first heading — he did that while the halyard man was handling the jib. Now for trimming the jib. The helmsman makes sure he's on the right point of sail, with the main trimmed properly. The crewman grabs the leeward jibsheet and takes three or four turns around the genoa winch. He hands the sheet's end to the helmsman, who will tail it — or else he tails it himself, if the wind is light enough to manage alone. He may try to take in as much of the sail as he can by pulling the sheet around the winch drum as it freewheels, but eventually, be inserts the winch handle and cranks the sail the rest of its way in to its appropriate trim angle. Some winches are *self-tailing*, meaning that their mechanism includes a self cleating device that maintains tension to pull the sheet against the drum for trimming. When the jib is trimmed exactly right, the sheet is secured with a few turns around the adjacent cleat, and coiled in big loops.

## COMING ABOUT

The tacking maneuver in a big boat bears little difference from the one in the small centerboarder. However, it is worth looking at the whole process to point out the important variations.

* At the command "Ready About," the crew of two take on their split function: the helmsman as skipper and mainsheet handler; the crewman as jib-handler.

* The jib man unwinds the jibsheet from its few figure-eight turns on the cleat, and prepares to cast the sheet off the winch drum. The helmsman makes sure the

direction he's about to tack toward is clear of traffic, and that all loose items are secure.

* At the command "hard alee" or "lee ho", the helm is put down to leeward and the boat starts its turn into the wind. No action is taken by the jib man until the jib dumps its wind and begins to luff. When the sail empties and begins to flutter, he casts off the sheet entirely from the winch drum. He makes sure the leeward sheet will run freely from its coil in the cockpit, and moves to the opposite side to begin hauling the jib around for the opposite tack.

* The boat turns through the eye of the wind and begins to pay off on the other side. The jib hangs briefly, looking somewhat tangled against the mast and shrouds. But the wind will help push it around as the boat falls off on the new tack. The jib man simply takes in the sheet, preparing the winch and handle for the trimming process. The helmsman has not had to do anything with the mainsheet; it has remained fastened to its own cleat throughout the operation.

* Finally, the jib blows free of the shrouds and mast and streams out to leeward. The jib man hauls the sheet in as before, pulling it around a freewheeling drum until the strain becomes too much, then cranking on the winch until the sail is properly trimmed.

* If the skipper wishes to fall off further, the jib can be slacked slowly by the jib man — with one hand lightly on the winch drum, the other paying out the sheet. The helmsman will also find the proper trim angle for the mainsheet.

* Both main- and jibsheets are belayed with a few turns on their cleats, and the extra line coiled and stowed neatly.

## JIBING

While a jibe in a small boat is a maneuver requiring quick thinking and precision, in a bigger boat it can be a true challenge. In a dinghy, you risk a banged head and possibly a capsize if things don't go well; but in a big boat, a severe knockdown can result if the wind is heavy, or gear can be broken — or a crewman can be seriously injured if his head gets in the way of a fast-moving boom.

The best solution is never to jibe in a stiff breeze when under-manned; or jibe only when you have practiced the maneuver sufficiently to feel confident in yourself and your crew.

Here are the steps to a safe jibe:

* The boat is running almost straight downwind. The command "prepare to jibe" is issued.

* The helmsman slowly begins to trim the mainsheet. The crewman casts off the turns he's made in the jibsheet around its cleat and prepares to cast off the turns from the leeward winch.

* When the mainsheet is gathered in so that the main boom is at about the proper attitude for a beam reach, the command "jibe-ho" is given, and the tiller is slowly eased to windward — in other words, the boat is steered so that its stern will pass *very* slowly through the eye of the wind.

* The helmsman gathers some more mainsheet in, and prepares for the quick passage of the boom overhead. The command ". . . watch your heads!" or ". . . duck!" might be appropriate.

* The helmsman prepares to slack the mainsheet quickly away as the boom passes over and hits the end of its sheet travel on

*The tacking procedure for a big boat is essentially the same as that for a dinghy. However, the movement of crew weight is not as important since there is no danger of capsizing.*

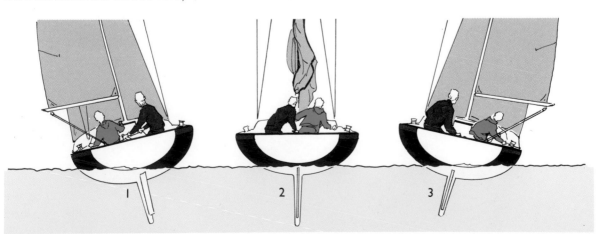

the opposite side. This is to cushion the shock on the rigging. The jib man casts off the winch turns and prepares to take up his sheet on the opposite side.

* The boom comes across the cockpit abruptly as the wind backs around the sail all at once. The helmsman eases the sheet to cushion the shock, and allows the mainsail to continue taking slack until it is to the point of trim appropriate for the offwind angle he wants to sail. As the main shifts sides, it uncovers the jib, which is in turn blown forward and around the mast. The jib man's job is to keep the jib from snarling the headstay, and to bring it safely around the mast with the leeward sheet.

* With the maneuver completed, the helmsman cleats his mainsheet and squares away on his new course. The jib man gets his trim right, cleats off and coils his sheets neatly for the next maneuver.

## SHORT-TACKING

Should you find yourself in a narrow stretch of water where your course takes you through to windward, you may have to beat upwind. This would involve many tacks through the narrow passage, particularly against a foul tide.

Picture yourself handling, in short order, 10 or 15 of the tacking maneuvers described earlier. It can be trying.

There are several approaches to making it easier:

* The most obvious step may seem to be to douse the jib and attempt to sail upwind through the narrow spot on mainsail alone.

If short-handed, this can be the least taxing on crew, but it seriously inhibits the efficiency of the boat, and might not provide enough power to get you through against a foul tide, for example.

* This is when a self-tacking or "club-footed" jib — one that has its own boom and traveler and needs no trimming during a beat — comes into its own.

* If the passage is long, involving many tacks, you can replace a big genoa with a small working jib. The smaller sail will make the tacks simpler by eliminating the need for getting the jib around the mast and free of the shrouds, and will be much easier to handle on the winch.

* Lastly, if you simply must use the genoa, the helmsman should tail the jibsheet; as he will not need to do anything with the mainsheet on a beat, and the jib man will have his hands full with the winch work.

## DOUSING SAIL

The day over, you'll want to sail into a sheltered spot and lower sail. The procedure is as follows:

* Take most sail down. Head up slightly, luffing all sail, and have the crew go forward and let go the jib halyard. The crewman should let the halyard slip through his hands, or slack it away steadily around the winch, as he gathers the sail aboard and piles it gently on the foredeck. He must take care not to snag the sail on any projections — such as the anchor stock or foredeck cleats.

* The crewman detaches the jib halyard and secures it to the rail, ready to be clipped

*Jibing a big boat is a potentially dangerous maneuver. The correct procedure for a safe jibe is: (1) crew tends jib while helmsman hauls mainsheet until boom is central; (2) stern steered slowly through eye of wind, boom passes overhead; and (3), jib and mainsail trimmed on new tack.*

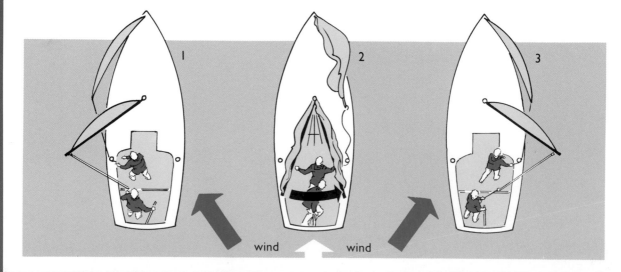

wind    wind

on again if the engine fails at the last minute.

* Then the jib is secured to the lifelines, or bagged, leaving the luff hanked on to the forestay.

* With all sail but the mainsail down, the skipper makes sure no sheets or lines are trailing in the water, and starts the engine. He puts the engine in gear and swings slowly upwind until he is aimed directly into the wind. He applies enough power to maintain steerageway, and trims the mainsail all the way in tight.

* The crewman on deck hauls the topping lift up tight and cleats it off. He then prepares to drop the main. He casts off the main halyard from its cleat and awaits the command to let go.

* On command, the crewman lets the main halyard run freely, and helps guide the sail down so that it falls on the near side of the boom and neatly on deck. The helmsman keeps the boat pointed directly to windward and helps guide the main down.

* The crewman on deck begins to furl the mainsail by "bagging" it or "rolling" it

inside itself, starting from the bottom up. The process of furling begins forward. As the forward part near the mast is done, the crewman secures it with a sail tie. He then moves aft to do the rest of the sail. With a larger crew, several people can be stationed along the boom to furl and secure sail. The result of this process is called a "harbor furl", which can be improved upon later when securing the boat for the week. Some racing sailors prefer to fold their sails neatly on the boom in a more formal fashion — but as mentioned in a previous chapter, these folds must be staggered so as not to crease the sail permanently.

* With the jib bagged or secured and the mainsail down and furled against the boom, the boat is relatively secure but sail can still be raised at a moment's notice. Once securely anchored or berthed the sails can then be properly bagged and the mainsail cover put on.

And don't forget the fresh water washdown when you're back in port. Nothing keeps a boat looking new like a good scrubbing.

*The correct procedure for dousing sail : (**1**) release jib halyard and gather sail aboard; (**2**) detach jib halyard and stow sail neatly; (**3**) main halyard released, sail gathered; and (**4**), mainsail furled against the boom.*

121

# 12 | ADVANCED SAIL TRIM

*This cruising genoa needs a little more halyard tension.*

The most important rule is that a sail should be trimmed only so far as to capture the apparent wind.

To windward, the luff of the sail is kept drawing just enough to eliminate the flutter that indicates wind getting around the lee side. On a reach, it's the same thing. And on a broad reach or run, the sail is simply a pocket designed to catch the push of the wind. Essentially, these rules hold true of almost any sail you'd hoist in almost any condition.

These are *basic* rules, not designed for extracting the absolute maximum out of your rig, but rather for the casual purposes of cruising. Those interested in racing or "performance cruising" should examine the techniques for more carefully controlling sail shape.

What follows is not meant to be the last racer's word on shape-control. For that, your own boat and a good measure of experience are the best teachers. Consider this an introduction, a source of ideas to help you improve your performance.

## SAIL SHAPE AND WIND STRENGTH

Without going into all the aerodynamics involved, let's look at some simple rules for setting up sail shape in various wind conditions and points of sail.

Typically, when on a hard beat in moderate to heavy winds, you need to set

up your sails so that they are relatively "flat" in their angle of attack on the wind. You do not want baggy sails when going to windward in heavy wind. Sheeting our sails in tightly helps flatten them, but there are other ways.

As you fall off from your hard beat, you will want to allow a bit more bagginess in your sails, until you are running downwind, at which point of sail you'll want enough draft to catch the wind, but not so much that the boom lifts and gets out of control. Paying out the boat's sheets does much to make her sails baggy, but — again — there are other methods.

What is needed now is an appreciation of a sail's *draft*, or the degree to which its *camber* — or cross-sectional curvature — can be controlled.

## SAIL SHAPE CONTROL — THE MAIN

A cruising/racing sloop or cutter probably doesn't have many lines and gadgets to control sail shape; not when compared to a pure racing machine.

For hard windward work on the average keelboat, when the mainsail needs to be flat, there are several ways of controlling draft. Some or all of these might be present on a small performance centerboarder, but they're more likely to be available on the bigger and more complex boat.

*Perfect sail trim is essential if this ocean racer (**above**) is to build up a lead at the start of an Admiral's Cup race, but the cruising sailor (**left**), dinghy in tow, need not be quite so concerned, although he should still seek a measure of performance.*

The mainsheets of older boats usually were positioned at the aftermost tip of the boom. Because of this, they had little effect on the shape of the middle sail. Many of today's designs have the mainsheet practically amidships, or at least at the center of the boom. When the sail needs to be flattened at the center, the mainsheet can be hauled tighter so as to bend the boom downward and consequently help to flatten the sail.

123

*The combination of working jib and full main provides ample power for this 32ft cruiser in the conditions, but she could find herself overpowered to windward without a reef.*

Two very common sail controls, the outhaul and cunningham, are almost always available on the cruising keelboat. Because both stretch the sail's fabric on the bias, both are capable of taking the belly out of the length of sail they stretch: the outhaul stretches the foot, and therefore can eliminate draft toward the sail's bottom; the cunningham stretches the sail's luff, and reduces draft at the leading edge.

The *boom vang* is another method for controlling sail draft by manipulation of the boom rather than the sail itself. However, it is not usually as effective as the centrally located mainsheet on a windward beat, but is normally used when running off the wind, a point of sail where the angle of mainsheet — even if on a car/traveler system — prevents it from being as effective. The vang can be located on any of a number of fittings mounted on deck, usually outboard of the boat's centerline, or at a point at the foot of the mast.

The vang reduces draft by limiting the boom's lift when off the wind, and also keeps the boom end under control during rolling oscillations in sea conditions produced by a following wind.

When a sophisticated performance boat is going to windward on a hard beat while carrying a large racing headsail, some extra tension will be needed on the backstay to offset the force of the jib or genoa on its headstay. Without this the headstay would sag, distorting the luff of the jib.

The backstay tensioner is a device that exerts tremendous force on the rig and compression on the mast through its screw mechanism and/or its hydraulic cylinder.

The tensioner system also removes some draft from the mainsail, by bending the mast so as to conform to the main's luff shape. When the spar is bent to conform to the curving shape of the luff, and the sail is trimmed close-hauled, as a result much of the belly is taken out of the sail. Again, keep in mind that the backstay tensioner is a piece of gear used almost exclusively by racing craft.

When running off the wind, or when reaching in light airs, there are times when it's wise to increase the draft of the mainsail. To do this, make sure your mainsheet is properly trimmed (not too tight — you don't want to bend the boom at the middle), and make sure your downhaul or cunningham is slack. Couple that with some slack in the outhaul, and you can greatly increase the draft at the middle of your main.

## SAIL SHAPE CONTROL — THE JIB

Headsails are similar to mainsails in that, in light airs, more draft is appropriate, either on or off the wind. In heavy windward work, the more uniform the shape, and the flatter the sail (up to a point where it is over-trimmed and the boat heads toward a stall), the better.

Because the standard working jib or genoa has no boom, the process of controlling its draft is much simpler.

We have already mentioned one way to increase luff tension on a jib: the backstay tensioner. Another important draft-controlling aspect of jib trim is where its sheet is positioned and angle it is led aft.

On most modern boats, genoa *tracks* are positioned on the deck, both port and starboard. These tracks enable you to position the jib blocks at any point you choose along the tracks. This is handy for changing headsails, as the clew point for a large genoa will be in a very different location from that of a smaller one.

Fine adjustments in fairlead position can also be used to adjust the way a genoa draws. If the block and car are too far aft for the sail being used, the sail's leech will belly causing wind to spill off the sail's most effective working sections. If the block and car are too far forward, the jib's leech will be too taut and its foot will be baggy. This will cause the jib's leech to "hook" inward and backwind the mainsail, reducing efficiency.

Ideally the jibsheet should come away from the clew and toward the lead position

*The helmsman watches the tell tales on this genoa in light airs (**left**), trying to keep the boat moving, but he might do better to bear away a little.*

*Sheet position is critical to headsail shape (**below**). One way of fine-tuning the sheeting angle is to use a barberhauler (**bottom**).*

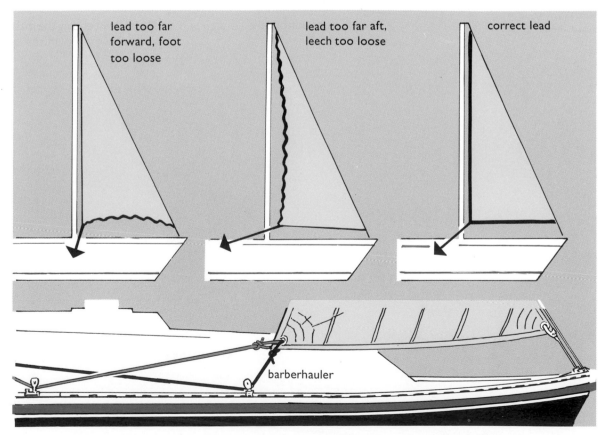

lead too far forward, foot too loose

lead too far aft, leech too loose

correct lead

barberhauler

in a direction more or less at right angles to the stay on which the headsail is hoisted. This angle can vary slightly according to the specific cut of the jib involved.

This exact positioning is not always possible, however, so there is one more method of fine-tuning the sheeting angle on a headsail. The *barberhauler* is simply a line led from the clew of a headsail almost vertically downward to the boat's rail track and to another block or light tackle arrangement (see opposite). By leading the genoa's sheet slightly more aft than is proper, and by applying some tension on the barberhauler, you can adjust the lead angle between the barberhauler and sheet lead and thereby control the sail's draft.

### LIGHTWEIGHT, HEAVYWEIGHT

In the past several decades of yachting, sails to handle extremely light winds have been developed. *Ballooners*, *spinnakers*, *drifters*, *bloopers*, *reachers*, and so on, have all contributed to racing and cruising performance.

All share two things in common: first, they have more draft than their corresponding heavy-air partners; and second, all are made of relatively lightweight fabric, responsive to light winds.

The typical 30-foot cruising boat designed for coastal work will carry the normal sail complement of working jib, genoa, and mainsail — plus one or two other sails designed for light airs.

**Mainsail** This is the most bulletproof standard sail aboard the boat. The design and weight of the sail makes it suitable for almost all conditions, and it can be reefed, so that in really extreme conditions its size can be reduced.

**Working jib** For all points of sail. A fabric weight comparable to the mainsail. Suitable for heavier wind conditions.

**Genoa jib** The term usually applied to the No I jib — usually made of lighter cloth with less stabilizing resin than the working jib. For windward and reaching work. The genoa may overlap the mainsail by half, or more, depending on its designation.

**Reacher** For all points of reaching in light to moderate conditions. Sometimes with a high-cut clew, sometimes cut close to the deck like a genoa, this sail is usually very light. Hanks to the headstay like a genoa, and used like a genoa.

**Spinnaker** For off-the-wind work.

*The "gun mount" or fixed spinnaker pole (**below**) is a novel answer to spinnaker handling, and enables the sail to be controlled at all times.*

Effective on broad reaches and downwind runs, but experienced sailors carry some flatter-cut spinnakers on beam and close reaches. Very light sail. Most common designs require separate pole to push one clew out to windward for stability. Some cruising-types are cut so that no pole is necessary, however.

Of course, on a racing boat there will often be many more bags of sails. The first additions to any sail locker usually will be a set of jibs. These will fill the gap between the No 1 genoa and working jib, and will apply to strengthening wind conditions with flatter cuts and heavier cloth.

Then other light-air sails will be introduced. Perhaps a blooper, which is hoisted alongside a spinnaker to increment downwind horsepower. And then a drifter, which is a full-cut genoa made of extremely light cloth and designed for close reaches and windward work.

The list is practically endless, which is why dedicated racing crews must share their quarters with an extraordinary volume of sailcloth.

*The cruising chute (**below**) is a cross between a big genoa and a spinnaker.*

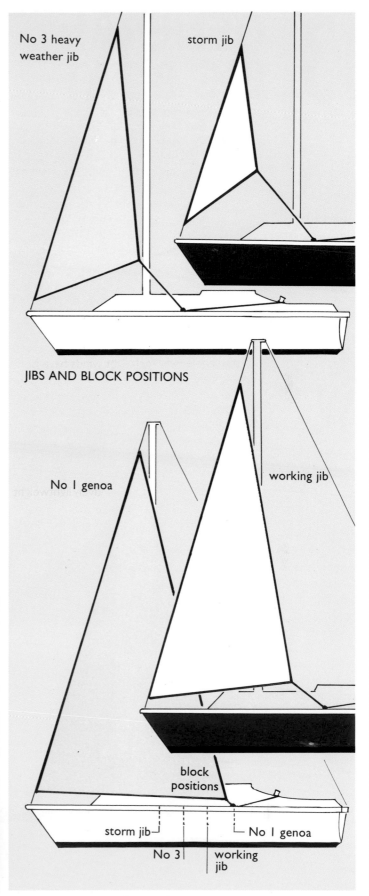

JIBS AND BLOCK POSITIONS

# 13 | GENERAL BIG BOAT SAFETY

*Losing a mast can happen to anyone (**below**). A well equipped cruising yacht complete with life raft (**below**).*

**W**hile the cruising/racing keelboat is quite safe by virtue of its freeboard (the height of its deck above the water), its rough-water ability, and its stability due to its keel-mounted ballast, it presents some particularly important safety considerations.

* First, because it is heavy in comparison to the centerboard dinghy, its gear is more highly loaded and its power far greater. Its sails convert far more wind energy into motion and therefore store much more power. If a shroud should let go or a seam in a sail rip, a great deal of force would be loosed in sometimes unpredictable directions. It is one thing to lose a dinghy mast in a gust, or to capsize in a small boat with full flotation — and quite another to have a tall rig collapse on deck in a tangle of wire and sail cloth, or to take a knockdown in a heavy wind.

* The crew of a big boat is often larger than that of a small one, so there are more people for the skipper to organize.

* A bigger boat spends more time on open water, sometimes many miles from safe harbor, therefore changes in weather and sea conditions are always a threat.

What follows is a list of some common situations requiring a good measure of safety-consciousness, along with recommendations on how best to deal with them.

## SAFETY SCENARIOS

**Dockside dangers** A 30-foot cruising boat can weigh somewhere near 10,000–17,000 pounds and carry a great deal of momentum.

When docking, it is wise to move through the routines slowly, and all close maneuvering should be done under power, unless the traffic is thin or non-existent and the dock or mooring clear enough of the shore or obstructions to make rounding up under sail a relatively straightforward operation. Remember, with full momentum on, a larger boat requires a lot of power to slow to a stop, and may not be able to stop even within several boatlengths or more.

Make sure to inform crew members to keep hands and feet out from between dock and boat, and do not ask any crew member to fend off a possible impact. Use your boat's soft fenders, or send a crewman to the dock with a line to snub around a cleat to help slow the boat's forward motion (see below).

Always have plenty of docklines at hand, and make sure you have a crewman forward during all docking and mooring maneuvers.

**More wind** On a day when reefing sail is not practical because the wind is mostly moderate with only occasional strong gusts, take care to luff in the gusts so that the rig and hull are not overburdened. You will develop a good feel for what your boat can take, but it's usually wise to sail her heeled no more than "rail-down", or where the water surges at the leeward rail but decks are dry. As your skill develops, your approach will no doubt become less conservative — but it's wise to start with some limits in mind.

Of course, when the wind gets very strong, it is always wise to douse a larger headsail and replace it with a smaller one, or reef the main, or a combination of the two.

**Guest aboard** If you have a crew consisting of guests who may not have a thorough background in sailing, keep things conservative. Don't try to crowd on sail in a blow, for instance, or try to make a passage in record time. Keep fancy sailhandling to a minimum; you don't need spinnakers and spinnaker poles to attend to while you're entertaining the boss and his wife.

Make sure you have sufficient lifesaving equipment for all those aboard, and show your guests where the lifejackets are, and how to put them on. Make sure to ask how many can swim, and issue those that can't with their own lifejackets to wear at all times when aboard. Remember, a larger boat can't turn abruptly to pick up a man overboard; it could take a while to get back to someone who's fallen in.

Make sure all aboard are briefed on safety

*With fenders and lines ready (**far left**), a crewman prepares to take a line ashore while another fends of amidships (**left**).*

129

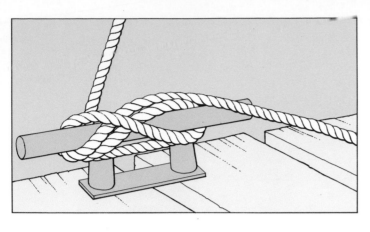

*A dock line securely made up on a mooring cleat with a locking turn.*

*Life raft (**1**) and horeshoe life ring (**2**) with flashing light, activated when inverted.*

procedures *before* the need for any arises.

**Fire hazards** The auxiliary engine in a large keelboat is a potential hazard, especially if it uses petrol as a fuel. Gas fumes tend to gather in a boat's bilge, and a skipper must make sure the boat is thoroughly ventilated before starting the engine or working near the bilge.

Fire extinguishers should be placed in key locations throughout the boat. If your boat has a galley stove, make sure there's a fire extinguisher nearby but *not* above the stove; in a flare-up, the extinguisher must be accessible, not engulfed in flame. It is wise to mount an automatic extinguishing system (CO2 or Halon 1301) within the engine compartment for on-the-spot protection, but also important to have hand-operated extinguishers nearby.

A petrol-engined boat should have forced-air circulation for the bilge — a blower to pull fumes out of the lowest point in the bilge area, but it's a good idea to have the same system in a diesel boat.

**Distress** The most important piece of safety gear aboard may be your bilge pump.

Do not trust merely one to do the job. Your boat should have an electrical bilge pump, driven off the ship's battery system, an additional manual pump and even a third pump, this one driven off the engine and capable of pumping the greatest volume possible with the power available.

There may come a time when long-distance communication is required to get help in a crisis. Learn how to use the VHF radio, and know the common distress frequencies.

Always check your transmitting capabilities at the beginning of a sail. Ask for a radio check on the common-traffic channel, and always ask the respondant for his approximate position, so that you know how far you've managed to transmit. In any routine communications, take note of your communications range and the quality of your reception and transmission.

Have a suitable signal-flare system aboard. No less than ten skyrocket flares, plus another ten hand-held flares are considered adequate. Day signals consist of smoke flares and/or bright shapes or flags.

If you spend long periods of time far offshore, a reputable inflatable liferaft is a good idea. If you do venture offshore, but not that frequently, then your normal ship's tender (your dinghy) could serve in an emergency. Whichever you choose, you should have a kit made up for the chance that you'll have to take to your raft or dinghy. The kit should include, at very least, *(1)* A strong waterproof light. *(2)* A complete first-aid kit. *(3)* A complete flare kit. *(4)* Throwable lifesaving device. *(5)* Some

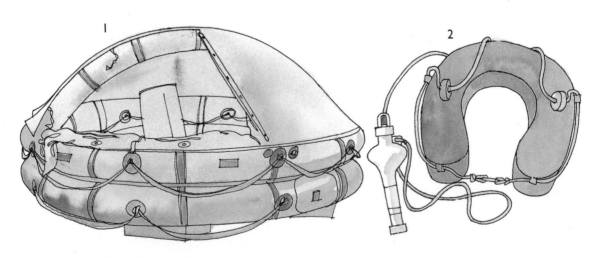

1

2

lengths of synthetic line. *(6)* Minimal rations. *(7)* A portable EPIRB -- or emergency position–indicating radio beacon. A list of required safety items may be obtained from the U.S. Coast Guard (see page 47).

**Man overboard** Make sure your crew knows what to do in a man-overboard situation. Have a horseshoe lifering and danbuoy nearby to pitch to the man overboard. One crew member should be assigned solely to the task of keeping an eye on the swimmer. The watchman should continually point to the man in the water, giving the helmsman verbal direction in his maneuvers.

You should also have a good plan for hauling the man back aboard. This is often the hardest part, and it is wise to plan for any eventuality and practice, practice, practice. A good idea is to design a simple sling system — perhaps using the boom vang, topping lift, mainsheet, or some separate tackle — for strapping around the man in the water and swinging him aboard (see right).

**Getting lost/Poor visibility** In fog, your position soon becomes doubtful, even though you've been keeping track on your chart, so it's important to know the tides and currents and the times of high and low water in the area you're cruising. It's also important to know where the best harbor of refuge is. Even in known waters, the visibility can be so poor that you'll find yourself faced with several choices: *(1)* Anchor until the fog clears. Proper fog signals must be sounded regularly and clearly. *(2)* Turn around and steer a reciprocal course in the hope of sailing back out into the clear. *(3)* Hold your course, but slow down by reducing sail, and keep sounding your fog signals. Try to keep track of your speed and course so as to keep a running estimate on your position. If you're in open water, this might be the best procedure of all.

It is wise to carry aboard a radar-reflective shape to hoist aloft in case of reduced visibility. Commercial vessels all have radar, and such a shape could enhance your visibility in traffic lanes, but, keep a vigilant lookout at all times.

**Running aground** This happens to almost everyone eventually. It can range from a soft grounding on a sandbar, to a hard on a reef or rocky coast.

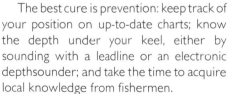

The best cure is prevention: keep track of your position on up-to-date charts; know the depth under your keel, either by sounding with a leadline or an electronic depthsounder; and take the time to acquire local knowledge from fishermen.

If you should go aground, your gear should include a *kedge*, or heavy anchor with stout line long enough to set for hauling off the bar or reef. If you boat has a standard Danforth or plow, either can be used as a kedge, provided it is heavy enough.

The kedge is taken out in the ship's tender to a point in deeper water, and set.

*Recovering a man overboard is a skilled operation. This crew practice hoisting the victim aboard in the bight of the headsail (**left**).*

*A number of clever devices are now on the market for recovering a man overboard. This rigid loop (**left**) is designed to lasso the man in the water.*

*A radar reflector (**above**), correctly hoisted in the "catch water" position, will produce a clear blip on an approaching vessel's radar screen.*

Strain is taken, and the boat is pivoted or othewise hauled off. Sometimes, it helps to heel the boat to reduce draft. This can be done by sending one or two agile crewmen out on the boom as it is swung far to one side. Another anchor may also be set out to the side and the main halyard attached to its line. Then the halyard is hauled and the boat further heeled until the kedge can spin her off the bottom.

The best answer, of course, is a tow from another boat but that's not always possible. Lastly, one can wait until the tide floats the boat clear, but only if the grounding occurred at less than full high tide.

Careful helmsmanship alone is no guarantee that another boat will not hit yours, but you stand a better chance of avoiding collision if you are completely familiar with the Rules Of The Road and exercise due caution and common sense.

A good understanding of weather, including a late radio forecast, is no guarantee that a big storm won't swing down on your area and catch you at sea.

The best way to have a good safety record — while continuing to push back your horizons in a bigger, more complex vessel — is to use all your senses (including your reason), to make sure your boat is equipped for any eventuality, and to educate yourself and your crew.

Preparedness is at the heart of good seamanship.

*Aground on the edge of a shoal, this cruising ketch has hoisted all sail. The crew is now attempting to heel her down (thereby reducing her draft) and sail her off.*

133

The crew of this racing boat are trying everything in an attempt to free her, but it looks as though they're in for a lengthy wait.

# 14 | SPECIAL SAILS

*A spinnaker transforms the downwind performance of this staid cruising yacht.*

The workhorse of all light-air sails is the spinnaker, and it is found on almost all types of boats — from the small performance planing dinghy to the ocean-going maxiboat.

## THE SPINNAKER

The spinnaker is a large, baggy, lightweight sail designed to be presented before the wind. It works in much the same way as huge squaresails did on the clipper ships of the last century — it catches the wind in its huge pocket and lifts up off the deck as it bellies out, pulling the boat along with it.

**Hoisting the spinnaker** The boat must first be brought into a position to hoist the spinnaker. If you know that a course change will bring your boat onto a downwind point of sail — either a very broad reach or a straight run — then it's time to begin preparations.

*Setting up* Begin by getting the spinnaker pole set up on deck. Decide first which angle you'll be taking the wind when under spinnaker; the pole must be set on the side closest to the wind. On a very broad reach, for example, with the wind slightly on your starboard side but well astern, the pole must be rigged to starboard.

The first step is to attach the pole topping lift — a halyard run through a small block about half way up the mast. Another line is

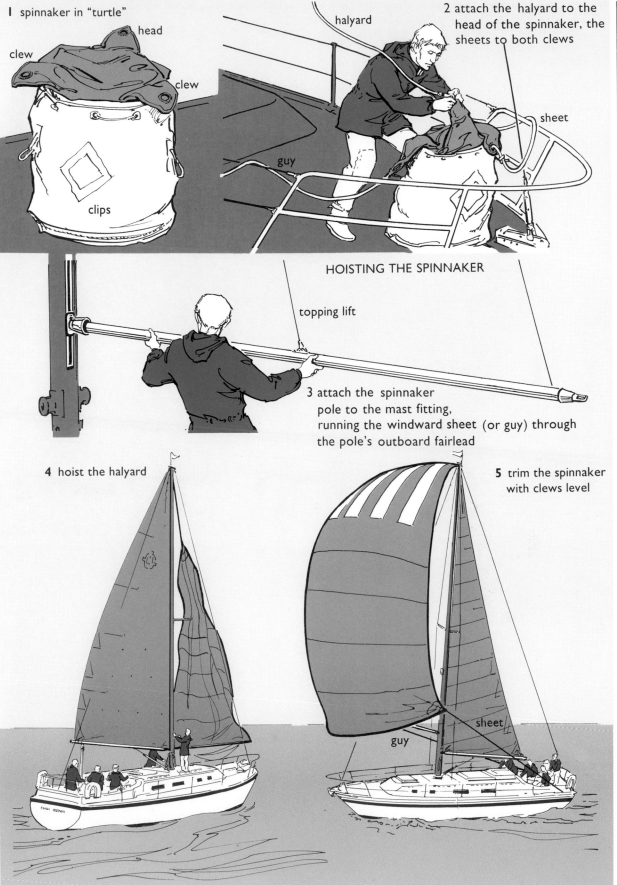

1 spinnaker in "turtle"

head

clew

clew

guy

clips

2 attach the halyard to the head of the spinnaker, the sheets to both clews

halyard

sheet

HOISTING THE SPINNAKER

topping lift

3 attach the spinnaker pole to the mast fitting, running the windward sheet (or guy) through the pole's outboard fairlead

4 hoist the halyard

5 trim the spinnaker with clews level

sheet

guy

This spinnaker (**right, below right**) is being hoisted from a sock and is under control all the time. It can be doused at a moment's notice if the wind pipes up.

The consequences of a classic broach under spinnaker (**below**). While the sail flogs, the helmsman tries frantically to get the boat under control and prevent the spinnaker wrapping round the forestay.

then rigged from the bottom of the pole, about half way out its length, to a block on the foredeck and then led aft. This is the spinnaker pole foreguy, which keeps the pole under control in much the same way as a boom vang does to the main boom.

*The sheets* The spinnaker sheets are simply lengths of light, strong line that are attached to the twin clews of the sail by bowlines or snap shackles (see Appendix B "Knots"). The leeward sheet can be laid out, with its hauling part in the cockpit, near the winch on the side that will be used for trimming the sail. The windward sheet is taken through the end of the spinnaker pole that will be swung outboard for hoisting, then the sheet is led aft to a winch.

*The sail* Bring the spinnaker up on deck in its bag. It should have been bagged with its huge central "belly" at the bag's bottom, and its head and two clews at the top. Place the bag as far forward on deck as possible.

Make fast the spinnaker sheets — the leeward one to the leeward clew, the windward one, called the afterguy, passing through the pole-end and to the windward clew. Then attach the spinnaker halyard, making sure both your spinnaker sheets run outside your shrouds and that your spinnaker halyard is clear of any standing rigging aloft.

So far, the sail is still in its bag. Only its corners are rigged.

*Setting up the pole* Just before you change course, attach the inboard end of your spinnaker pole to its fitting on the mast at about chest height. Make sure the fitting is adjusted so as to be tight on its vertical track. Using the topping lift, raise the pole so that it is about level with the deck and points directly forward (it will swing against the headstay lightly). Adjust the guy line so as to pull the pole only slightly aft and away from the headstay.

*Hoisting sail* Change course now by falling off the wind and steady on your new course. Now the command is given to "hoist away". The halyard man hoists the sail quickly but surely, making sure that it feeds safely and easily out of its bag. The leeward sheet man (usually the helmsman) makes sure his sheet is not fouling any rigging. The windward sheet-and-guy man watches the angle of the pole and the fairness of his sheet.

Once the sail is out of the bag, the halyard man makes sure that it is not twisting itself about the headstay or winding itself up. The sail is mostly in the lee of the mainsail at this point and is relatively easy to handle.

Now the sail is hoisted completely, and the halyard cleated off. The next step is to slowly trim the leeward sheet while also trimming the afterguy to keep the pole from lifting from its level position. As the sheet is trimmed, the sail will begin to fill with wind, and the leeward sheet man should begin trimming as well.

As both sheet and afterguy are trimmed back, the halyard man should remain on the foredeck to watch the progress, and instruct the trimmers. When trimmed properly, the middle seam of spinnaker should align with the mast with both its luffs full and showing no sign of collapse. Allow the foot of the sail *some* degree of belly when before the wind; you don't want to stretch it against the headstay.

**Jibing the spinnaker** This maneuver should be performed with extreme care and deliberation. The goal in a jibe is to get the wind around to the opposite side of the boat; and that means swinging the boat's stern through the wind, trimming the main in and letting the wind catch it and take it around, *and* swinging the spinnaker's pole around to attach it to the opposite clew.

You have already seen how to jibe without a spinnaker, and this maneuver is no different. The main boom is handled the same way as always. The foredeck action, however, is quite another matter.

One method of spinnaker jibing, usually done on smaller keelboats, is called the "end-for-end" method:

*Step one* Foredeck man goes forward; helmsman proceeds with jibe. As boat is turned directly downwind, helmsman eases pole guy, and foredeck man detaches pole from mast housing and walks end over to other sheet, where he snaps it on. Now the pole runs from clew-to-clew on the spinnaker, and hangs on the topping lift.

*Step two* Boat sails through jibe, with main boom swinging to opposite side. Foredeck man detaches pole from original afterguy (now on the new leeward side) and attaches that end to the mast fitting. The pole guy is then tensioned to stop pole lifting.

## JIBING THE SPINNAKER

137

*Step three* Sheets are adjusted for new point of sail.

Note that a spinnaker is designed to be trimmed so that its foot is as parallel to the horizon as possible. This can be achieved by adjustment of the pole guy and topping lift, the trim of the pole itself, and the vertical position of the pole fitting on the mast.

**Dousing the spinnaker** The easiest way to take down a spinnaker is in the lee of the mainsail. Here's the drill:

*Step one* Sail the boat slightly more to windward if you're on a run, or otherwise get her on a broad reach.

*Step two* Lower the topping lift, slack away on the afterguy (windward sheet) and let the pole rest against the headstay briefly. (This procedure is for small boats only; in larger boats it can result in damage to the foresail and pole!) Haul on the pole foreguy to pull the pole down and away from the headstay slightly.

*Step three* Grab the leeward sheet and work the sail back behind the mainsail by handling it along its foot. When you've got the middle in your hands, gather the sail together along the foot. For this, you'll need to pay out the sheets.

*Step four* Slack away slowly on the spinnaker halyard, bringing the sail down in a vertical bundle behind the shadow of the main. When you get to the middle of the sail's belly, about halfway up, begin stuffing it into the bag. Keep slacking as you bag, making sure to bag the lower part of the sail at the same rate that you're bagging the upper part. When you're finished, you should have the two clews and the head at the very top of the bag, just the way you started. Detach the sheets and secure. (Spinnakers that are too unmanageable to be bagged while being lowered are normally bagged later.)

## ROLLER FURLING HEADSAILS

At the opposite end of the spectrum from the spinnaker is the roller-furling headsail. Its strong points are that it is easy to use for a short-handed crew, requiring only minimal cockpit control and no foredeck work.

All roller-furling jibs unroll by means of trimming the sail's sheet. They are furled by

*The spinnaker rig (**below**): topping lift (**1**); spinnaker pole (**2**); downhaul (**3**); guy (**4**); sheet (**5**).*

*A boomed-out headsail (**above**) is a more manageable alternative for long-distance cruising.*

A typical cruiser roller reefing/furling jib (**far left**). The drum is mounted just above the tack fitting (**left**) and the line runs back to the cockpit.

means of pulling on a pendant that extends from the drum at the base of the roller-stay.

## STORM SAILS

Most of your early sailing work will be inshore, but if you should plan to be offshore for any length of time, you will want to consider storm sails as important items of ship's gear.

The time to use storm sails is when your deepest mainsail reef still exposes too much sail to the wind, and when your smallest jib is too big to handle the blow.

**Storm trysail** In a heavy blow, the mainsail is either taken off the mast and boom and stowed below, or lashed with extra sail ties to the boom. The luff of the traditional trysail is usually attached to the mast with lacings to avoid stressing the sail track, and to allow the main to remain rigged. Some newer systems use the mainsail track, providing it is strong enough, but then the main must be de-tracked or the rig provided with a track switching system to allow the two sails to coexist. The main halyard is used to tension the trysail's luff, and the sail's clew is taken back aft, its sheet led through a block secured to a padeye on deck or to the gunwale sheeting track. In almost all conditions, the trysail is sheeted flat.

**Storm jib** The storm jib is sheeted just like a normal working jib, its sheet led aft through the fairlead and to the cockpit. It is hanked to the headstay with snap-hanks, or sometimes hoisted on its own heavy luffwire to keep it further inboard.

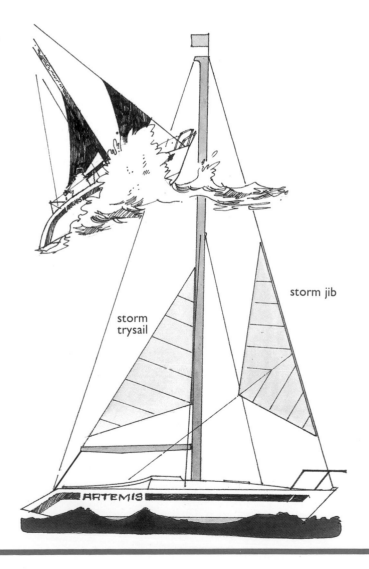

storm trysail

storm jib

ARTEMIS

139

# 15 | HEAVY WEATHER SAILING

*Reefed down and prepared for heavy weather.*

It will be a few years before you run into any serious sea conditions, but you should prepare so that you feel confident in your abilities when you finally decide to venture offshore. When sailing along the coast, it is usually possible to find shelter in a protected harbor before the weather has changed to affect the sea.

However, there are situations to be careful of now. When you and your boat are ready to venture offshore, you eventually will risk exposure to the full force of wind and wave. Here's what you need to know immediately, and some advice on what to expect when you get really adventuresome later on.

## HANDLING A SQUALL

The best way to handle a squall is to know when to expect it, and to head for cover before it hits. Tracking the storm visually is the best way to know whether it's going to pass through your area, and augmenting your own observations with those of local radio broadcasts can create a reasonably good picture of the expected pattern of weather.

If you're too far from land to take cover, and the storm is headed your way, however, you must be prepared.

* Expect a short period of turbulent weather, with winds possibly as strong as

60-80 mph, hard pelting rain, some possible hail, and lightning. Secure all loose gear topside and below. Close all belowdecks openings — ports, hatches.

* Even if your boat is adequately grounded against lightning strike, suspend a length of chain from the amidships shrouds into the water, taping the contact point. Make sure to connect the chain to the masthead (upper) shroud.

* As the squall approaches, check that no lines are in the water, switch on engine and douse all sail and furl it securely. Do this far enough in advance to allow plenty of time to get yourself and your crew settled.

* Break out the foul-weather gear, and unpack the lifejackets and make sure each crewman knows he's got one. Run through a quick fire-safety drill, making sure everyone knows where the extinguishers are and how to use them. Turn off your radiotelephone and temporarily disconnect its antenna.

* With the engine running at about half-speed, point the bow directly into the roll cloud as it approaches. Send everyone else below. If there is moderate vessel traffic about, the helmsman must remain topside. If there is heavy traffic, one lookout should also remain on deck. Any crew topside should wear safety harnesses.

* As the wind hits, make sure the vessel has steerageway against it. More throttle may be needed. If the engine was not started, the skipper should attempt to steer the boat in the direction she tends to move in. She will actually "sail" on nothing but the bare mast alone — but probably not too handily, and certainly well off the wind. A yacht under reduced sail — reefed main and storm jib, for instance, could get knocked down. Until you are better at gauging relative wind strength, a skill that can only come with experience, rely on engine power if a squall threatens.

## TO WINDWARD IN A BLOW

Even inshore, the sea can kick up quite fiercely under the right conditions of wind and tide. When you're heading into it, a lot depends on your skill as a helmsman.

The typical 30-foot cruiser begins to labor in seas that are about equal in height to her freeboard amidships, and not quite as far apart as she is long. That's when the situation is just awkward enough to stop her forward motion if she is not sailed properly.

The best technique in windward sailing in a rough inshore chop is to bear off a little, keeping the seas off the bow to present more of the boat's side to the waves.

The surface of the sea usually has a pattern — a repeating cycle, a rhythm. Larger waves come in groups, followed by periods of relatively smaller seas when you can work the boat more to windward, bearing off only when those seas too big to breast come rolling down.

In restricted waters inshore, a rough sea can be problematic for a number of reasons:

(1) You could get caught off a *lee shore*. This is when the wind and sea overcome a boat and drive her toward a land mass. Always have an alternative course of action planned to avoid a lee shore. If there is no safe harbor to leeward, reach off some

*Under deep-reefed main and storm jib, this cruiser can still make progress to windward.*

141

Wrapped up well, this crewman (**top**) faces a cold watch ahead as dawn breaks. Cloud formation over a headland (**above**) indicates bright but squally weather. Too much sail spells trouble for this cruiser (**right**).

distance to get into the clear and ride it out.

(2) Maneuverability is greatly reduced in heavy seas. Traffic and/or obstructions may be hard to avoid.

(3) Your crew's effectiveness may be greatly impaired. Seasickness is often unavoidable, despite a number of new treatments.

The most prudent course of action in an inshore blow is to seek shelter as soon as you find the conditions uncomfortable. The best technique is to alter course off the wind, taking the seas on your quarter as on a broad reach, and head for the nearest harbor in that direction — even if it means not making your destination that day. Of course, you could also slog directly into it if your engine has enough power and the seas do not threaten your safety, but this can be uncomfortable and can often be avoided with proper passage planning.

## OFFWIND HELMSMANSHIP

Every boat behaves differently when sailing in a rough sea off the wind. But all share some common general traits.

* In a quartering sea — that is, when the boat is broad-reaching in rough conditions and the seas are approaching from off the boat's after quarter — the waves will try to push the boat's stern off the wind and steer her broadside. If the push of the waves is not counteracted by the helmsman, the sails will reinforce the boat's natural tendency to round up into the wind. This is called *broaching*. The beginnings of a broach can be felt in the tiller or wheel as an increase in weather helm, and a helmsman must be ready to counteract it .

* In a following sea, the danger of broaching still exists, although the boat's helm is usually much lighter. Since the wind and waves are astern, there is no constant pressure on the stern to swing off into a broach — although if the helmsman is not attentive, the stern could get off the wind and be pushed by a wave. A broach to windward could lead to an accidental jibe.

The best way to avoid the dangers of broaching and being overpowered by wind and wave on a broad reach or run is to reduce sail. The slower a boat is moving downwind, the more time a helmsman will have to counteract broaching forces and control the boat.

The mainsail is the sail that contributes most to weather helm, because its area is largely distributed abaft the hull's center of lateral resistance. Therefore, if sail is to be reduced at all to avoid broaching, it should be the mainsail (or mainsail and mizzen on a ketch).

## REEFING

Every sailor has his own rules about when to reef. The best answer is experience. Learn what your boat can take, and make sure you reef *before* conditions make it dangerous.

The practice of reducing sail in heavy conditions really starts before the wind reaches unmanageable levels. As your boat begins to labor under full main and genoa, for instance, douse the big jib and hank on your working jib. The reduction in sail area will ease the boat immensely.

On a boat with roller-furling headsails, the jib can be rolled half way, reducing its area and easing motion. On a ketch or schooner, some sails can be doused and others left hoisted to keep the rig balanced under reduced canvas.

Eventually, however, a reef will have to be taken. Here's the way it's done aboard a typical 30-foot sloop or cutter, with slab or "jiffy" reefing.

*Step one* Sail has been reduced to full main and working jib or staysail. The object is to reef the mainsail. First ease the boat onto a close reach and let the mainsail luff so the boat's motion is not uncomfortable for working on deck. (There are times when you reef the mainsail *before* going to the smaller jib.)

*Step two* Hoist the main boom by several degrees with the topping lift; pay out the mainsheet as you hoist. Cleat off topping lift.

*Step three* Slack away on the main halyard until the tack reefing grommet is at the reefing pendant or hook at the gooseneck. Slip the reefing hook/pendant through the tack grommet and take up on the main halyard to produce the proper luff tension. Make up the halyard.

*Step four* Haul on the leech reefing pendant until the leech grommet is snug against the boom and the proper foot tension is achieved. Cleat the pendant.

*Step five* The helmsman steers the boat

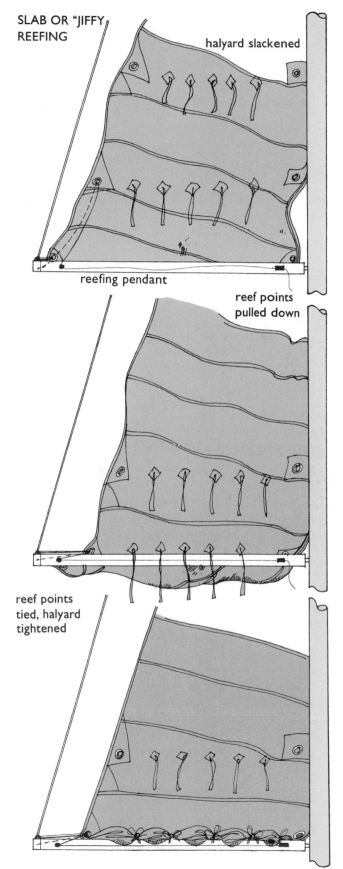

SLAB OR "JIFFY" REEFING

halyard slackened

reefing pendant

reef points pulled down

reef points tied, halyard tightened

more into the wind, hauling the boom inboard. The deck crew slacks away on the topping lift.

*Step six* With the boat close-hauled, the deck crew ties the reef points to bundle the doused portion of mainsail against the boom. The reef points are passed around the sail and tied around the footrope, not the boom. The boat may now be steered offwind again.

### AND, SOMEDAY, OFFSHORE

When things get really rough you are on your own. Blue-water sailing is something you study for. The skills involved are beyond the scope of this book, but here are a few tips on handling heavy weather offshore.

**Battening down** Ports and hatches should be closed and secured whenever there is danger of seas breaking around or over the boat's decks.

**Bearing off** Just as in an inshore blow, it is wise not to struggle to windward in a big sea offshore. Let her fall off to a broad reach or run and ease her motion, and remember to mind the helm against broaching. Reaching broadside to a really big sea is not a good idea, as a breaking crest could knock the boat down, and water could come aboard.

**Slowing her down** Ocean waves whipped up by strong winds get far larger than those described thus far. Some ocean voyagers have experienced waves taller than their masts, with a span many boatlengths between crests. In such a sea, or in a more typical scenario where seas are perhaps 10 or 15ft in height and slightly more than two boatlengths apart, you must slow your boat's speed.

The first way to do this is to reduce sail. Hank on the smallest working jib, and reef the main as far as necessary. When that is still too much sail, secure all plain sail and rig the storm sails. Trim the storm sails to handle your offwind point of sail, just as you'd handle main and jib.

**Even slower** If the waves and wind are still driving the boat too fast and there is a danger of broaching, stream some gear astern to act as a brake.

One typical answer is to stream a long line (or *warp* in seaman's terms) astern in a loop or *bight*. The bight itself should be four to five times the length of your boat, which means the warp needs to be 400ft long or more. It should be stout rope — perhaps ¾in in diameter. One end is made fast to a heavy cleat or winch to starboard, the other end is made fast similarly to port, then the line is dropped astern and paid out until the entire loop is streamed.

When venturing far offshore, it is wise to carry a warp designed and rigged just for streaming. Some sailors stream old automobile tires, others rig a spare anchor to the belly of the warp to weight it down and give it more drag in a sea.

**Lying ahull** If there just isn't quite enough sea room to keep running off in a gale, whether streaming warps or not, then a

*Classic techniques for weathering or riding out a gale. Streaming a long loop of rope astern (1). Hove-to with jib backed (2). Lying ahull with all sail stowed (3).*

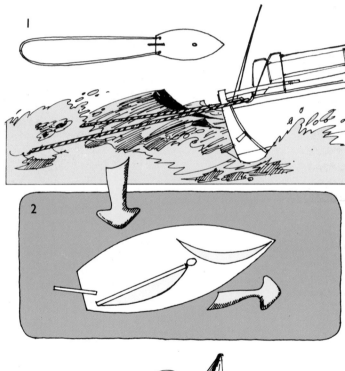

boat must be stopped at sea. One way to do this is to lie ahull — which simply means that all sail is taken off, the hatches are battened and the boat is left to her own devices. Sometimes, a skipper will want to experiment with lashing the tiller or wheel in several positions until he finds one that will steer the boat into an optimum attitude against wind and sea.

**Heaving-to** If lying ahull still creates too much drift, and there isn't enough sea room, then heaving-to may be the answer. Heaving-to is the act of stopping her with her bow headed into the wind and sea, and requires either storm sails or *sea anchor*.

With storm sails hoisted: the storm jib is hauled around to the windward side and sheeted tightly. It is *backwinded*. The trysail is trimmed flat, and the helm is lashed at an angle determined by trial and error to be best for the particular storm situation. Thus, the forward motion generated by the trysail is counteracted by the backed jib, and the boat slowly moves sideways, with her bow to weather.

**Under sea anchor** A sea anchor (sometimes called a *drogue*) is usually a cone-shaped canvas bag, open at both ends. Its wider end is held open by a wire hoop and braces, and has a bridle attached. Its trailing end sometimes has a tripping line attached. The anchor's bridle is mated to a long line and streamed over the boat's bow, like a normal anchor. Any sternward motion (*sternway*) tugs at the sea anchor, and the boat's bow is kept headed to weather.

*Adequate clothing is essential for offshore sailing.*

*The first reefing line (**below**) leads from the leech cringle back along the boom. The power of a breaking wave is simulated in this test tank (**bottom**). The helmsman must concentrate hard as a crest rises astern (**right**). Note the safety harness line clipped to a secure fixing.*

# 16 | PLANNING A CRUISE

*Well wrapped up against the cold, this crew can enjoy the conditions but still be ready to respond in an instant to the skipper's commands.*

The successful and competent cruising skipper must be able to navigate precisely, see to the care and repair of all his vessel's systems, provide sustenance for himself and his crew, know how to avoid and/or deal with hundreds of types of difficult situations, understand the tides and currents and weather over a broad geographical area, and finally ... be a capable and cautious sailor.

It has been evident throughout this text that if sailing involves a single most important aspect, that aspect is preparation. Or, more appropriately, *preparedness*.

### THE RULES

A cruising boat needs space enough belowdecks to accommodate the care and feeding of her crew, enough tankage to supply fresh water to her galley and head and fuel to her engine, a hull suitable to the conditions she'll be facing in her travels, and a rig strong enough and fitted with sufficient sail to power her hull to a degree of acceptable performance.

**The first rule of cruising** The best piece of cruising equipment is the mind of the sailor.

It is also the most adaptable piece of gear. If the sailor is able to embrace the idea of a cruise in a cockleshell, then a cockleshell will become a fine cruiser. If a sailor is able to go without an enclosed, comfortable head with a proper toilet, but use a bucket instead, then he can do without the head. If a sailor needs only a small primus stove, then he can make do without a large and complex galley.

In short, the individual doing the cruising can go a long way toward simplifying his or her life by adapting himself to the task.

*Corollary* The best cruising boat is one just large enough for the needs of her crew.

Never over-estimate your needs when starting out. Buy a boat that you can handle easily, rather than a large, less-easily handled one with all the comforts of home.

**The second rule of cruising** Plan to sail only half as far as you think your cruise will allow. The best part of cruising is learning about people and places, and a sailing boat lets you see the world from a completely new perspective.

*Corollary* Decide how much gear and stores you must have along on your trip, and leave half of it at home.

Too many cruisers burden themselves with clothing, food, bedding and hardware that they never use. Limit yourselves. Any boat — particularly a small one — is sensitive to weight, and burdening her with needless food and equipment will slow her down and possibly make her inept in tough going.

**The third rule of cruising** A friend is not necessarily a good shipmate, and a shipmate is not necessarily a friend.

Take care in selecting your crew for an extended cruise, especially if your boat is small and her quarters cramped. Remember, you will be sleeping and eating (and other things) within mere feet of each other.

It helps to have as crew people who are already sailors, and who already know and accept some of your more disagreeable traits, and it pays if you have a similar knowledge of them. Mutual respect and trust are also worth much aboard ship.

## THE RIGHT BOAT

The cruising sailboat is large enough, yet small enough. She is handy to maneuver, but fits her crew.

For most people, the sloop-rigged keelboat of moderate displacement and size is the answer. She's 30ft long or so, with perhaps 10–11ft of beam and 4–5ft of draft.

She weighs quite a bit less than 6 tons fully loaded, has a small inboard engine and carries perhaps 400–500 square feet of sail in main and jib.

She has a cockpit that is capable of draining off any water that comes aboard in the form of rain or spray, and a cabin with a small galley, an enclosed head, and several berths for her crew. She also has stowage for a modest amount of cruising gear and comestibles.

The rig will be simple: main and working jib, plus one genoa of ample proportion; no running backstays or backstay tensioner; mainsheet placed at aft end of boom and requiring only manual trimming; two genoa winches, two mast-mounted halyard winches; two pairs of lower shrouds, and one upper shroud per side running over single spreaders; tiller steering.

The working gear will be minimal so as

*This modern double-ender (**below**) makes a striking contrast with this obviously well traveled and over-burdened cruising boat (**bottom**), with the accumulated gear of many years.*

147

## THE TYPICAL CRUISING BOAT

*A well found cruising yacht, either long or short keeled, should have gear adequate for any weather, self draining cockpit, sturdy hatchboards, lifelines and sufficient safety equipment.*

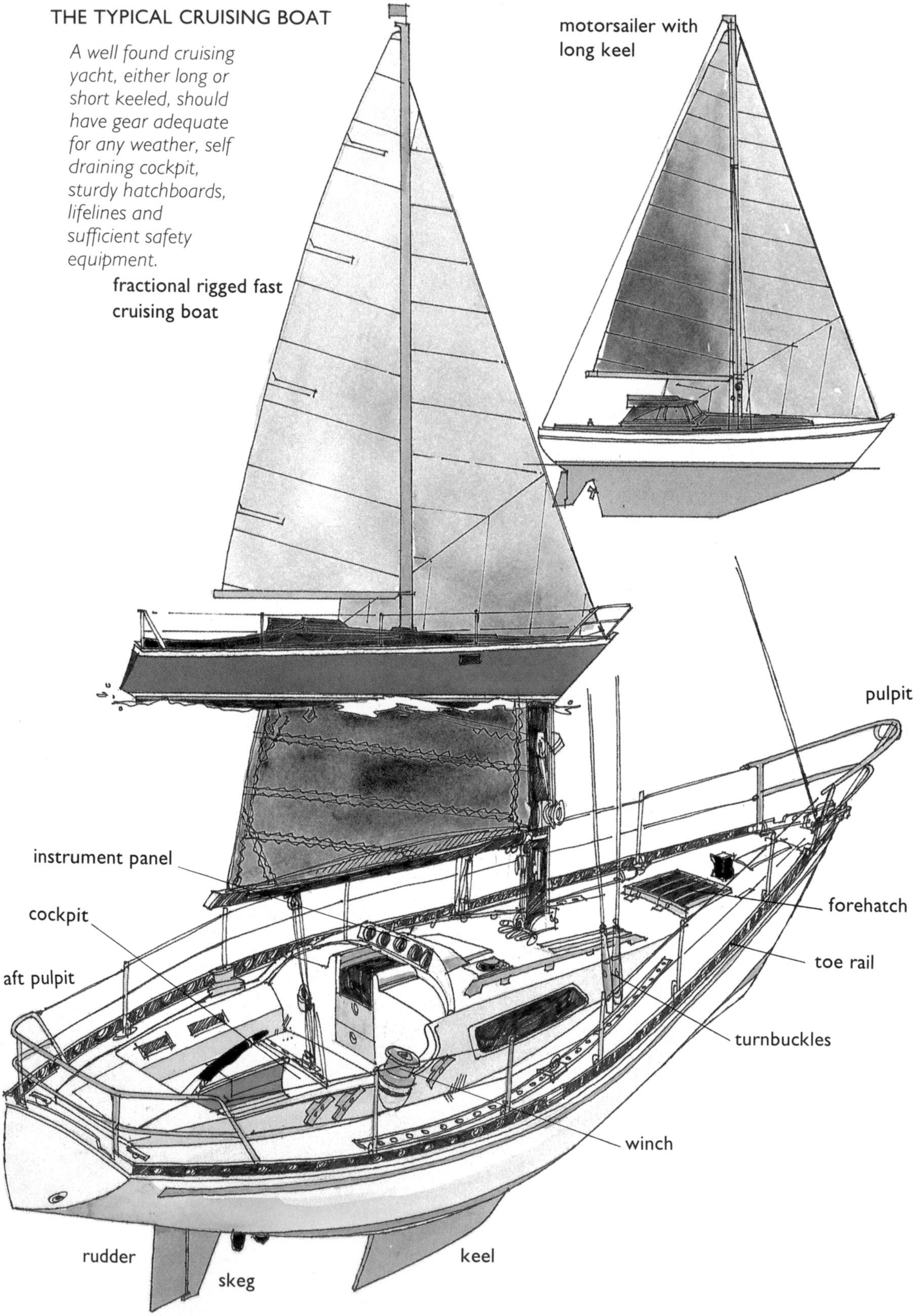

**motorsailer with long keel**

**fractional rigged fast cruising boat**

pulpit

instrument panel

cockpit

forehatch

aft pulpit

toe rail

turnbuckles

winch

rudder

skeg

keel

148

not to get in the way of the real purpose of the boat — to provide space for the simple pleasures of cruising on the open water: Deck space should be clear for lounging; cockpit provided with comfortable seating while under sail *and* at anchor; foredeck clear for handling lines and anchoring.

## HOW MUCH IS ENOUGH?

In this boat, almost any cruising distance is possible, given enough time and skill. Good sailors have circumnavigated the world on boats smaller than this.

But be conservative at first. Become familiar with your boat's abilities and shortcomings; and learn to adapt to the cruising life. A typical cruising family will start with a weekend trip, and then perhaps spend an entire week aboard. During the first two or three years of day- and weekend-cruising, much will be learned.

With each step, each lengthened stay aboard, the crew learns more. This kind of acclimatization is more likely to engender harmony and a love for the sport than a quick move into more ambitious trips.

Of course, weather can affect the length and harmony of any cruise. Just because your boat relies on wind, do not choose the season with the most of it.

Plan on making reasonable runs each day, with enough allowance for relaxing in port and foul weather.

A small cruiser is capable of perhaps five knots (5 nautical miles per hour) optimally (1 nautical mile = 1.152 land miles). Therefore, it is reasonable to expect that the boat could make trips of 20-25 miles per day with relative ease, allowing time for the other joys of living aboard. Plan on traveling at this rate *every other day*, and plot your destinations accordingly.

Acquire a *chart* (a "map" of the coastal area, more precisely detailing the contours and features of the water rather than the land) of your general region, and roughly plot the day's runs according to your time allotment.

*Use a small-scale chart to plan your cruise, but remember to be realistic about the distance you can comfortably cover.*

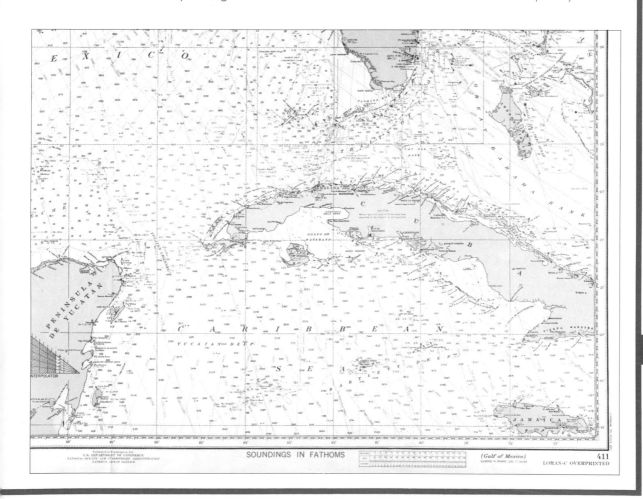

SOUNDINGS IN FATHOMS  (Gulf of Mexico)  411  LORAN-C OVERPRINTED

# 17 | **PREPARATION**

*Acquire a large-scale chart of the area you intend to visit.*

Once you've got the overall picture of where you want to go and what kind of sailing you'll be doing, it's time to marshal the stores and equipment you will need.

## CHARTS

When you are sure of your general route, study the itinerary. For this, you'll need more and better charts.

There are two general types of charts: *small-scale*, and *large-scale*. Small-scale charts cover large geographical areas, and thus the many coastal features depicted lack detail in favor of the overall picture. Navigators coming in from sea use small-scale charts on their approaches to coastlines, as do ships who are running coastwise far offshore. They are interested only in overall contour and principal features.

Large-scale charts cover small geographical areas, and thus are able to convey a good degree of detail on the bottom contours and coastal features of the area depicted.

Because you'll want to see more detail of the harbors and coastline along which you'll be cruising, you'll need mostly small-scale charts, plus one or two large-scale ones for planning purposes.

The small-scale charts of the harbors

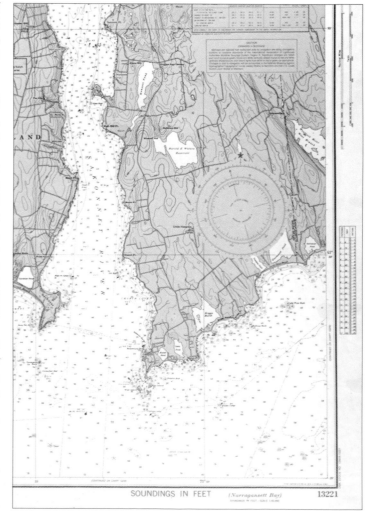

SOUNDINGS IN FEET *(Narragansett Bay)*    13221

150

you'll be visiting show protected anchorages, landmarks, and the buoyage system.

For now, in the planning stage, you should use the charts to picture the places you'll be visiting. Set them against a background of the weather you expect during the time of year for which your cruise is planned. Where will you anchor in a southwest blow? Where can you expect to get fuel? Use the charts to get some advanced idea of what to expect.

Charts can become obsolete if you don't update them regularly. Government publications are issued for this purpose, which give notice of changes on buoy and marker locations, channel improvements and shifts, and light/signal corrections. All your charts should be checked by a chart agent periodically for error and conformity to these publications.

Some skippers roll their charts and stow them in oblong cubbyholes at or near their boat's navigation station. Others fold them and stow them flat in drawers. Rolling charts makes it hard to work with them on a flat surface; yet folding creases them and can wear them out more quickly.

Whether your boat has a proper navigation station or not, she should have some provision for chartwork. The dining table, a large counter space, or simply a board that can be carried up to the cockpit — any of these can make good working surfaces.

Spend the time to buy the proper charts for your planned cruise, and care for them the best way you can.

## SUPPLIES AND GEAR

There are several categories of gear necessary for cruising competently. Each

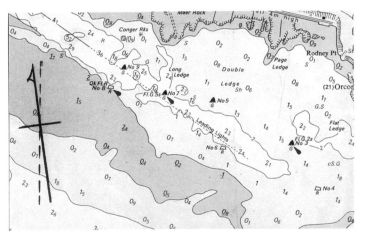

*The navigator's skill lies in relating his own observations and readings from instruments like this satellite navigator (**right**) to the chart (**above right**), continually updating his position and planning ahead (**above**).*

*Hand-bearing compass (**1**), safety harness (**2**), tools (**3**), storm lamp (**4**), sail-repair kit (**5**), spare shackles and key (**6**), signal flag (**7**), binoculars (**8**), cleaning gear (**9**).*

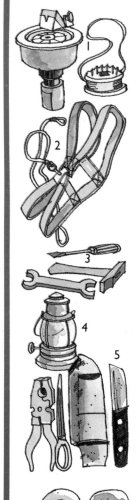

category serves a particular general area of need: ship's work, sustenance, comfort.

**Ship's work** (1) Cleaning gear: a plastic bucket; a sponge-fiber mop; two or three large synthetic sponges; spray cleaner; ammonia; salt-water liquid soap; a ship's hose for attaching to dockside fresh-water taps; metal polishes for stainless steel, brass, and bronze; vinyl treatment; and a supply of clean cotton-waste rags. (2) Docking gear: six heavy warps or docklines — two at least the length of the boat overall, and four more at least twice the length of the boat; four or five fenders; three or four utility lines of greater dimension than the docklines, and each at least twice the length of the boat; fender boards — at least one. (3) Safety gear: lifejackets for each crew member; throwable device; waterproof light with lanyard; bright hand-held searchlight; gas-powered horn; fog bell; fire extinguishers; radiotelephone; am/fm radio receiver; radar reflector; emergency visual distress signals; first aid kit; lifelines and safety harnesses. Lists of required safety gear may be obtained from the U.S. Coast Guard (see page 47). (4) Maintenance gear: complete tool kit for simple carpentry and machinery work; spare engine parts — V-belts, ignition parts, sparkplugs, water-pump impellers, oil filter, fuel-filter element, hose clamps, fuses, etc.; engine shop manual; various dunnage — wooden plugs carved to fit various through-hull fittings; assorted nails, screws, bolts, etc.; several pieces of canvas or sailcloth; sail-repair kit; one large roll of duct tape; rigging knife and line-splicing tools; stainless steel siezing wire; diving mask and fins; kit of underwater epoxy glue; small cans of touch-up paint and brush with thinner; spare parts for stove; stove fuel; cleaning gear for galley

work. (5) Anchoring gear: two anchors; sufficient anchor line; appropriate anchor-stowage gear. (6) Navigation gear: charts; two clear-plastic triangles, or parallel rules; 2 pencils; pair of dividers; ship's compass; hand-bearing compass. Note: electronic navigation tools like Loran and RDF can successfully complement and extend the navigator's tool kit. Of these, more later.

**Sustenance** (1) Complete galley cooking gear: two saucepans; a pressure-cooker; frying pan; teapot; coffee pot or filter funnel; all utensils. Note: all should be stainless steel. (2) Complete dining set: place-settings for full crew, plus two guests. Note: dishes can be plastic, napkins paper. (3) Bedding: enough for crew. Note: cotton sheets are more comfortable than poly-filled synthetic sleeping bags. Great comfort can be had by encasing quilts in cotton covers. (4) Bathing set: large plastic pan; bottle with spray nozzle; bath towels and cloths. Note: an on-deck showerbag suspended from the rigging is a good way to provide pressure-water shower on boats without the tankerage or electric pumping system.

**Comfort** (1) Topside cushions: complete cockpit cushion set — vinyl covered; movable deck cushions. (2) Sun protection: cockpit sun awning; sun-screen lotion for protection, salve for sunburn. (3) Entertainment: am/fm stereo tape player with tapes; insulated foam drink holders; books, magazines. (4) Sport: swim ladder; diving mask and fins; sketch pad; deck of playing cards.

## FOODSTUFFS

Each cruising family will have their own selections of favorite foods. The amount of food — especially perishable items — that can be brought along at one time will depend on the stowage capacity aboard, and on the amount of cool-stowage space.

**Non-refrigerated stowage** Many meals can be made with vegetables and dried foods requiring no icing or refrigeration. Potatoes, onions, and other root vegetables will keep indefinitely if stowed in a cool, dark place. Even eggs will keep unrefrigerated — especially if sealed in wax or varnish. Dried smoked fish and pork will keep similarly, but should be eaten within several days of purchase unless sealed from the air.

Plastic bags designed to thermal-seal can be used to store some uncooked, smoked, or dried foods for long periods.

Obviously, canned foods are ideal aboard ship, as they can be stowed almost anywhere and will keep indefinitely.

Dried/de-constituted soups and freeze-dried foods are available for those concerned about the weight of provisions aboard.

**Refrigeration** Most cruising boats have an icebox, rather than the refrigerator unit to which we are accustomed at home. The icebox is usually top-loaded with block ice, and the foods packed around the block or blocks and on shelves within the thickly insulated space. The icebox is designed to drain its melt either into the boat's bilge or overboard.

On some newer boats, direct-current (usually 12-volt, battery-derived) powers a small refrigerator. This is the same compressor-equipped type as the home model, but smaller and somewhat less effective. Except that no ice is required, the dc refrigerator behaves much like the icebox.

In packing the icebox or refrigerator, the items to be kept coolest should be packed lowest. Meats and cheeses can be put in sealed plastic containers to keep them dry, and nestled next to the ice in an icebox. Green vegetables can be put inside plastic bags along with a damp paper towel to keep them crisp.

Never leave a cool box open for more than a few seconds. Know what you want to get out of stowage, open the box, reach for it, then close the box to keep the cool air inside.

Frozen foods can be convenient aboard, especially if stowed deep inside an icebox next to the ice: They will normally keep a long time if stowed cool and inside a heat-sealed container (like a thermal freezer-sealed plastic bag). Entire meals or main courses can be cooked at home, sealed in thermal bags, frozen, and then stowed aboard for a cruise. However, it is recommended that these frozen meals be eaten relatively early in the cruise.

In your cruise-planning, determine how many meals you'll want to eat aboard, and how many times you'll go ashore for lunch or

dinner, then pack only as much as you'll need. Remember that you do not have to pack for the entire cruise if you'll be stopping along the way. In fact, one of the pleasures of cruising is going to town to replenish supplies at the local shops.

Bring along snacks and soft drinks, too, as there will be times when things are brisk under sail, and putting a full meal together is difficult. In this connection, make sure that breakfast on the day of a particularly long passage is sufficiently nourishing, and consider filling a large thermos flask with hot soup to supplement the quick snacks.

In general, you can be as elaborate or as simple as you want to on a cruise. With some imagination, extremely satisfying meals can come from relatively basic ingredients. The quality of your meals need not depend on how well-equipped your boat's galley is or how large her lockers are.

*When provisioning for a cruise, check all cardboard boxes (**above**) for insects. Fridge and icebox (**below**).*

153

# BASIC PILOTAGE

C ruising means navigation of some sort, whether it be simple daytime buoy-to-buoy sailing or difficult offshore passagemaking with complex position-finding procedures.

In our scope of study, we will include the simpler, common-sense methods of inshore navigation. These will include: steering by compass, basic chart use, and methods of determining position by referring to fixed markers and time/speed computations.

This is *pilotage*, the practice of navigation which is most basic to the understanding of all forms of the science. By understanding fully the points contained here, you will be capable of conservative inshore cruising. To go any further, you are encouraged to seek more detailed information in texts dedicated to the art and science of navigation.

## THE MAGNETIC COMPASS

The compass is an ancient tool based on the simple principle of inter-polar magnetism. The earth's poles are as the poles of a magnet, causing properly balanced and charged masses to align between them. The card of a modern magnetic compass is such a mass, its "N" mark always pointing toward the earth's magnetic north pole.

There are a few imperfections, even in the modern ship's compass:

*The compass is still the navigator's most important tool, but because magnetic north is invariably some degrees to the east or west of true north, a few simple sums are needed to relate compass to chart.*

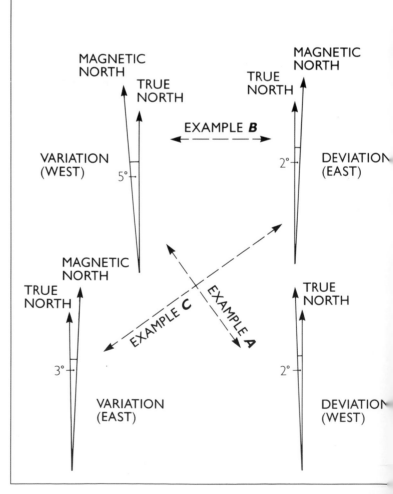

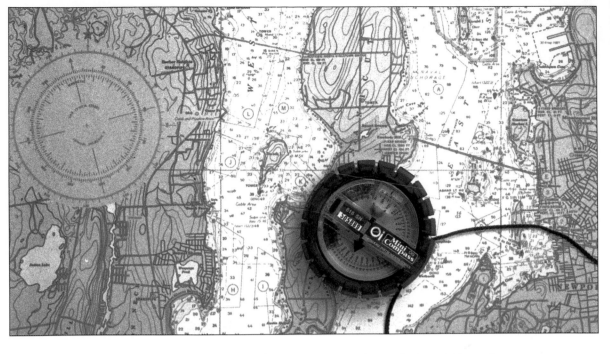

## EXAMPLES

|            | A    | B    | C    |
|------------|------|------|------|
| Variation  | 5°W  | 5°W  | 3°E  |
| Deviation  | 2°W  | 2°E  | 2°E  |
| **Total error** | **7°W** | **3°W** | **5°E** |

### TRUE TO COMPASS

|                  |       |       |
|------------------|-------|-------|
| True course      | 163°  | 110°  |
| Variation        | 5°W   | 5°E   |
| (Total error)    | (8°W) | (3°E) |
| Deviation        | 3°W   | 2°W   |
| **Compass course** | **171°** | **107°** |

### COMPASS TO TRUE

|                  |       |       |
|------------------|-------|-------|
| Compass course   | 163°  | 110°  |
| Variation        | 5°E   | 7°W   |
| (Total error)    | (7°E) | (5°W) |
| Deviation        | 2°E   | 2°E   |
| **True course**  | **170°** | **105°** |

### AIDE MEMOIRE

*Error East, Compass Least* (less than true)
*Error West, Compass Best* (more than true)

\* Because magnetic north is not the same as true north, and because the discrepancy between the two varies from place to place on the earth, the pilot must know this discrepancy and account for it at all times. The difference between magnetic and true north is called *variation*.

\* Because no two boats are exactly alike, their internal mass, positioning of large metal components (such as engine, steering system, electronics, etc.) — and therefore their magnetic nature — can affect the compass card by drawing it away from its proper alignment. The difference between magnetic north and the compass's north is called *deviation*.

\* Information on variation is always available to the coastal sailor. A representation of the compass directions is printed on the chart. This *compass rose* has both true and magnetic directions indicated, with variation taken into account. Therefore, almost all your shipboard piloting can be done using magnetic compass directions.

\* But since each boat's deviation is different, each skipper must account for it in his own way.

Note that both variation and deviation are expressed as "east" or "west". When the chart's indicated variation puts magnetic north to the west of true north (to the left, or counterclockwise), variation is west.

*Some navigators prefer to use magnetic courses, relating actual compass readings to the inner circle of the compass rose on the chart.*

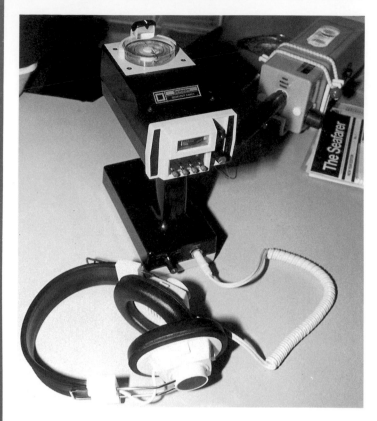

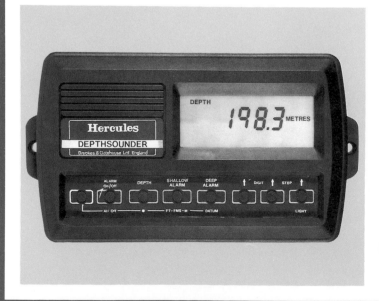

*The radio direction finder (**above**) gives reasonably accurate bearings of fixed radio signals transmitted at regular intervals.*

*Readings from the depth-sounder (**below**) can be related to the bottom contours to give an idea of a ship's position.*

When your boat's compass puts ship's north to the west of magnetic north, deviation is west. Of course, either or both can be east, too.

The first thing to do is to adjust your compass to remove deviation. There are compensating magnets placed around the circumference of a compass housing that can be moved to achieve this. For now, it is wise to hire a professional compass adjuster to come aboard and *swing* your boat's compass.

The adjuster runs your boat, with all her normal gear aboard, at several known landmarks and along headings he is sure of. He then moves the internal magnets until several cardinal directions line up with the corresponding magnetic directions.

A compass adjuster should be able to reduce or eliminate deviation in the compass. When this is accomplished the magnetic compass rose on your chart and the vessel's magnetic compass are sufficient for inshore piloting.

In steering by compass, you match the desired course heading on the floating compass card with the fixed line on the housing called the *lubberline*. The best way to think of the lubberline is that *it is the bow of the boat*; the compass card is simply the earth with all its magnetic directions. You steer the boat through the selected directions.

The compass is used not only for steering, but also for determining directions from your position, or *bearings*. To find the compass bearing of a distant object — landmark or vessel — you simply sight at that object over the top of your compass.

To be precise in your sighting, you should use a device called a *pelorus*, which mounts atop your compass and provides sighting vanes through which to pinpoint the object.

However, if your steering compass is not in a position to use for sighting, an auxiliary *hand-bearing compass* is needed. This smaller compass may have a sight vane, and is portable. Note that you must compare your adjusted steering compass with the hand-bearing compass and note accuracy before using.

## THE NAUTICAL CHART

The nautical chart is the detailed representation of a region's coastal features and sea-bottom contour and composition. It also has the magnetic and true compass directions surprinted in several places for the use of the coastal navigator.

The chart also has a detailed set of positions for all navigation markers in existence for its region. Buoys and towers and lighthouses and daymarkers — all are positioned as accurately as possible on the chart. Channels are depicted, along with harbor anchorage areas, dumping grounds, commercial port anchorages, and so on.

Many nations have had their own buoyage and light system, each differing to some degree, but all are now connected via a relatively new set of international colors and shapes. Take the time to learn the general rules, as well as the standards in your own cruising area. Learn what the different colors of buoys mean, and how each is depicted on the chart.

By using a chart and proper piloting techniques you can determine your course, position, and progress through your chosen cruising area.

**Course plotting** This is the most basic chart function. The tools needed for this are simple — a set of parallel rules, a pencil, and a chart.

*Example* Your trip today will take you from the harbor at Fairhaven to the small creek just below Low Bluffs. There is a buoy just outside Fairhaven, from which it is a straight line to the fixed marker outside the entrance to the creek. Use the Fairhaven buoy as your "departure" point.

*(1)* You need to know the course from the buoy to the marker, so you place your parallel rules along the course line, and draw it in lightly in pencil.

*(2)* Then you maneuver the parallel rules by stepping them slowly toward the chart's compass rose, making sure not to lose the directonal orientation of the rule on the chart.

*(3)* Finally, you bring whichever edge of the rule is convenient to the point at the center of the compass rose, and you read the magnetic direction of your course heading off the edge of the rose, writing it at the

*Taking a fix. Compass bearings to silo on Willie Head, tower on Short Shoal, and cupola on far shore, when laid down on chart, produce a set of crossing lines. The fix is at that region where the lines cross most closely.*

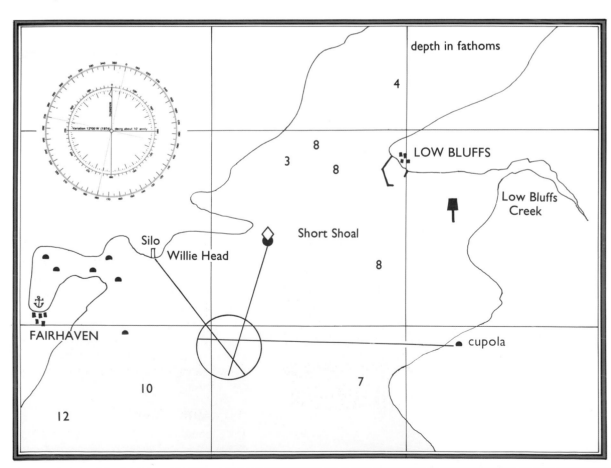

157

beginning of your course line.

**Distance finding** This is a corollary to the plotting of a course. In order to predict the time it will take to sail or power to your destination, you need an accurate measurement of the distance.

*Example* You want a good measurement of the distance between the anchorage at Fairhaven and the creek at Low Bluffs.

*(1)* You use your dividers, the two-legged plotting tool designed to "step off" distances on a chart. Set them at a short known distance — say ½ mile — and walk them from the anchorage at Fairhaven to the buoy outside, making sure to follow all the contours of the channel. The setting for the dividers is obtained off the chart's scale or from the left or right edges of the chart, where *each minute of latitude is equal to one nautical mile.*

*(2)* Then, you take a larger measurement from the scale or chart-edge and step off the distance between the buoy at Fairhaven and the marker outside the Low Bluffs creek.

*(3)* Finally, a few short steps through the channel to the anchorage inside the creek. Then you add all the distance recorded for the total.

**Position finding** Because your chart gives you the exact positions of landmarks and navigational markers, and because you have the ability to take bearings on these points, you can find your position accurately on the chart.

*Example* You are less than halfway between Fairhaven and Low Bluffs, when the fog begins to roll in and your visibility becomes limited. Rather than rely on an estimate of your position along the course-line you have drawn, you decide to take bearings before the fog gets too thick.

*(1)* Choose identifiable markers or landmarks around you that can be matched to the chart.

*(2)* You find the buoy marking Short Shoal and the silo of the farm just south of Willie Head. You estimate that your position puts you at a right-angle juncture between the bearings to these points; in other words, they are not opposite each other, but will provide a favorable triangulation. It is important to try and choose marks that do not fall roughly along a line with your assumed position, for the oblique angle at which such bearings cross will fail to be distinct enough to yield a good position.

*(3)* You use your hand bearing compass to find the magnetic bearings to both points.

*Transferring position lines using a parallel rule (**left**). All distances are taken (with a pair of dividers) from the adjacent latitude scale at the side of the chart being used (**below**).*

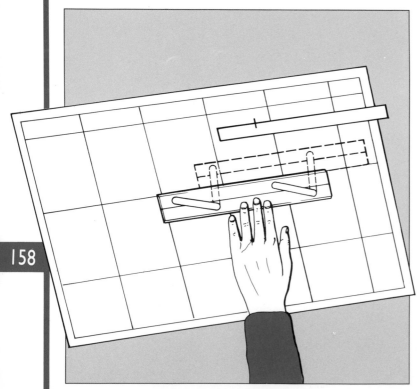

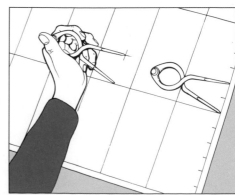

Then, after aligning your parallel rules or triangles with the appropriate directions on the chart's magnetic compass rose, you manipulate the rule or triangles to each point on the chart (the buoy and the silo) and draw a line in pencil that intersects your course line.

*(4)* The intersection of the two lines is your position, but remember that positions of buoys on charts can be approximate.

*(5)* To check yourself, find a fixed marker (or buoy if a marker is not available) and get its bearing. If your plot of its bearing falls on top of the intersection of the two other lines, then your position is verified.

The position as determined on a chart is called a *fix.*

Several notes: a bearing can be taken on almost anything that is visible on a chart — not just on fixed navigational marks. Distinct land features, shoreline contours, charted structures (like our silo), and other prominent features can be used as long as they are clearly identifiable. Further, it is recommended that you plot at least one fix per hour of travel, even in good visibility.

## DEAD RECKONING

This refers to the logical computation of course, speed, and distance as transferred from full-scale to chart and the reverse.

There are many things to take into account when creating a dead reckoning plot, and the more you know, the better your plot will be:

* Boat speed: of course, you need to know what speed you are making through the water. A speed indicator such as sumlog is a good device for measuring. You can also take fixes and compute your speed between them by a simple time/distance calculation. The projection of this calculation is useful in dead reckoning as long as other factors remain unchanged. These factors would include:

* Tidal stream: the strength (its speed in knots), and the direction in which it flows, and the times of its change in each area.

* Wind: its direction and strength.

**The DR plot** The basic method for setting up a dead reckoning plot is to draw your course line or lines, then predict your speed capability for each leg of the plot according to what you know about your boat's own character, the expected prevailing wind conditions and the rate and direction of the tidal stream.

*Example* You are continuing along a

*(1) A good triangulation gives a reliable fix. (2) Angles which are too narrow give an unreliable fix. (3) A range and a bearing give a good fix. (4) A range sited to keep approaching yachts away from isolated dangers such as rocks.*

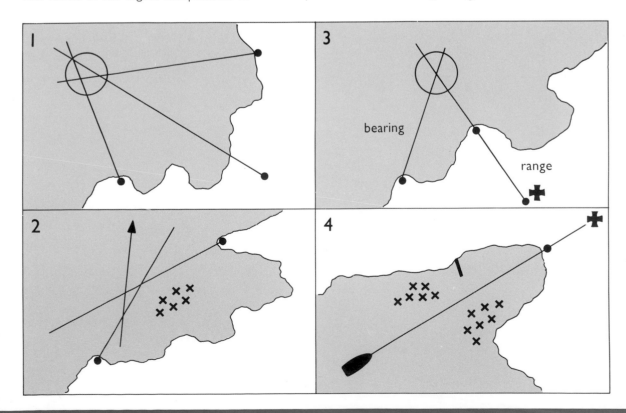

course to Low Bluffs, after having fixed your position. The fog has drifted in, and although you can see a great deal of water around you the shoreline is obscured. Your job is to continue along, predicting when you will arrive at the several buoys along the way, and when you will arrive at the final destination.

*(1)* Examine the tidal stream information printed on the chart (marked by diamonds at various key points on the chart) and relate them to the times of High Water. If the chart does not provide tidal information, check a tide table. You may find that you have a tidal stream of 2 knots helping you along in the direction of travel. Unfortunately, that stream will drop off and soon change against you — in perhaps two hours. For now, though, add 2 knots to the speed indicated on the sumlog to get the actual speed over the bottom.

*(2)* You *compute* your speed by determining the time it took to travel from your departure point outside Fairhaven to your recent fix.

$$\text{Knots} = \frac{\text{Distance (nautical miles)}}{\text{Time}}$$

*(3)* Project your present speed and course along the course line on the chart, accounting for the favourable current. Each hour of progress is noted with a tick in pencil along the course line and labelled with the "DR" (dead reckoning) time of arrival at that point. Ex: 0900 DR, 1000 DR, 1100 DR, and so on.

*(4)* At regular intervals, you may need to adjust the DR plot. Things to take into account will be: change in sumlog-indicated speed; change in tidal stream; wind shift.

**Tidal stream vectors in DR** Note that when the tidal stream in our above example changes in a few hours, it will come directly against us. If its speed is listed at 2 knots on the chart or in the tides and currents book, then you will lose a 2-knot boost and pick up 2 knots' worth of resistance to your forward motion over the bottom. That means a four-knot difference in speed to figure-in to your DR from the estimated time of current change.

However, as with all things, there are more complex situations, like cross tides.

*Example* If the current shifts so as to present itself from one side or the other of the direction of travel, then it will act to move you sideways, or *set* you, and you must compensate for its action by a corresponding change in course.

*(1)* The best way to figure course-compensation for a shift of current outside our course line is to draw a vector diagram. An arrow of a length to represent the boat's speed is drawn, and another to represent the current's relative direction and speed is drawn. A third line is drawn from the base of the boat's arrow to the base of

*Plotting a course is the first step in planning a passage, but it is only a rough guide to be updated by accurate position fixing as the passage progresses.*

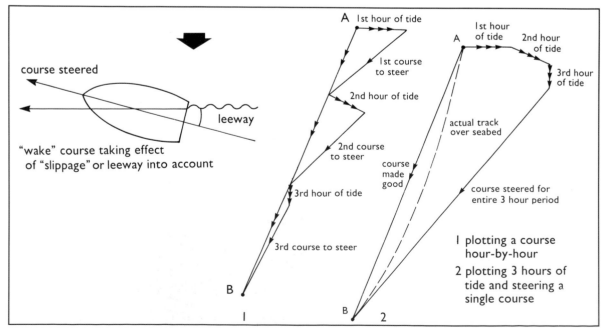

course steered

leeway

"wake" course taking effect of "slippage" or leeway into account

A 1st hour of tide

1st course to steer

2nd hour of tide

2nd course to steer

3rd hour of tide

3rd course to steer

B

1

A 1st hour of tide

1st hour of tide    2nd hour of tide

3rd hour of tide

actual track over seabed

course made good

course steered for entire 3 hour period

B

2

1 plotting a course hour-by-hour

2 plotting 3 hours of tide and steering a single course

the current's arrow. The angle formed between the boat's arrow and this third line is the angle and direction of the compass-heading change required to maintain present course while accounting for the current's set.

(2) In addition to a heading change as noted above, there will also be a change in real boat speed. The third arrow may be thought of as representing *time*. In the example, the first arrow was drawn five scale nautical miles long to represent a speed of five knots (five nautical miles per hour). The second line expressed a current of two knots coming at right angles from the starboard side. The third arrow, extended from the base of the boat's arrow to the base of the current's arrow, was longer. Its new length, when compared to the length of the first arrow, shows the percentage of increase in time it will take to travel five nautical miles.

(3) Note that the third arrow also may be thought of as representing speed, whereby to compensate for an adverse tidal stream and maintain both the original DR course and speed, the boat's speed through the water must be increased.

The sailor will either estimate the percentage or calculate it and apply the time differential to the boat's speed, reducing it. An easy example: the third arrow turns out to be one fifth longer than the first —

meaning that the 5 nautical miles will take 12 more minutes to cover on the current-compensated heading. Or . . . the boat is now traveling one-fifth as fast, or 4 knots.

Spend some time familiarizing yourself with vector problems, and learn to apply the time/speed/distance relationship — particularly with tidal vectors. You will soon be able to apply what you've learned to almost any DR situation involving the several outside forces affecting your boat. If she makes leeway under sail, or if the tidal stream in your area is particularly strong or variable, then a vector estimate to quantify it will go a long way toward improving your DR plotting.

*A harbor entrance with sand bar (**above**) demands precise navigiation.*

*Taking tides into account when planning a passage (**below**).*

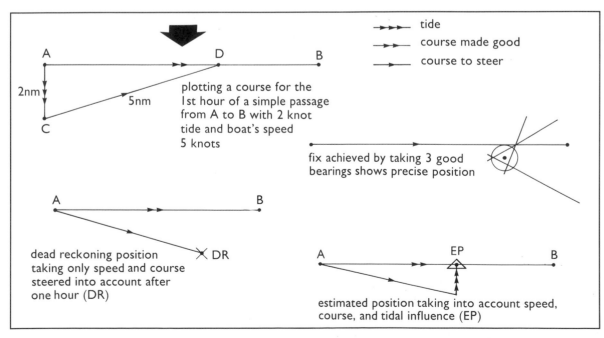

tide
course made good
course to steer

A    D    B

2nm

C    5nm

plotting a course for the 1st hour of a simple passage from A to B with 2 knot tide and boat's speed 5 knots

fix achieved by taking 3 good bearings shows precise position

A    B

dead reckoning position taking only speed and course steered into account after one hour (DR)    X DR

A    EP    B

estimated position taking into account speed, course, and tidal influence (EP)

# 19 | WEATHER ROUTING

In the early days of sail, when man relied on primitive materials and techniques, traders became skilled at detecting weather patterns. They had to, simply because their craft were handicapped by the inability to go to windward. They were forced to wait for favorable winds before making sail.

For the cruising sailor of today, much has changed. Better materials and refined technology and design have replaced the old ways, and the modern cruising yacht is weatherly and capable in rough going.

But you must remain constantly aware of the weather in your area, and listen to the forecasts.

## UPWIND, DOWNWIND

There are several basic rules. They are the same as those airplane pilots use when planning a trip across country, and almost the same ones deep-sea navigators use, though far less stringent.

*(1) A tailwind today is a headwind tomorrow.* A fine downwind start in the normal prevailing winds of summer, can mean a hard push back upwind at the end of a cruise. Because a beat to weather takes much longer than a nice broad reach or run, learn to allow time for it.

Note your weather reports. Listen for cyclic changes in wind. Often, when a front

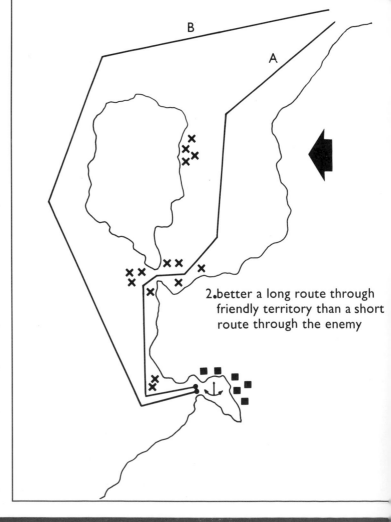

2. better a long route through friendly territory than a short route through the enemy

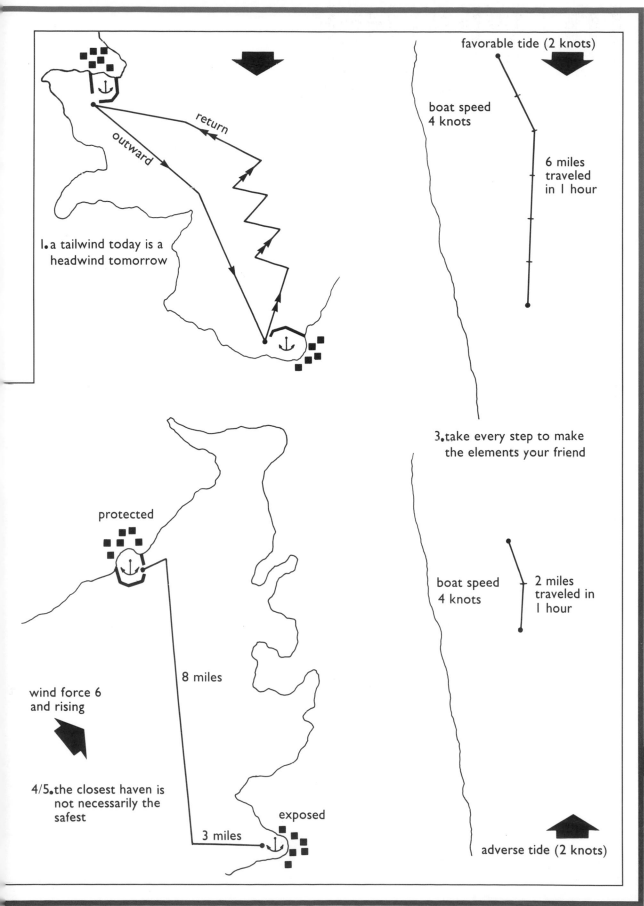

1. a tailwind today is a headwind tomorrow

favorable tide (2 knots)

boat speed 4 knots

6 miles traveled in 1 hour

3. take every step to make the elements your friend

boat speed 4 knots

2 miles traveled in 1 hour

protected

8 miles

wind force 6 and rising

4/5. the closest haven is not necessarily the safest

3 miles

exposed

adverse tide (2 knots)

moves through, the wind can veer or back half-way around the compass from its normal direction. You may be able to take advantage of this and make a fair sail for home.

(2) *Better a long route through friendly territory than a short route through the enemy.* If the wind favors one side of a passage, even if the way is longer, it is best to take it.

Stay away from lee shores in a blow; hug those shores that serve to block a strong and unfavorable wind.

(3) *Take every step to make the elements your friend.* If you have a contrary wind, try to make the tide your ally; and vice versa.

If waiting a few hours will get the tide in your favor, then wait. But if that wait puts you in danger of being caught out in that afternoon squall, then maybe you should go now. Weigh the options carefully.

(4) *There is no shame in retreat.* You may be halfway home, and a big blow can threaten to close your passage. Turning back to your previous port may be the only answer. However:

(5) *Any port in a storm.* More sailors find more new ports-of-call this way. If the weather threatens to close your passage and

*Typical logbook entries enable the navigator to keep a check on the courses steered by his crew, who must in turn be scrupulously honest.*

## LOGBOOK ENTRY

**Yacht Venus on passage**
from: Fairhaven
to: Low Bluffs

Friday 13th April

Crew:
A. Morgan, T. Ridley
S. Paul

| TIME | LOG READING n miles | COURSE TO STEER M° | COURSE STEERED M° | WIND/SEA | BAROMETER | REMARKS |
|------|------|------|------|------|------|------|
| 1200 | | | | S.W. Force 4 | 1001 | Left marina, headed down channel. Engine on. |
| 1230 | 0 | 85 | 85 | S.W. 3 slight | 1001 | Engine off at Fairhaven buoy. Sails up. Weather bright, wind decreased. Forecast more wind. |
| 1300 | 2.5 | 85 | 85 | S.W. 3 slight | 1001 | Mid channel buoy to st'b bearing 165°M. Set N°1 Genoa. A.M. very seasick in bunk. |
| 1400 | 7.9 | 85 | 80 | S.W. 6 Choppy | 999 | Wind freshening. N°1 Genoa down at 1345. Steering difficult. T.R. on watch. |
| 1500 | 12.8 | 95 | 95 | S.W. 6 rough | 998 | Low Bluffs bearing 065°. Engine on tick over. Big tanker to port. |
| | | | Engine hours 2½ 8 galls. | | | |

stop your forward progress, check your chart for a harbor close enough and protected enough to offer sanctuary. Look for good holding ground for your anchor (mud, silt, soft sand), and land high enough to offer at least some wind protection.

## LOCAL KNOWLEDGE

There are books that supplement charts by providing more detailed information to the sailor. These cruising guides describe regions favored by sailors, facilities in those areas, harbor conditions, and local knowledge important to the newcomer.

A good guide can help a crew challenged by foul weather find a comfortable way out. Before you begin a cruise, check your local chandlery and purchase the appropriate guide(s) for the region you plan to sail.

Learn to ask questions. No one begrudges a sailor information if he asks in honesty and without guile. Sometimes cruising guides lack details on particular channels and particular tidal behavior. Local fishermen and skippers might know what you should expect in a particularly bad stretch during the full ebb of the tide. If a stretch of coast is locally known for gusty conditions when the wind is out of a particular quadrant, the natives should be able to help.

In other words, when sailing in unfamiliar waters — especially in less-than-desirable conditions — give yourself the benefit of all the information you can glean. It could provide the raw material for important decisions later.

## COMMUNICATIONS

Remember your radio. If you are cruising some distance from home, have two: an AM/FM receiver for the essential information bands, and a *transceiver* for transmitting and receiving.

There may come a time when a call from a quiet harbor to a vessel outside on the open water will reveal more than remote and impersonal weather reports.

Make a habit of listening to the regularly scheduled weather forecasts, and log them in your logbook morning and evening, and to back up the official reports, take three daily readings on your own *barometer*, noting both the pressure and the trend and degree of change. Log these indicators as well.

By monitoring the radios, and keeping a good log, you will have that much more information at the ready if and when it is needed in a decision.

Common sense goes a long way toward developing a safe cruising style. As in all other things, begin conservatively, and begin to stretch your adventures only at the pace of your advancing skill. This is particularly true of managing your cruise in concert with the elements. Nothing can replace experience in this regard.

*The barometer or barograph can give prior warning of bad weather, but keep an ear cocked for local weather forecasts.*

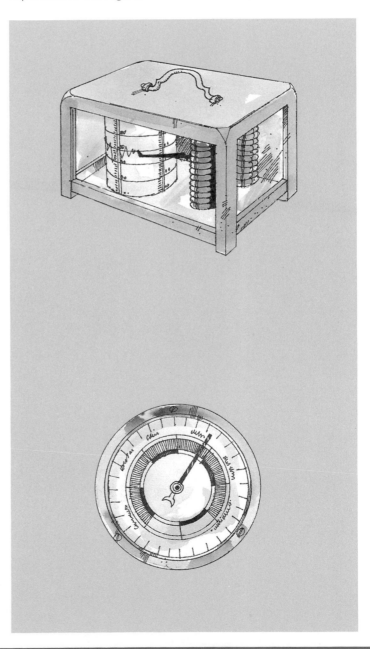

# 20 | THE SHIP'S POWERPLANT

A modern auxiliary under the cockpit, well sound-proofed and with adequate servicing access.

The following is a brief survey of the things you'll need to know about your cruising boat's engine, its management and maintenance. The chapter may get you started in your mechanical education, but it is by no means designed to inform you thoroughly.

Rather, you will be able to use the things you learn here in conjunction with any number of good texts on the subject of marine propulsion, and with your own engine's operations manual.

## THE BASICS

The sailboat auxiliary is either an inboard or outboard engine.

The outboard is most often a lightweight (aluminum alloy) engine mounted to a bracket or inside a well in or on the after quarter of the boat. The engine itself, or *powerhead*, is mounted with its *crankshaft* in the vertical plane, and is usually shrouded under a lightweight hood. From the crankshaft, a protected vertical shaft descends to the engine's *lower gearcase*, where power is transmitted at right angles to the *propeller shaft*, a short shaft that exits the lower gearcase to turn the propeller. If the outboard has any gearshift mechanism at all (some don't), it will be a simple *dog-clutch* mechanism designed to actuate two sets of gears inside the lower gearcase.

The inboard is usually mounted to hull framing belowdecks and deep inside the hull, on the fore and aft centerline of the boat. It is usually made of cast-iron, and may be diesel- or gasoline-fueled. The engine is not unlike that in a car. Its horizontally disposed crankshaft is mated to a transmission usually designed to change gears via a hydraulically activated clutch assembly. From the gearbox, power is transmitted via the *propeller shaft* through a watertight seal called a *stuffing box* to the propeller.

## COOLING

With all the heat generated by combustion, a marine engine must be cooled, and what better way to cool it than by using the water it operates in.

Marine inboard engines typically are cooled with water that is pumped through a set of passages cast-in to the engine block. The water circulates in one of two ways:

*(1) Open (raw-water) system* This system takes water from the outside of the boat, through a valved hull fitting, and through a strainer before pumping directly into the engine's cooling system. Once the water cools the engine block, it is dumped into the exhaust system behind the engine itself, where the force of escaping gases pushes it through the silencer (muffler) and out through the exhaust fitting and astern.

*(2) Close (fresh-water) system* This system brings water through a hull fitting, strains it, then pumps it through a *heat exchanger*, where it passes over and around a set of copper tubes through which pumps the engine's coolant (usually glycol-based antifreeze). The seawater draws the heat out of the antifreeze just the way your car's radiator draws heat. The antifreeze continues to circulate through the engine and heat exchanger, maintaining an even operating temperature. The seawater dumps into the exhaust behind the engine, and is evacuated with exhaust pressure.

Note that the exhaust of an inboard engine must be *high-looped* to raise it above the boat's waterline and break any backflow that could develop because of the relatively low position of the engine. Also note that some method of breaking the potentially dangerous syphon that could develop because of the below-the-water water intake must be provided (usually a vent). Unless the high-loop and syphon-blocking measures are taken, any water either pushed by wave action or syphoned back to the engine through the exhaust could find its way into the cylinders through open exhaust valves and cause severe damage.

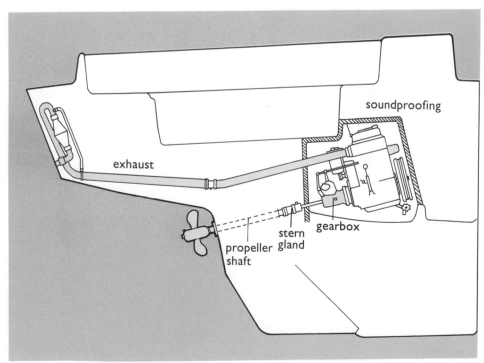

*A typical diesel installation showing the looped exhaust system which prevents water from running back into the cylinders. Cooling water often exits via the exhaust system.*

soundproofing

exhaust

gearbox

stern gland

propeller shaft

In outboards, cooling is relatively simple. All outboards pull seawater through intakes on the lower unit, pump it via a small impeller pump up water channels and into the cooling passages of the aluminum powerhead and push it back to sea through both an exhaust-dump and a small idle passage at the rear of the powerhead.

## MAINTENANCE

Keeping in mind the four basic elements of the internal combustion engine, along with the peculiarities of the marine cooling system, there are specific items of maintenance every skipper can see to that will help insure efficiency and longevity from his machinery.

*(1) Combustion* Fuel should be kept fresh. Outboard oil/petrol pre-mixture should be maintained according to manufacturer's specifications. Diesel fuel should pass through a filter/water-separator before passing into the injection system. Gasoline (outboard or inboard) should pass through at least a basic particulate filter before intake.

Note that filter elements should be checked and/or changed frequently and the settling bowl in a water separator should be watched for any signs of the collection of water.

Make sure your spark–plugs are fresh each year. And have the ignition system timed and/or its integrated circuitry inspected and replaced as recommended.

*(2) Exhaust* The routing of the exhaust system can be crucial in an inboard installation. Make sure all connections and clamp fittings are made tightly and are leak-free. Keep an eye on the color of the exhaust gases. Too much smoke, either from a diesel engine or a gasoline engine, can mean excessive combustion of oil, dirty fuel, insufficient air, or any of these. Note that outboards typically push more smoke than inboards, but it is characteristically blue-ish when the engine is running properly.

*(3) Intake* Keep your engine's air intake system clean and clog-free. This involves simply cleaning the air filter, just the way you do with your automobile's.

*(4) Compression* Make sure your engine's lubrication system is kept clean. Oil breakdown can lead to rapid wear of piston rings and valves, which in turn can lead to loss of compression. At each oil change (the interval for which is recommended by the manufacturer), change the oil filter.

Make sure your instrument panel is equipped with an oil-pressure gauge and alarm system.

An engine's compression can be checked using a *compression gauge*, checking each cylinder against manufacturer's original specification. If any one cylinder shows much less compression than any of the others, component wear must be suspected, and a re-build may be in order.

*The four most common propulsion systems allow flexibility of installation to suit all boat types.*

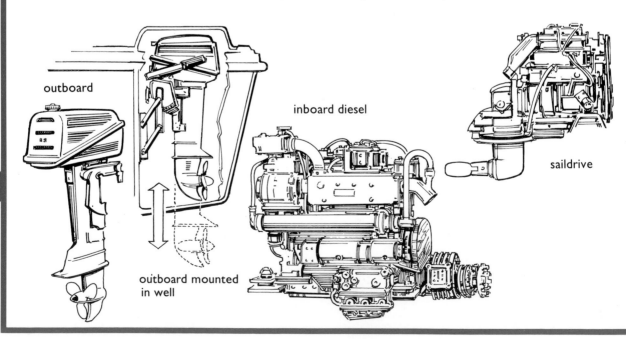

outboard

outboard mounted in well

inboard diesel

saildrive

(5) *Power transmission* Your inboard's transmission needs regular maintenance, especially its lubrication system. Check your transmission's oil level at recommended intervals; and make sure its coolant system (usually a portion of the raw-water circuit) is not leaking — either into the transmission itself, or into the bilge.

On an outboard motor, check the heavy-grade gear oil in the lower unit for water contamination. Any traces of milkiness indicates seawater slipping past the water pump shaft seal. Many outboards can operate perfectly well with some water in the gear oil, but it is wise to change the oil at least once a season, and replace the seal as recommended by the manufacturer.

(6) *Cooling* As mentioned, check the continuity of your exhaust system, making sure cooling water is passing freely and regularly out the pipe astern. Examine the hoses frequently for wear due to vibration — especially around the hose clamps.

At the intake point, make sure the valve at the through-hull fitting is clear of obstruction, and that the on-line strainer is not clogged. Check all the clamps in the intake system for tightness, and make sure the hoses are free of wear.

Check tightness and wear of V-belts driving water pump(s), making sure they're doing their job.

Make sure coolant in any closed system is filled up to specified level. Have a water-temperature gauge and alarm built into your instrument panel.

## LOG IT

To keep a running check on all aspects of your propulsion system, maintain an engine log. Listing dates of oil change, coolant top-off, transmission oil change, ignition work, and other maintenance can help remind you when the routine chores are due.

Further, you will want to keep a record of the rpm you run your engine at while cruising, and the amount of fuel you burn at normal levels of operation. Add to those figures the speeds you are able to make good at cruising speed, and you will be able to track your boat's performance.

Not only is this a good thing from a maintenance standpoint, but it will help you to estimate and log speeds for your dead reckoning plots.

Though many purists will insist that an engine is unnecessary in a sailboat, and that a true sailor should be able to navigate anywhere without one, most sailors do rely on their powerplants.

A good engine helps when navigating in close quarters or during times when the situation calls for quick dousing of sail and a dash for that protected cover. Nothing beats that power when the wind dies and you're still a long way from home.

So take care of your engine. It will return the favor someday.

*Installation variations for outboard and inboard engines. While the outboard variation is simpler to maintain, it can be vulnerable to damage. Inboard systems, although harder to service, are more reliable.*

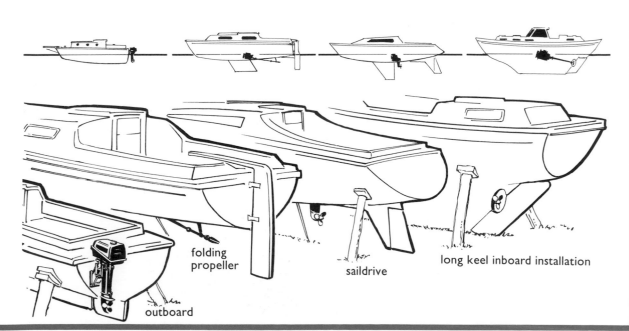

folding propeller

saildrive

long keel inboard installation

outboard

169

*Hook down and holding, it's time to furl sails and go ashore.*

One of the greatest joys of cruising is found at day's end, when the hook is down and the wind goes quiet — when the sun casts a warm light against the spars and sailing companions discuss the events of the day.

There is a freedom to lying at anchor, one not available to dock dwellers. You are out in the open, away from the traffic and hustle of the shore. If you know your own boat and her gear, and are proficient at anchoring technique, you often will feel safer on the hook than at a dock.

## GROUND TACKLE

In order to take full advantage of the many beautiful anchorages in the world's cruising areas, you must have complete faith in your anchoring gear — your *ground tackle*.

The anchor, of course, is important, but so are the other components. Line, deck fittings, chain, and shackles are among the other pieces of hardware involved.

The anchor itself has some major components: the *shank* is the shaft to which the anchor line, or *rode*, is attached by stout shackle. The *crown* is the end that attaches to the bottom, the *flukes* being the broad "shovels", attached to the crown, that dig in. Generally, an anchor has a cross-piece to help it orient itself on the bottom so as to dig its flukes in; this piece is called the *stock*.

**The anchor** There are many different types of anchor, each suited to a different bottom consistency and purpose.

*(1) Danforth* This is the world's most common anchor. It is a good general-purpose anchor, designed to orient itself properly on whatever bottom it finds. It does this by catching the bottom with either of two short flukes on its crown. These short flukes serve to rotate the large flukes downward, toward the mud or sand of the bottom. The anchor then digs its way in as the boat powers astern with tension on the rode. Because a Danforth is so well designed, it does not need to be quite so heavy as other types, and therefore is ideal for smaller boats with small crews.

*(2) CQR, or plow* The CQR is a rather heavy anchor that uses its weight to orient itself properly on the bottom. It has a single, plowlike fluke attached by a pin swivel to its stockless shank. The weight of the large fluke, as well as the shape of its edges, work the anchor into the bottom. The CQR type is good for rocky or coral bottoms, as its sharp fluke easily catches outcroppings or snags. However, it also works nicely in sand or mud. It's biggest advantage is that it is housed easily on a short sprit at a boat's bow. Many boats carry both Danforth and plow.

*(3) Yachtsman or standard or fisherman's* The yachtsman anchor is the simplest and one of the oldest designs available today. It is often called a *kedge* because it can be set — by simply dropping it, using its weight to bury in the bottom — and hauled upon to work a boat off a grounding. The yachtsman is among the heaviest of all anchors. But perhaps that is why it remains popular, even in competition with the newer high-tensile lightweights. Its weight is as much a factor in its holding power as any design feature. Because its stock is at right angles to its flukes, the flukes are able to dig in. However, only one fluke ever finds bottom, and it is a narrow one at that. This makes the yachtsman anchor best in hard mud, hard sand, gravel, or a mixture of gravel and weed — places where a Danforth would be less than ideal.

**The rode** An anchor rode for a cruising boat normally consists of two components: the line, and the chain.

*(1) The line* Anchor line should be *plain-*

*This plow (**right**) is stowed on the stemhead roller ready for instant use, while a Bruce anchor (**below right**), used as a kedge, sits in a special stern chock.*

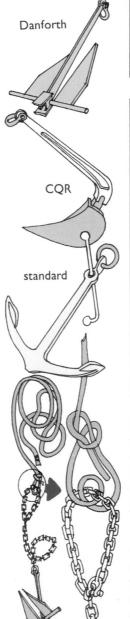

Danforth

CQR

standard

ZLARIN

*laid* synthetic rope — that is, it should be twisted from three strands, each consisting of many nylon fibers. The diameter of the line will vary with the size of the vessel it serves, with ⅝in being the average for boats just under 30ft, and anywhere from ¾in to 1in and up for larger vessels.

*(2) The chain* A length of plain-link chain should always lead away from the anchor shank. There are two reasons for this: first, the bottom can present snags and abrasive surfaces that might chew through fiber line; and second, it helps to add weight to the anchor-end of the rode, to help the anchor

*A bow anchor well with a small hand-operated anchor winch and plenty of room to stow chain and rode. The main anchor should weigh roughly 1lb for every foot of length, but the best rule is "the heavier the better".*

bury itself in the bottom. The length of chain normally specified can run anywhere from 6ft for a small boat to 10 or 12ft for a larger cruising vessel.

Note that many cruising boats carry anchor rodes comprised entirely of chain. The advantages of this will be explained shortly. The chain is always connected to both anchor shank and fiber rode with screw-pin shackles, almost always of galvanized steel. The galvanized coating helps lock the threads of a shackle, making for a positive connection.

**Deck gear** The size of a boat dictates how complicated its deck gear must be. On some larger boats, *electric windlasses* haul on all-chain rodes and raise and lower 75-lb CQRs with great ease. On small cruisers, the mate or skipper manually hauls the 15-lb Danforth with its short length of chain.

Perhaps the best anchor-handling item is a *stemhead anchor roller*. This can only be used for stockless anchors, like the Danforth or CQR, because the roller itself is used to house the anchor while at sea. By simply passing a lashing around the anchor's shank, the rig can be secured.

While CQR anchors all must be housed in bow chocks, Danforths may be brought up on deck and laid flat in deck mounts or stowed below. Yachtsman anchors can be partially dismantled (by rotating their stocks) and stowed flat in deck mounts.

Anchor rode should be led below through a *deck* or *hawse pipe*. This pipe is guarded from water intake by a cap that

allows the line to feed out. Finally, stout hardware on the foredeck must be sized suitably for the ground tackle a boat needs. Deck cleats must be large enough to handle the strain and diameter of line used. *Fairleads* must be of a size to handle the diameter of line and must lead the line clear of any obstructions on deck.

Perhaps the best anchor or mooring connection on any boat's foredeck is a *samson.post*. This is a post that penetrates the deck itself and mounts deep inside the boat, down in the structure of framing forward. It gains tremendous strength by tying into the boat thus, and therefore provides the best purchase for anchoring, as well as for towing. The upper end of a samson post can carry a windlass or a single crossbar for belaying the rode.

## ANCHORING TECHNIQUE

To set the stage for dropping anchor, a skipper first must find a proper spot. In the beginning, this will take much thought, but after awhile, you will get better at picking the best location.

There are some basic criteria for locating the best anchoring position:

*(1) Protection* A harbor with high ground in the way of the wind's direction. Or a spot within a harbor best sheltered from the weather.

*(2) Depth* A spot with enough depth to accommodate a vessel's draft at mean low tide, and with enough depth all around within a circle whose radius is described by the boat's anchor rode. Depth can be determined by examining the soundings on a chart, and then by testing the exact location with electronic depthsounder or weighted line (*leadline*).

*(3) Holding bottom* A spot with the proper bottom characteristics for the anchor being used.

*(4) Swinging room* A spot clear enough of other boats and natural obstructions to allow 360-degree swinging around the anchor, within a circle whose radius is described by the boat's anchor rode. And a spot that permits enough anchor rode for secure holding. A skipper should look at all the other boats within the anchorage and determine which of them have similar characteristics to his own. Other sailboats

make better neighbors than powerboats do, as sailing yachts will respond to tidal stream more readily (because they have deeper keels), and powerboats will respond to wind (because they have less in the water and more tophamper).

Once a skipper locates a spot with all the above characteristics, he then may prepare to anchor. The following are the steps of the procedure, using one anchor:

*(1) In position* The skipper brings the boat up into the wind, either under sail or power. If under sail, he must allow himself the room to sail away again if the anchor fails to bite and the boat drifts too close to other anchored boats. For this reason, it is wise for the beginner to anchor under power during the learning stages.

Under sail, the boat must coast to a stop at the position where the anchor is to be dropped; under power, the engine is reversed and the boat stopped. When over the drop point, the boat should be pointed directly to windward.

Note that sometimes other boats will be lying with their bows toward the direction of the *tidal stream* rather than the wind. In such a situation, sailing up to anchor becomes more complicated and less desirable.

*(2) Letting go* The foredeck crew then

*Anchor down, but the crewman can feel it dragging (**below**).*

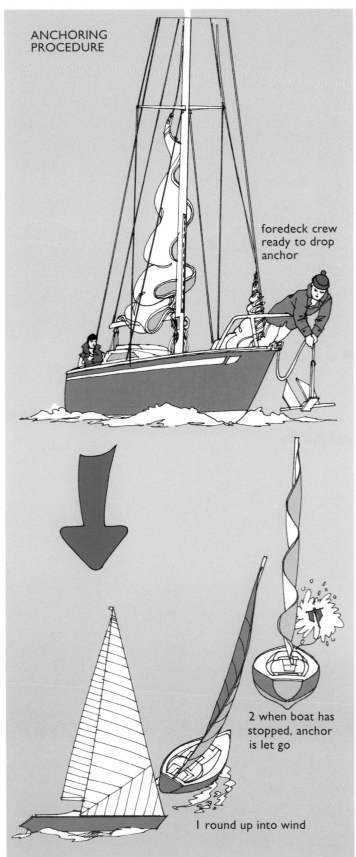

ANCHORING
PROCEDURE

foredeck crew
ready to drop
anchor

2 when boat has
stopped, anchor
is let go

I round up into wind

*This small cruiser, left at anchor in a gentle offshore breeze, is now in danger from an onshore breeze and breaking waves which are putting a great strain on its ground tackle.*

lets go the anchor, letting it down so as to keep the rode clear of the anchor's stock and flukes. Once the anchor is on the bottom, the crewman signals the helm.

*(3) Backing down* The engine is then reversed; or the boat begins to drift astern with the wind on her rig pushing her. If under sail, the jib is dropped, and the main is sheeted loosely so as not to fill. As the rode comes taut, the bowman lets it slip from his grip, applying a slight tension. Once the anchor is approximately one boatlength away, the bowman gives the rode a sharp tug to get the anchor positioned in the correct attitude. The boat continues to back.

*(4) Allowing enough scope* Scope is the amount of rode let out. It is important to pay out a scope that is correct for the depth of the water. Experts agree that a ratio of seven-to-one is appropriate for most conditions. That is, seven feet of rode for each foot of depth, from the *foredeck to the bottom*, taking into account the change of tide. If possible, always set out enough scope for *high tide*. The easiest way to determine correct scope is to take note of the approximate distance the anchor falls before it strikes bottom, then multiply by seven. As you become more experienced, you will learn to gauge scope by looking at the angle of your anchor rode as it becomes taut at the bow.

*(5) Setting the anchor* Just before the proper scope is achieved, the bowman should take a wrap of rode on the windlass capstan or the bow cleat or post. He then

should take some strain, slowing the boat's rearward motion. He will feel the anchor begin to dig in as he applies pressure. If the flukes are skipping on the bottom, he will feel short tugs on the line; if the anchor digging, he will feel a steady increase in pressure. When he feels the anchor bite, he must take more turns on the fitting to stop the rode from paying out.

If the maneuver has been done under sail, it is completed and sail may be taken down and furled. But if you've anchored under power, the engine should be reversed again and run in reverse for several minutes to make sure the anchor has hooked itself firmly in the bottom.

*(6) Taking bearings* When all is secure, it is wise to take a set of anchor bearings. These can vary from a formal set of compass bearings on fixed shoreline features, to a casual lining up of landmarks and other boats. In the middle of the night and during a squall, a skipper must be able to glance about and determine if he's dragged anchor and changed position.

## DRAGGING ANCHOR

There may come a time when a squall or a tidal change or a drastic change in wind direction causes an anchor to break its hold on the bottom. When this happens, there are several things to do.

*(1)* First, you needn't worry about sleeping through a dragging, as most skippers learn to feel it when something changes in the middle of the night. If a squall blows through, the noise and commotion is enough to wake you; and if a wind shift takes you around and starts moving you down the anchorage, the boat's motion should change enough to get your attention. Of course, if you sleep through all that, the sound when you bounce off the next boat is sure to wake you.

*(2)* Second, you should keep calm. Examine your landmarks (anchor bearings) and determine how far you've gone and how fast you're dragging. Wake your crew calmly, and instruct them to dress quickly.

*(3)* Get yourself into the cockpit and start the engine, first making sure there are no stray lines in the water to foul the propeller. Determine where the anchor is right now. It may be under the boat or dead

astern, in which case, you might be able to get clear and turn her by pushing the helm over. It's usually best to give the helm a push to leeward; you might be able to get her to round up into the wind. However, and luckily, most boats tend to drag anchor with the bow slightly toward the wind, so it may be possible to maneuver with the engine.

*(4)* Shift to reverse once you've determined where the anchor is. Get someone forward immediately to handle the rode. Once the boat is backing, try to slip more scope and get the anchor to set. If other boats are too close, see the next step.

*(5)* Shift to forward and get the bow pointed to windward. Have the bowman haul on the rode until the boat's bow is directly over the anchor. Haul in the anchor until it is clear of the water and dangling, ready to drop again.

*(6)* Power to a new spot in the clear, making sure you adhere to the original criteria for finding a spot. Drop anchor and go through the normal procedure for setting.

Note that before a storm it is wise to pay out more rode than is usual. If an anchor turns in a windshift, or if the wind becomes too much for its holding power, more scope should enable it to dig in again of its own accord.

Also note that a Danforth is particularly prone to turning out in a strong wind shift — especially one of more than 90 degrees. A CQR, on the other hand, is excellent in drastic shifts, as is a yachtsman.

*Hoisting the anchor — a job for strong arms and straight backs (**below**).*

## RE-SETTING

bowman hauls on rode until bow is over anchor

anchor hauled in

anchor dangling and ready to drop again

175

*With plenty of room to maneuver, this cruiser sets her mainsail (**1**) and sails up to her anchor which is retrieved by the crewman on the foredeck (**2**). Once clear of the water, the crewman signals to the helmsman that he is free to bear away (**3**) and order the jib to be set.*

## TWO ANCHORS

Strong shifts of wind or current can cause anchors to turn out of the bottom and perhaps foul or not set again. For this reason, and in some places in particular, it is wise to anticipate the shifts in wind or current and set one primary anchor, with another set for the shift.

**Breasting** When two anchors lead out in opposite directions from the bow, a boat is said to the *breasted* between two anchors. The technique for breasting is as follows:

(1) The boat is run toward the direction of primary wind or current. Approximately three boatlengths from the position the skipper wishes the boat to come to rest, the first anchor is dropped and its rode paid out freely.

(2) The boat is allowed to continue past its eventual position until it is approximately four boatlengths beyond the first anchor.

(3) At that point, strain is taken on the first rode, and the boat's motion is slowed as the first anchor is set. The boat is permitted to continue forward, while it is also turned so the stern swings slightly away from the first rode passing aft.

(4) The first anchor bites, and forward

*Two anchors are necessary where space is restricted (**below**), such as an estuary, or where a tide change is expected that will swing the boat through 180 degrees.*

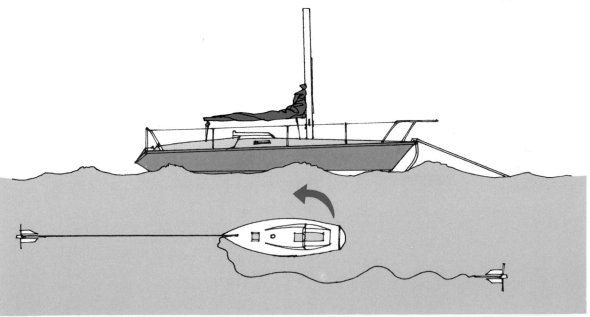

motion is stopped just as the boat reaches a point three boatlengths past its intended position — six boatlengths past the first anchor.

*(5)* The second anchor is dropped, with the boat ready to back away from it. The engine is reversed, and the boat is backed away from the second anchor in a direction toward the first, but with its stern well clear of the first's rode. Slack in the first rode is taken up slowly as the boat backs.

*(6)* The second anchor is set normally, and the boat positioned between the two anchors.

**Bow and stern** Bow-and-stern anchoring is done in precisely the same manner as breasting, with the exception that the first anchor may be set off the stern, and its rode controlled so as to keep it completely clear of the propeller.

In bow-and-stern anchoring, the stern rode is made fast to a fitting at the transom, and the boat is kept in line between the two anchors.

Note that in breasting, the boat is allowed to swing between both rodes, always keeping her bow toward wind or current. In bow-and-stern anchoring, each end is alternately presented to the wind or current.

Both breasting and bow-and-stern anchoring can be accomplished in other ways. A good alternative is to anchor in the primary direction first, and then take a second anchor out in the dinghy to its proper position. Strain can be taken and the second hook set with some maneuvering. Here's where a good heavy kedge can be worth its weight in gold, as it can simply be taken out and dropped, with just a few tugs required to get it set.

Anchoring may seem complex, but if it is done right it will produce a feeling of self-sufficiency quite unlike that produced by any other endeavor. When coupled with a lovely harbor, a pretty sunset, good companionship, and a hot meal, the reasons for cruising at all become absolutely clear.

*Lying to bow and stern anchors (**below**) will stop the boat swinging to the tide or wind.*

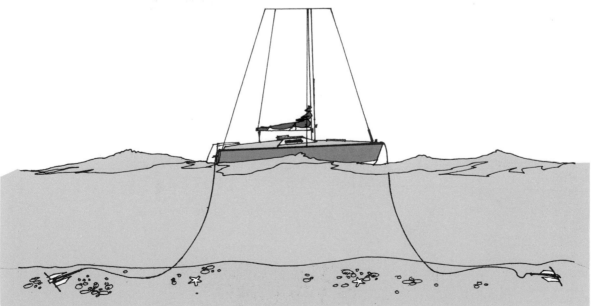

# 22 | MAINTENANCE

*Fitting out — a time to renew and repair made easier with a generator and power tools.*

If there were a single useful philosophy to pass along to the beginner, it would be this:

*The boat is the center of the sport. It is a system of great importance, one to which you may entrust your life someday, and so it must receive the utmost care.*

I have discussed the maintenance of a ship's propulsion machinery and looked at the elements of proper sail care. I will now complete the picture with a look at the hull and rig, and the things you can do to ensure their continued good operation.

## THE BOTTOM

The single most loathed job in all of boat maintenance is the care of the bottom. Not only must a skipper get under the boat in all kinds of awkward positions, but he must also scrape and sandpaper the old dry paint and apply new paint — all of which exposes him to certain toxins. Not a friendly proposition.

The job of maintaining a good finish on the bottom is an important one for two reasons: firstly a smooth finish can improve a boat's speed and efficiency; and secondly an effective paint job with a high-quality *anti-fouling* paint can help keep marine growth (algae, weeds, barnacles) off the surface.

Most boats kept in salt water rely on a basic oil-based copper-filled paint, applied at the start of each season. The process for applying this is as follows:

(1) Wear a particle mask — either a fine-weave fabric mask or a full-face protector. Goggles should be worn if the mask leaves the eyes unprotected. Bottom paint contains poison.

(2) With a sharp right-angle paint scraper, scrape all loose paint from the bottom, being careful not to dig or score the surface. (Do not scrape a fiberglass hull; use sandpaper only.)

(3) When scraping is complete use medium-grit sandpaper (dry-type) and sand entire bottom. (If in an area where extraneous dust is undesirable, use wet-type medium-grit paper.)

(4) Mix paint thoroughly, making sure all copper material is held in suspension. Have your paint shop shake the paint, but also use a short length of wood or metal and continue to stir frequently while applying the paint.

(5) If the boat is planked wood, use soft seam-filler before applying paint. On any boat, wipe down the surface before painting.

(6) Apply bottom paint generously with a roller, filling-in and touching up with a brush. The first coat dries quickly; and the second coat should be applied immediately after the first.

Do read the instructions on the paint tin to determine how soon a boat must be launched after painting. Most common bottom paints must touch seawater within two or three days from application, while some new types can go 60 days or longer.

It is best to paint the *boot-top* (the narrow band just above the waterline) before finishing the bottom, as painting the bottom *up* to the stripe is usually easier than painting the stripe *down* to edge against the bottom paint. Use "enamel-type" antifouling paint on your boot-top.

On some boats, bottom paint may have flaked away from the ballast of the keel. If that material is exposed, it should be primed before applying bottom paint. There are many materials made for this purpose, and it's best to consult your chandlery for the best available for your purpose.

All boats have small zinc plates bolted to the bottom to help ward off the destructive action of electrolysis. The zinc plates on your boat should look worn and eaten-away, showing that the zincs are being electrolyzed instead of allowing your boat's other underwater metals to succumb to the destructive process. Replace any worn zincs with new ones.

Note: *Never paint your zincs; the coating would prevent them from contacting the water as they should.*

## TOPSIDES

The sides of your boat's hull above the waterline are called *topsides*. Most fiberglass boats have a hard coating of tinted, polymerized resin on the topsides, called *gel-coat.*

Gel-coat requires little maintenance. It needs wax each year to help resist fading, and it should be repaired when it is scratched or damaged.

To repair a surface blemish in gel-coat, use a kit designed for the purpose. Most chandlers carry them. It is important to watch the temperature on the day of application, and make sure it is within the specifications of the manufacturer. Most gel-coat repair kits allow the applicator to grind and/or polish shortly after drying.

There may come a time when painting is the only way to renew a boat's topside finish. this is always true on a wooden boat, where yearly painting is usual, but even fiberglass boats need to be painted — especially when their gel-coat fades and dulls.

On both wooden and fiberglass boats, a process of sanding and filling is required to gain a smooth, even surface for painting. The materials and methods for sanding and filling vary and so it's wise for the beginner to consult instructional guides on the subject, or to inquire of the yard's expert personnel.

Once the hull is fair, the choice of paint is up to the owner. There are three major classes of topside paints:

(1) Alkyd enamel — normal oil-based paint, designed to hold up through one season's use in normal weather conditions. Does not necessarily need special primers. (Least expensive.)

(2) One-part polyurethane — high-gloss polyurethane-based paint designed to last perhaps two or three seasons. Must be applied over special primers. (Mid-priced.)

oil turnbuckles

dismantle and grease winches

check roller reefing gear

replace navigation lights and other bulbs

top up and check battery

179

(3) Two-part polyurethane — an extremely high-gloss coating designed to last from three to five years. Must be applied over special primers and surfacing materials, and is usually recommended for professional application. (Most expensive.)

The last two systems are most often used on fiberglass boats, as they show superior adhesion to the prepared gel-coat. Both can be touched up, though with some difficulty.

Alkyd enamel is usually used on wooden boats, as swelling and shrinkage of planking and moisture retention in wood usually do more to deteriorate surface paint than normal weathering, and painting therefore must be done annually.

### BRIGHTWORK

Often, some wood on a boat is left unpainted — natural. This *brightwork* must be treated with preservative or sealant, or eventually it will suffer the ravages of salt water and sun.

*Oil* There are numerous types of oil available with which an owner may coat his brightwork. Teak is especially common on newer boats, and this wood is perfectly suited to oiling.

When oiling teak, make sure to rub small amounts of oil in thoroughly with a terrycloth rag. Doing this frequently (about once a month) will keep the teak rich-looking and well sealed.

*Varnish* Varnish is another sealant, but has properties that make it more permanent. However, because teak usually has natural oils present in its grain, it is one wood that should not be varnished.

Varnish dries into a hard, glossy surface. Unlike oils, it must be built up coat after coat, with the varnisher making sure to sand lightly between coats. A good varnish job can last a long time, with a simple touch-up (a light coat or two) all that's required each year.

Varnish works well on seasoned oak, softwoods, and on mahogany.

Note that there are many types of varnish, from the traditional spar varnish to the new hi-tech clear polyurethanes. Ask your chandler for his recommendations.

### RIG MAINTENANCE

Since the rig must support all your sails and absorb all the stresses of sailing throughout the season, it's important to examine it thoroughly at the beginning of the year.

*Mast* On an aluminum mast, check all mast-mounted fittings and tangs. Make sure there is no cracking of the extrusion around tangs and bolts, and make sure that none of the stainless fittings are showing signs of cracking around their fastenings.

On a wood mast, do all the above, but also check for cracks and separations in any glue lines, and cracks or gaps in mounting blocks and at the mast's butt. Refinish the mast as appropriate each year.

Check all mast wiring by examing by eye for deterioration in the wire casing, and set up a battery to test the masthead light, spreader lights, and any other mast-mounted lights. Replace any worn or ineffective wiring.

Oil masthead main-halyard sheave, and replace pin and/or sheave if worn.

*The masthead and standing rigging should not be neglected. A mid-season check by bosun's chair will ensure that masthead fittings and shackles have not worked loose nor standing rigging frayed at the terminals or swages.*

Examine and oil or replace (if necessary) any other blocks — spinnaker, jib, topping lift(s), etc.

*Standing rigging* Examine closely the swaged terminals on all wire. Look for small cracks at the swaged collars, and have the entire shroud or stay replaced if swages show signs of bad cracking.

Look for elongated clevis holes on all swaged ends, as well as on any other terminal end. Elongation reflects serious strain and distortion of the alloy.

Check wire and terminals for signs of rust. Rust could indicate a developing problem. Clean it away and examine closely for cracking at terminal.

Examine turnbuckles for stretching or elongation at clevis holes and threads. Check holes and body for cracking, damage. Replace whole unit if necessary. Lubricate threads with moisture-penetrating lubricant (or . . . anhydrous lanolin works well). Make sure cotter pins are inserted in clevises of correct size for terminals and turnbuckles in rig when set up.

*Running rigging* Make sure all blocks are lubricated with moisture-penetrating lubricant, or with anhydrous lanolin. Check that all fittings requiring cotter pins have fresh ones.

Make sure swivels and blocks are without too much play. If axles or swivel pins seem worn, consider replacing part.

Check all line for chafe and wear. Repair any unraveling, and replace any questionable line.

Lubricate all winches according to manufacturer's instructions. Make sure that boom, spinnaker pole, and any other spars are examined as thoroughly as the mast.

Lubricate and check any roller-furling gear. Check furling pendant for unraveling and signs of wear.

Check all wire halyards for burrs, and replace if flattened or pinched at any point.

## ONGOING MAINTENANCE

Of course, the foregoing is simply a survey of the things to be mindful of during maintenance season. There are many things that must be attended to on an ongoing basis as well such as the ship's powerplant and support systems.

Here are some of those things, in no particular order:

*Decks* If teak, keep scrubbed. Oiling teak decks is alright, but too much oil will make them slippery when wet.

If fiberglass, keep clean.

If canvas-covered wood, keep painted, using porch-and-deck enamel if possible, as it flexes more than marine paint. Keep canvas sealed, especially at edges; and replace canvas if it begins to tear and/or deteriorate.

If leaking develops, search for source(s). When found, mark source and attack when dry with surface sealers and/or deep-penetrating sealers. Check with local chandler on best material for purpose.

*Ship's electrical system* Maintain good check on battery charge. Keep all external light fixtures well sealed from moisture. Keep all internal wiring terminals, switches, and busses sprayed with moisture-penetrating lubricant.

*Bilges* Keep bilges as clean as possible. Clean bilge pump intake screen frequently. Use oil-absorptive sponge or emulsifier to disperse and absorb stray oil.

*Lockers* Keep stowage spaces dry and clean. Keep dry food stores enclosed and sealed in plastic containers. Bars of fragrant soap placed in each locker space helps keep boat "sweet" smelling without overdoing it. In winter season, keep mildew-absorptive bags aboard.

*Underwater* If possible, scrub the boat's bottom once in the middle of the season. Also, make sure propeller remains free of barnacles.

As you can see, maintenance, is an ongoing fact of life aboard a boat. But it can be one of the more enjoyable parts of your life under sail.

Use your good common sense about every aspect of your boat's many systems. Ask the advice of your yard and of friends you respect. Read more about the specifics you're concerned with. Through the years, you will develop your skills and insights until you become a fine seaman. And when you do, you can pass along what you've learned.

Most importantly you will understand what Water Rat meant when he said " . . . there's absolutely nothing . . not a thing . . half so worthwhile as simply messing about in boats."

gelcoat repairs

polisher

paint

brushes

eye protection

protective gloves

181

# APPENDIX A: RULES OF THE ROAD

Due to the limited scope of this book, some of the material contained herein is designed simply to begin your acquaintance with the serious subject of safety afloat. Matters such as the Rules of the Road or coastal piloting for example should be explored in greater depth. It is for this reason that we include in this Appendix some of the pertinent rules governing the flow of marine traffic at sea and in restricted waters. Other vital matters, such as the rules governing sound signals and lights and shapes, are not included. Therefore, we strongly recommend that additional sources, such as Chapman's *Piloting, Seamanship and Small Boat Handling*, be sought out.

The rules are in sections: General; Steering and Sailing Rules; Lights and Shapes; Sound and Light Signals; and Annexes concerning location, rigging, requirements for equipment etc.

What follows is an abridged version of the main rules. Explanations are made in parentheses.

## GENERAL

### RULE 1
### APPLICATION

These rules shall apply to all vessels on the high seas and waters connected therewith, navigable by seagoing vessels.

### RULE 2
### RESPONSIBILITY

Nothing shall exonerate any vessel or the owner, master and crew from the consequences of any neglect. In complying with these rules due regard shall be given to all dangers of navigation and collision and to any special circumstances which may make a departure from these rules necessary to avoid immediate danger.

## STEERING AND SAILING RULES
### Section 1 — Applied in any condition of visibility

### RULE 5
### LOOK-OUT

Every vessel shall maintain at all times, a proper look-out by sight and hearing as well as by all available means appropriate to the circumstances.

(This is probably the single most important rule. On yachts you must be aware of the blind spots such as behind the leeward side of the headsail or behind the structure if keeping watch for long periods from an inside steering position. It is also important to preserve night vision from bright interior lights, cigarette lighters and deck floodlights because 100 per cent night vision is lost in a fraction of a second yet takes many minutes to recover. Note also the reference to hearing. In fog, for example, a look-out away from engine and exhaust noise is invaluable.)

### RULE 6
### SAFE SPEED

Every vessel shall proceed at a safe speed so that she can take proper and effective action to avoid collision.

(Many factors should be taken into account here: level of visibility, traffic density, maneuverability of vessels, depth of water, presence of background lights at night and state of wind, sea and tide.)

### RULE 7
### RISK OF COLLISION

In determining if the risk of collision exists, the following shall be among the considerations taken into account: if the compass bearing of an approaching vessel does not alter appreciably, and/or if a very large vessel or a vessel with a tow is approaching at close range.

(Here there can be no substitute for taking a bearing on an approaching vessel and monitoring any change closely.)

### RULE 8
### ACTION TO AVOID COLLISION

Action to avoid collision shall be positive, made in ample time and with due regard to good seamanship.

(This often means making your intentions clear early. In giving way to one vessel do not increase the risk of collision with another. In confined waters such alterations of course may often take small craft out of the buoyed deep water channels.)

### RULE 9
### NARROW CHANNELS

A vessel proceeding along the course of a narrow channel or fairway shall keep as near to the outer limit of the channel as is safe and practicable on her own starboard side. A vessel less than 20 meters (65.6 feet) or engaged in fishing, shall not impede the passage of any other vessel and any vessel shall if possible avoid anchoring in the channel.

(Definition of a narrow channel is purposely avoided.)

### RULE 10
### TRAFFIC SEPARATION SCHEMES

A vessel so far as practicable shall avoid crossing traffic lanes, but if obliged to do so, shall cross as nearly as practicable at right angles to the general direction of traffic flow. A vessel less than 20 meters (65.6 feet) or a sailing vessel shall not impede the safe passage of a power-driven vessel following a traffic lane.

(This last part may seem in conflict with the idea that power gives way to sail, but it should be obvious that a small vessel ought to keep clear of a larger one in an area of high traffic density. Also take special note of the instruction to cross at right angles. This means the yacht's heading, i.e. course steered, should be at right angles to the traffic lane, not her course over the ground. There are two reasons for this. Firstly simple geometry tells us that even if a yacht crabs sideways on a tide, she will cross through the lane quicker if she steers straight across rather than steering into the tide. Secondly her aspect, particularly her lights at night, will show others that her intention is to cross at right angles. Traffic separation lanes are becoming increasingly frequent so our behavior in them warrants extra thought.)

**Section 2 — Conduct of vessels in sight of one another**

## RULE 12

### SAILING VESSELS

When two vessels are approaching one another, so as to involve the risk of collision, one of them shall keep out of the way of the other as follows:
(i) When each has the wind on a different side, the vessel which has the wind on her port side shall keep clear.
(ii) When both have the wind on the same side, the vessel which is to windward shall keep out of the way of the vessel to leeward.
(iii) If a vessel with the wind on the port sees a vessel to windward and cannot determine with certainty whether the other has the wind on the starboard side, she shall keep out of the way of the other.

## RULE 13

### OVERTAKING

Notwithstanding anything contained in the rules of this section, any overtaking vessel shall keep out of the way of the vessel being overtaken. A vessel shall be deemed to be overtaking when coming on another vessel from a direction more than 22.5 degrees abaft her beam. If a vessel should be in doubt as to whether she is overtaking or not, she should assume this is the case. Any subsequent alteration of the bearing between the two vessels shall not make the overtaking vessel a crossing vessel within the meaning of the rules.

(This rule makes abundantly clear its priority over other Sailing and Steering

rules. It also cautions the helmsman to assess the effect of a course alteration before it is made.)

## RULE 14

### HEAD-ON SITUATION

When two power-driven vessels are meeting on a reciprocal course or nearly reciprocal courses, each shall alter her course to starboard so that each shall pass on the port side of the other.

(For the purposes of the rules, a yacht using her auxilliary engine is considered a power-driven vessel.)

## RULE 15

### CROSSING SITUATION

When two power-driven vessels are crossing so as to involve the risk of collision, the vessel which has the other on her starboard side shall keep out of the way and shall, if the circumstances of the case permit, avoid crossing ahead of the other vessel.

## RULE 16

### ACTION BY GIVE-WAY VESSEL

Every vessel which is directed to keep clear of another vessel shall, so far as possible, take early

and substantial action to keep well clear.

## RULE 17

### ACTION BY STAND-ON VESSEL

a) Where one of two vessels is to keep out of the way, the other shall keep her course and speed. The latter vessel however may take action to avoid collision by her maneuver alone, as soon as it becomes apparent to her that the vessel required to keep out of the way is not taking the appropriate action.
b) When, from any cause, the vessel required to keep her course and speed finds herself so close that collision cannot be avoided by the action of the give-way vessel alone, she shall take such action as will best aid to avoid collision.
c) This Rule does not relieve the give-way vessel of her obligation to keep out of the way.

(This rule may seem contradictory in that it requires the right of way vessel to maintain her course and speed but allows her to take avoiding action and ultimately requires her to avoid collision. The key is that it allows the right of way vessel to take avoiding action if the give-way vessel fails to act in

accordance with the rules. Thus a yacht should not hold on into danger just because the rules say she has right of way. Yachts even in daylight may be difficult to spot from a merchant ship and may not be sighted in time for the early action required of the give-way vessel by the rules to be taken.)

## RULE 18

### RESPONSIBILITIES BETWEEN VESSELS

Except where rules 9, 10 and 13 otherwise require:
a) a power-driven vessel underway shall keep out of the way of a vessel not under command: a vessel restricted in her ability to move; a vessel engaged in fishing; a sailing vessel.
b) a sailing vessel shall keep clear of a vessel not under command; one restricted in her ability to maneuver; or one engaged in fishing.
c) a fishing vessel shall keep clear of vessels not under command and vessels with restricted ability to maneuver.

(This is really a very logical rule requiring more maneuverable vessels to give way to those less so.)

# APPENDIX B: KNOTS AND ROPEWORK

Ropework is a way of life for the sailor, day in and day out. Its maintenance, repair, and replacement are the bread and butter of his routine.

For the inshore sailor, the relatively small demands of shipboard seamanship dictate a less evolved, simpler level of marlinspike skill. Some elementary knots and the basics of fiber rope splicing are all that one needs to manage a small cruising boat in protected waters.

Learn these, then; they are the basics from which you will build a more complete body of skill.

## FIGURE OF EIGHT

*This knot is used to stop a rope slipping through an eye or block. It is equally simple to tie and undo.*

1

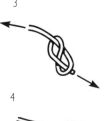

2

3

4

## REEF KNOT

*Originally used to tie reefing lines, the reef knot is formed from two half hitches. To untie a reef knot (**right**), simply hold one end of the rope in one hand and the "standing" part in the other and "push" the knot off.*

6

7

8

1

2

3

4

5

## SHEET BEND

*This knot can be used to join together two ropes of unequal thickness or to fasten a line to an eye. It is easily undone by bending it in the center and pushing the bight down on the half hitch.*

1

2

3

4

5

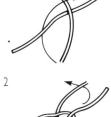

## ROUND TURN AND TWO HALF HITCHES

*Widely used to secure a heavy load to a spar, ring or any standing object. The rope can be secured with two half hitches.*

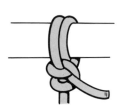

1

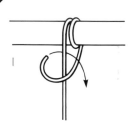

2

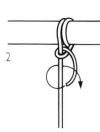

3

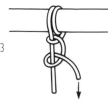

## CLOVE HITCH

*Particularly useful for temporarily tying small items. However, the knot only holds well when under constant strain at right angles to the standing object.*

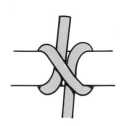

1

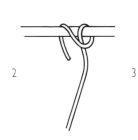

2

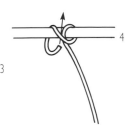

3

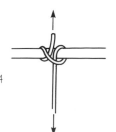

4

## BOWLINE

*A simple knot for forming an eye at the end of a rope.*

1

2

3

4

5

## ROLLING HITCH

*This knot is used to tie a rope to a spar when the strain on the knot is parallel to the object to which it is tied.*

1

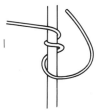

2

3

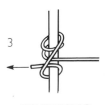

## WHIPPING

*A method of finishing the ends of rope with twine to prevent them from unraveling.*

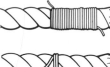

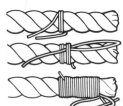

## EYE SPLICE

*Used to form a fixed loop in the end of a rope. It is much stronger than any knot.*

*1 Form required eye. Tuck middle strand under one strand of standing part. Tuck second strand of end part over next strand of standing part and pull tight.*

*2 Flop splice. Tuck last full strand under remaining strand. Pull tight.*

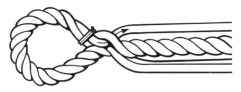

*3 Continue tucking each strand alternately going over and under strands in standing part. Pull tight after each tuck.*

*4 After five tucks are completed, cut off loose ends.*

# GLOSSARY OF SAILING TERMS

Cross-references are indicated by words in *italics*

**abeam** at right angles to the *beam*.

**about, going** changing direction by crossing the wind bow-first.

**ahull** an un-tethered drift with sails furled and helm secured.

**anchor** implement that chains the ship to the bottom.

**apparent wind** the wind as a combined vector between the true wind and that created by the motion of the boat.

**athwartships** at right angles to the *centerline*.

**backstay** any single wire supporting the *mast* from the *stern*.

**batten** wooden or plastic stiffener for a sail.

**beam** measurement of the width of the boat.

**bearing** a direction.

**beating** sailing against the wind by *tacking*.

**belay** make a line fast.

**bend on** tie or fasten.

**bilge** curved part of the *hull* below the *waterline*, inside or out.

**binnacle** container for ship's *compass*.

**block** a pulley.

**boom** *spar* that takes the foot of a sail.

**bow** front end of a boat.

**bowsprit** *spar* projecting from the bow.

**broach** turn sideways to wind and wave.

**buoy** floating navigational marker.

**burgee** small pennant or flag.

**centerboard** retractable *keel* to stop a boat's *leeward* drift.

**chain plate** metal fitting to hold the *shrouds*.

**chart** navigational map used only at sea.

**cleat** fitting to which a rope may be belayed.

**clew** aft bottom corner of a sail.

**close-hauled** sailing close to the wind with sails pulled in.

**compass** navigational instrument for finding geographic directions.

**compass error** combined error produced by magnetic forces of *deviation* and *variation*.

**cringle** loop or eye on the edge of a sail.

**cutter** single-masted boat with more than one *headsail* and with the mast right amidships.

**daggerboard** *centerboard* that does not pivot.

**dead reckoning** the process of predicting and fixing position by course, speed, and distance run.

**deviation** *compass* error produced by magnetic disturbances aboard ship.

**dinghy** small open boat for sailing, rowing, etc.

**displacement** weight of water displaced by a boat, always equal to boat's weight.

**douse** drop sails quickly.

**downhaul** rope used to set up downward tension or haul down a sail or *spar*.

**draft** depth from the *waterline* to the lowermost projection of the *hull*.

**ease** decrease the pressure on a sail.

**eye of the wind** direction from which the wind is blowing.

**fairlead** fitting through which a line runs easily.

**fall off** turn away from the direction of the wind.

**fix** boat's position established on a *chart*.

**fore-and-aft** lengthwise.

**fore-and-aft rig** sails set in a *fore-and-aft* line. Not *square-rigged*.

**foremast** *mast* nearest to the *bow*.

**freeboard** height of the boat's side from deck to *waterline*.

**furl** tightly roll up a sail.

**gaff** *spar* that secures the head of an old-fashioned *fore-and-aft* sail.

**galley** a boat's kitchen.

**genoa** large *headsail* overlapping the *mainsail*.

**gooseneck** sliding and pivoting fitting that connects the *boom* to the *mast*.

**grommet** rope or brass ring in a sail or piece of canvas.

**gudgeon** a *rudder* support.

**gunwales** upper edges of a boat's sides.

**guy** adjustable steadying rope on a boat's rig.

**halyard** rope or wire used for hoisting sails.

**hard chines** intersection of straight sides with a flat or V-bottom.

**hatch** a covered opening in the *deck*.

**hawsepipe** metal pipe through which the *anchor* chain passes.

**heads** toilet.

**headway** forward movement of a boat.

**heel** a boat's angle to the horizontal.

**helm** *tiller* or wheel.

**hike** to lean over the high side of a boat when it is *heeling*.

**hull** the body of a boat.

**jib** triangular sail set farthest forward.

**jibing** changing direction with the wind aft.

**kedge** small *anchor* used for maneuvering.

**keel** centerline backbone at the bottom of a boat.

**ketch** two-masted sailboat with tallest mast forward of amidships, shorter one forward of *rudder* position.

**knot** one *nautical mile* per hour.

**lateen** *rig* with a triangular sail secured to a *yard* hoisted to a low *mast*.

**leeboard** board on the side of a boat to stop its drifting to *leeward*.

**leech** outside edge of a sail.

**leeward** down wind.

**leeway** sideways drift of a boat.

**life-jacket** garment worn to keep a person afloat in water.

**lifeline** line attached to a harness or a boat for safety.

**logbook** book in which daily records of a voyage are kept.

**lubberline** *compass* mark indicating *fore-and-aft.*

**luff** to get so close to the wind that the sail flaps. Also the forward edge of a sail.

**lug** *fore-and-aft* sail with a *yard* that partly projects forward of the *mast.*

**LWL** length at the waterline.

**magnetic north** direction in which the needle of a magnetic *compass* points.

**mainmast** principal *mast* on a boat.

**mainsail** boomed sail projecting *aft* from *mainmast.*

**mainsheet** line that controls the main *boom.*

**make fast** secure a line.

**marconi rig** triangular *fore-and-aft rig.*

**mast** vertical *spar* to which the sails and *rigging* are attached.

**masthead** top of the *mast.*

**mizzen** after *mast* on a ketch or yawl.

**nautical mile** 6,080 ft.

**outhaul** line used to pull out the foot of a sail.

**pintle** metal pin on which the *rudder* is hung.

**plot** mark course or position on a *chart.*

**point** direction on the *compass* card.

**port** left side looking towards the *bow.*

**port tack** when a boat sails with the main *boom* to *starboard* and the wind hits the *port* side first.

**reaching** sailing on a *tack* with the wind roughly *abeam.*

**reef** reduce the area of sail.

**regatta** boat races.

**rig** arrangements of *masts* and sails.

**rigging** ropes and wire *stays* of a boat.

**roach** curved section at the *leech* of a sail.

**rode** *anchor* cable.

**rowlocks** crutches on the *gunwale* that hold the oars when in use.

**rudder** vertical metal or wooden plate attached at the stern, whose movements steer the boat.

**run** sail with the wind aft.

**samson post** strong post on a boat to which mooring lines are tied.

**sandbar** ridge of sand in a river or sea; often exposed at low tide.

**schooner** *fore-and-aft rigged* boat with two or more

*masts*, the tallest of which is the aftermost, and is stepped just abaft amidships.

**scull** propel a boat by means of one oar over the stern.

**sea anchor** floating object dragged from the stern to hold a boat to the wind.

**shackle** strong metal link with a removable bolt.

**sheave** wheel inside a *block* over which a rope runs.

**sheet** line that controls a sail or the movement of a *boom.*

**shrouds** transverse wires or ropes that support the *mast* laterally.

**sloop** single-masted, *fore-and-aft rigged* boat, usually with two sails.

**snatch block** single *block* with a latched opening on one side.

**sound** (verb) to determine the depth of the water.

**sound** (noun) a body of water partially enclosed by an island or offshore bar.

**spar** pole, *mast,* or *boom,* etc., that supports a sail.

**spinnaker** large, light foresail set forward of the *mainsail* when running before the wind.

**spreaders** struts attached to the *mast* to spread the *shrouds.*

**sprit** *spar* projecting

diagonally from the *mast* to extend the *fore-and-aft* sail.

**spritsail** sail extended or rigged from a *sprit.*

**squall** sudden storm resulting from extreme thermal conditions.

**square rig** square sails extended by *yards* set across the boat.

**stanchion** metal or wooden post bolted to the deck to support guardrails or *lifelines.*

**standing rigging** fixed *shrouds* or *stays* of a boat.

**starboard** right side of the boat looking toward the bow.

**starboard tack** when a boat sails with *boom* to *port* and the wind strikes the *starboard* side first.

**stays** *fore-and-aft* wires that hold the *mast* in place longitudinally.

**staysail** sail set on a *stay* inboard of the forwardmost sail.

**steerageway** the slowest speed at which a boat can operate while still under control.

**step** piece of wood or metal to hold the heel of the *mast.*

**stern** after end of a boat.

**sternway** backward movement of a boat.

**storm jib** small sail at the *bow* used

in heavy seas.

**storm trysail** small heavy *mainsail* used in stormy weather.

**swinging the compass** determining the amount of *compass* error on all headings.

**tack** bottom forward end of a sail. Also the diagonal made with the wind by a sailboat.

**tacking** working to windward *close-hauled.*

**tailing** pulling on a *sheet* while the winch is manually operated.

**topping lift** line that runs from the *mast* to the *boom* to hoist it.

**transom** flat surface of a boat's *stern.*

**trim** to adjust the angle of the sails to accord with the wind. The way a boat sits in the water.

**true north** exact geographic north.

**true wind** wind direction without taking into account the motion of the boat.

**variation** difference between *true* and *magnetic north*, caused by anomalies in the earth's magnetic field.

**warp** heavy rope used for towing. Move a boat by means of a *warp.*

**windward** toward the wind.

# INDEX

## PICTURE CREDITS

Quarto Publishing would like to thank the following for permission to reproduce copyright material (abbreviations used — *t:top, l:left, r:right, b:bottom, c:center).*

**Adrian Morgan** 6, 7, 111, 16, 17t & b, 20, 32, 35, 48, 51l & r, 64, 73; 90, 91t & b, 92, 94l, 95bl, 98t & b, 99, 101, 102b, 104, 107t & b, 109t, bl & br, 110tl, 113br, 122, 123t & b, 125, 146, 147.

**Jonathan Eastland** 8, 11r, 14b, 34, 49t & b, 56, 78, 79t, c & b, 85, 89tr, 93t, 94r, 95r, 102t & c, 103, 105, 110bl & br, 111, 114, 115, 116t, 126.

**Patrick Roach** 88, 89tl, bl & br, 106, 108, 110tr, 111 inset, 112t, bl & br, 113l, 116b, 117t, 118, 124, 127, 129l & r, 131t & c, 132, 133, 134, 136t, c & b, 138, 140c & b, 141, 142b, 145r, 151l, 153, 166, 170, 171t, 172, 173, 175, 176/7, 178, 180.

**C Jarman** 128t & b, 130, 139l & r, 142t & c, 145tl & bl, 147c, 156t, 161, 171c, 174.

**R Kennedy** 14t.

**G Beauvais** 93b.

**R Godley** 95t.

**H Cowley** 151tr & br.

**M M Advertising** 156b.

## ACKNOWLEDGMENTS

Quarto Publishing would like to thank the following for their assistance in the research and production of this book:

**Laser, Banbury, Oxfordshire**
**J.D. Potter Ltd, Admiralty Chart Agent**
**Lakedale Marine, London**
**Phillip Cornick**